HIRED SWORDS

HIRED SWORDS

HIRED SWORDS

*The Rise of Private Warrior Power
in Early Japan*

KARL F. FRIDAY

STANFORD UNIVERSITY PRESS

STANFORD, CALIFORNIA

Stanford University Press
Stanford, California
© 1992 by the Board of Trustees of the
Leland Stanford Junior University

Printed and bound by CPI Group (UK) Ltd,
Croydon, CR0 4YY

CIP data appear at the end of the book

Published with the assistance of a
special grant from the Stanford
University Faculty Publication Fund
to help support nonfaculty work
originating at Stanford.

Original printing 1992
Last figure below indicates year of this printing:
04 03 02 01

For my grandfather, Arthur Freiheit,
who taught me to grow and to keep growing

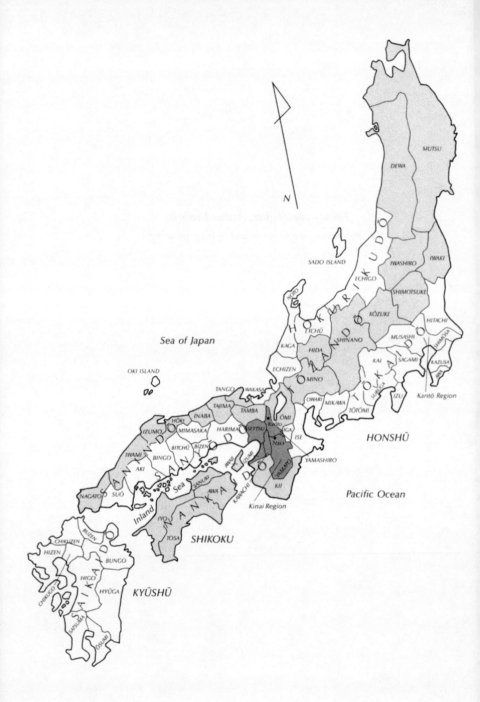

MUTSU

DEWA

SADO ISLAND

IWASHIRO

IWAKI

ECHIGO

SHIMOTSUKE

KŌZUKE

HITACHI

NOTO

ETCHŪ

HIDA

SHINANO

MUSASHI

SHIMŌSA

KAGA

KAI

SAGAMI

KAZUSA

ECHIZEN

MINO

OWARI

MIKAWA

SURUGA

IZU

AWA

Kantō Region

TANGO   WAKASA

ŌMI

IGA

TŌTŌMI

HONSHŪ

Sea of Japan

OKI ISLAND

TAJIMA   TAMBA

Kyōto

ISE

HŌKI

INABA

HARIMA

SETTSU

IZUMO

MIMASAKA

Nara

IWAMI

BITCHŪ   BIZEN

AKI   BINGO

AWAJI   IZUMI

YAMASHIRO

AKI

SANUKI

KAWACHI

KII

Pacific Ocean

NAGATO   SUŌ

Inland   Sea

AWA

Kinai Region

IYO

TOSA

SHIKOKU

BUZEN

CHIKUZEN

HIZEN

BUNGO

CHIKUGO

HIGO

HYŪGA

KYŪSHŪ

SATSUMA

ŌSUMI

ACKNOWLEDGMENTS

The academic equivalent to beginning a gothic novel with "it was a dark and stormy night" is without a doubt to preface an acknowledgment section with the statement that space does not permit thanking all of the people who made the project possible. But like a good many clichés, this one is both trite *and* true. And so to the many friends and relatives and colleagues on both sides of the Pacific whom I have neglected to mention here by name, *makoto ni rei o mōsu*.

My special thanks to the Japan Foundation and to the Social Science Research Council, whose grants funded much of the research on which this study is based; and to the Weter Fund of Stanford University, which helped pay the bills while I wrote up the dissertation on which the present volume is based. I am indebted as well to Professors Kanai Madoka and Masuda Takashi, and to the rest of the faculty and staff of the University of Tokyo Historiographical Institute, for giving me a place to work and for the time they took away from their own labors to assist me with mine.

I have been unusually lucky to have had a multitude of

friends and teachers to steer me through this very formidable project. A heartfelt thank you to Jeff Mass, for his diligent guidance in the preparation of this study; to my tutor, Sasaki Keisuke, for his display of superhuman patience during what must for him have been many frustrating hours of helping me hack my way through the underbrush of court documents and courtier diaries; to Cappy Hurst, who got me started in all of this; to Dick Spear, who reminded me when I needed it that the key to scholarly success is a judicious mixture of enthusiasm, curiosity, and cynicism; to Bruce Batten, for sharing with me several early drafts of his dissertation, on which I have drawn heavily; to Neil Kiley, for many afternoons and subway rides of conversation about rural Heian Japan and the Mino Genji, as well as for other innumerable hints and bits of advice, all of which helped me pull my own thoughts together; to Joan Piggott, for her enthusiastic support and encouragement throughout the project; to Michael Cooper, whose now-departed computer may, I fear, have choked to death on the dozens of superfluous "howevers" and "moreovers" that cluttered the article from which Chapter 4 was developed (the entire manuscript has benefited immeasurably from the excision of the stylistic foibles that he caught and called to my attention); to Arnie Olds, who produced the beautiful maps for this volume; to Prof. Sasama Yoshihiko and the Kashiwa Shobō, for graciously allowing me to reproduce several illustrations from *Nihon kōchū-bugu jiten*; to Katheryn Enniss, who produced the index; and to Peter Kahn, Barbara Mnookin, and Nancy Lerer of Stanford University Press, for their invaluable editorial help with the manuscript.

Many thanks to Roy and Ray Langley for uncountable burritos, pizzas, and burgers consumed with progress reports on the joys and frustrations of academia. Behind every completed

Ph.D. stands an indefatigable cheering section; it was Roy's and Ray's goading that helped me get through mine.

My greatest debt is to Chié, my wife and my best friend. She acted throughout as a sounding board for my ideas; tried—if not always successfully—to help me decipher some of the more opaque prose in the Japanese secondary literature, along with the readings of hundreds of mystifying Japanese names; and, most important of all, resisted the temptation to shoot, poison, or strangle me in the face of five years of preoccupation with my studies, and the many moments of short temper that it produced. I doubt whether I can ever make it all up to her, but I expect to have a lifetime during which to try.

K. F. F.

CONTENTS

Introduction *1*

1 The Emperor's Army *8*

2 Peasants and Professionals *33*

3 Warriors and Warbands *70*

4 The Contract Constabulary *122*

Conclusion: Reassessing the Heian Warrior *167*

Notes 181

Glossary 219

Bibliography 227

Index 257

Stanford University Press
Stanford, California
© 1992 by the Board of Trustees of the
Leland Stanford Junior University

Printed and bound by CPI Group (UK) Ltd,
Croydon, CR0 4YY

CIP data appear at the end of the book

Published with the assistance of a
special grant from the Stanford
University Faculty Publication Fund
to help support nonfaculty work
originating at Stanford.

Original printing 1992
Last figure below indicates year of this printing:
04   03   02   01

FIGURES

1. Idealized Organization of a 600-Man Regiment   *19*

2. The Japanese State in the Early 8th Century   *22*

3. *Haniwa* Figurine in Armor   *36*

4. Japanese Shield   *41*

5. Artist's Conception of an *Ōyumi*   *43*

6. Evolution of Central Military Institutions, 700–811   *65*

7. Provinces of Known *Ōryōshi* and *Tsuibushi*
   Postings, ca. 944–1180   *158*

8. Chains of Command in the Provincial Military
   and Police System of the 11th and 12th Centuries   *164*

HIRED SWORDS

HIRED SWORDS

INTRODUCTION

*War is a matter of vital importance to the State; the province
of life or death; the road to survival or ruin. It is mandatory
that it be thoroughly studied.*

SUN TZU, THE ART OF WAR

*In the beginning . . . no man was higher in birth than any
other, for all men were descended from a single father and
mother. But when envy and covetousness came into the
world, and might triumphed over right . . . certain men
were appointed as guarantors and defenders of the weak and
humble.*

THE BOOK OF LANCELOT OF THE LAKE

The light of the early morning sun over a bay called Dannoura,
near the straits between Honshu and Kyushu, on the twenty-
fifth day of the third month of 1185 revealed two mighty fleets
of warboats sailing grimly into one of the most celebrated battles in all of Japanese history. A beleaguered Taira Tomomori
was attempting a desperate stand against pursuing forces under
the command of Minamoto Yoshitsune.

At first Tomomori's flotilla acquitted itself well, but by late
morning, the tide had quite literally turned and was forcing the

Taira boats backward, trapping them between the rocky shore and the advancing Minamoto fleet, which made short work of them. Perceiving that all had been lost, Taira Tokiko took her eight-year-old grandson, the Emperor Antoku, into her arms and leaped into the sea. As they sank beneath the waves, they carried with them the Imperial Sword, one of the three imperial regalia; the blade was never recovered.

Thirty-four years later, the priest Jien pondered the meaning of the loss of this important symbol: "I have come to the conclusion that since present conditions have taken such a form, and soldiers have emerged for the purpose of protecting the sovereign, the Imperial Sword turned its protective function over to soldiers and disappeared into the sea."[1] For Jien, and for dozens of generations of historians who followed him, the sequence of events that climaxed at Dannoura marked a point of transition from the classical age to the military age; from an era of rule by the emperor and his court to one of primacy for Japan's warrior order.

Jien's "military age" was real. In his time, warriors had already achieved considerable autonomy from the imperial court in the administration of rural affairs; by the middle of the fifteenth century, political control of Japan had passed into the hands of these warriors, or *bushi*,[2] where it remained until the Meiji Restoration of 1868. But Jien's analysis of what happened at Dannoura was in error.

For the truth is that the Imperial Sword had "turned its protective function over to soldiers"—or rather, to warriors—long before 1185. During most of the Heian period (794–1185), Japan was guarded and policed not by the Imperial Sword, but by hired swords—the private military resources of a rising order of professional mercenaries. Born during the ninth century, this order had come to monopolize the application of arms in Japan by the early tenth century, the emperor

and his court having cast aside the original military institutions
of their state a century before. For a quarter of a millennium,
warriors fought the court's battles for it; and then, in 1180,
Minamoto Yoritomo, in what started as an essentially personal
quarrel with a hereditary enemy, Taira Kiyomori, began the
process that would lead to Dannoura and to the formation of
the Kamakura shogunate, Japan's first warrior government.

Yoritomo's feud with Kiyomori dated back to the 1150's,
when the Taira leader and Yoritomo's father, Yoshitomo,
found themselves fighting on the same side of a dispute between a reigning and a retired emperor. In the aftermath of the
ensuing Hōgen Incident (named for the Japanese calendar era
in which it occurred), Kiyomori reaped what Yoshitomo considered to be far more than his fair share of the rewards distributed to the victors. The enmity that this precipitated led to
the Heiji Incident (again named for the calendar era) of 1159,
a poorly conceived and clumsily executed attempt by Yoshitomo to eliminate his rival. This time, several days of bloody
fighting left Yoshitomo and most of his supporters dead and
Kiyomori as the premier warrior leader in Japan. For the next
two decades, Kiyomori's prestige and influence at court grew
steadily; a coup d'état in 1179 enabled him to assume virtual
dictatorial powers. But the Taira ship had no sooner come in
than it began to leak. Within the year, Yoshitomo's eldest son,
Yoritomo (whom Kiyomori had foolishly only exiled in 1159
when he might justifiably have executed him), issued a call to
arms that inaugurated the five years of civil warfare historians
call the Gempei War. In the course of this contest, which ended
with the destruction of the Taira at Dannoura, Yoritomo laid
the foundations for warrior rule in Japan.[3]

The birth, early development, and organization of the bushi
have been a major subject of research among Japanese scholars

since the turn of the century. But in the West, the subject remains nearly unexplored. Only a handful of articles on the premedieval Japanese military have appeared in English. The few Western-language treatments that do exist are to be found in survey histories or in monographs that come at the subject as background to the formation of the Kamakura shogunate. Such studies seek the roots of Japan's "feudal" age, emphasizing the rise of a proto-feudal class of armed landholders.

In their quest for the origins of Japan's medieval polity, early researchers were all too readily seduced by the apparent similarity of developments in Japan to the experience of northwestern Europe; medieval samurai and daimyō (regional military lords) were equated with knights and feudal barons. Accordingly, theories on the nascency of the samurai and their lords were heavily colored by conceptions of the conditions that had produced the knights and *their* lords.

So far as Heian military developments specifically are concerned, the standard view set out in Western textbooks and survey histories was formulated by Asakawa Kan'ichi during the early decades of this century and later expanded upon and popularized by George Sansom.[4] It describes the appearance, during the eighth and ninth centuries, of a new class of private landholders, who, by the tenth century, had begun to arm themselves and to gather around the wealthiest and most influential of their number for self-protection. This incipient warrior caste is said to have evolved rapidly and soon emerged as the de facto ruling power in the Heian countryside, although it remained nominally subservient to an imperial court that had become little more than an impotent, empty shell of a government.

According to this analysis, a warrior class was spontaneously generated during the middle years of the Heian period, just as one had been in Europe a few centuries earlier, in order to fill yawning holes in the military and administrative structures of the rural order. Asakawa and Sansom imputed these holes to two factors: the utter unfitness of early imperial military institutions, and the rampant growth in the provinces of privately owned estates or manors, which were immune from both taxation and administrative interference by the central government. Martial ineptitude on the part of the state, Sansom argued, was "inherent in the administrative structure, which gave little importance to military arrangements except for purposes of parade and display"; it was an unavoidable product of a central aristocracy that was predominantly civilian in outlook and fundamentally averse to violence and bloodshed.[5] The problems that inevitably arose from this situation, he claimed, were exacerbated by the appearance of the aforementioned private estates, which by the late ninth century had become so extensive and so independent of central supervision and control that the authority of the court in most provinces had virtually collapsed. The result was a breakdown of order in the countryside so severe that those who owned or administered the great estates were forced to develop private retinues of fighting men to protect their lives and property. Within decades of their inception, these bands of fighting men had undermined what little remained of centralized rule in the provinces, emerging as the true masters of the countryside.

In a landmark study published in the middle 1960's. John W. Hall offered two important adjustments to the picture painted by Asakawa and Sansom. First, he observed that the ancestors of the same provincial aristocrats who were taking up arms and becoming warriors during the Heian period had been at the center of military activity during the sixth and seventh centuries. Clearly then, said Hall, the growth of private military organizations during the ninth and subsequent centuries was not a new phenomenon, but rather the reassertion of what had formerly been the dominant pattern of Japanese life. Second, and more important, he challenged the conclusion that the militarization of the provincial elite was immediately or inherently disruptive to the existing order, arguing instead that the new warriors were simply officers performing military services within one or another of the established structures of public or private authority.[6]

Hall argued that at least one of the holes described by Asakawa and Sansom—the collapse of court authority and control in the provinces—might not have been as big as had been thought. In the past two decades, studies by other scholars have taken this idea much further—so much further that the imperial court is now seen not as an effete, tottering vestige, but as the dynamic center of a solid and highly centripetal polity.[7] Most specialists in the period now believe that, in contrast to Europe, where the knights sprang from the confusion of the waning Carolingian Empire and the onslaughts of Norse marauders, the genesis of Japan's bushi took place within a secure and still-vital imperial state structure. This, then, presents us with something of an anomaly: a provincial warrior order, organized into private military networks, is clearly visible in Japanese historical sources by the late ninth century; by the middle of the next century, this order had been handed a virtual monopoly of the country's martial resources; yet it was not until the twilight of the twelfth century that Japanese fighting men took the first significant steps toward asserting their independence from imperial court control. Why did they not do so earlier? Why did the bushi, the only effective soldiery of the age, remain obediently within the military chain of command of a court without any other military resources for nearly 300 years? And how and why did the court put itself in the potentially (and indeed, ultimately) precarious situation of contracting for its military needs with private warriors? It is on these and related questions that the following study is centered.

The failures of the central government in the area of military policy loom prominently in most previous treatments of Heian warriors: The court's inability to maintain an effective military and police system in the hinterlands forced provincial residents to take up arms for themselves; its inability to restrain this militarization of the countryside, combined with a general lack of interest in provincial and martial affairs, allowed the development of large, private warrior networks. According to this view, the court was ultimately doomed to perish by the sword because of its failure to live by it.

In the following pages, I will argue that it was largely court activism—not inactivity—in military matters that put swords in the hands of the rural elite. By tracing the development of Japanese military institutions from the late seventh through the mid-twelfth century, I hope to demonstrate that, from the inception of the imperial state system at the turn of the eighth century, court policy in both the capital and the countryside followed a long-term pattern of increasing reliance on the martial skills of the gentry and a diminishing use of troops conscripted from the ordinary peasantry. The emergence of a private, professional warrior order was at once a cause and an effect of this pattern. I will argue, moreover, that this pattern arose from the court's desire for maximum efficiency in its military institutions, and that throughout the Heian period, the court was successful in retaining for itself the exclusive right to sanction the use of coercive force.

1

THE EMPEROR'S ARMY

I don't know what effect these men will have on the enemy, but, by God, they frighten me.
THE DUKE OF WELLINGTON

God is ordinarily for the big battalions against the little ones. ROGER, COUNT BUSSY-RABUTIN

In the closing decades of the seventh century, the central court cast a waxing shadow over Japan's political landscape. Amid this gathering of power and authority, the imperial house and its supporters created an elaborate battery of military institutions modeled in large measure on those of T'ang China. Perhaps the best-known feature of this military system was its reliance on the citizen-soldier; the emperor's army was preponderantly an army of peasant conscripts.

Historians have not been kind in their assessments of this imperial military. It has generally been seen as over-ambitious, a malapropos system slavishly copied by an unsophisticated nation in awe of the splendor of the T'ang. In the words of Minoru Shinoda, it was an army "established on paper" that "could scarcely have been expected to work in the Japan of the eighth century."[1] It was, we are told, an experiment doomed to failure before it even began, and "undoubtedly," John Hall observes, "the least successful aspect of the Taika reforms."[2]

To be sure, the era of the peasant soldier was far briefer than the era of the imperial court itself. Before the eighth century was out, before even the capital at Nara was exchanged for Heian-kyō, and long before the age of "the Court at its zenith,"[3] most of the organs of the original system had been discarded, the peasants returned to their fields. But to call the military institutions created at the turn of the eighth century a failure in toto, to suggest they were a precocious folly that collapsed of their own weight, is to judge them too harshly. For the truth is that the armed forces, like most aspects of the imperial, or *ritsuryō*, polity, were a careful Japanese adaptation, not a wholesale adoption, of the Chinese system.* They were later abolished, not because they were utterly infeasible from the start, but primarily because the military and political demands of the late eighth century were different from those of a hundred years earlier.[4]

To date, no Western author has offered a thoroughgoing description of the imperial military system. This is owing, no doubt, to its long perception as a failure, an entity important only for the gap it left behind when it collapsed—for the detailed depiction of institutions of small consequence is the task of the antiquarian, not the historian. Yet to understand the fate of the imperial military, one needs to understand its structure. This, then, is our first order of business.

*The term ritsuryō refers specifically to the legal codes that defined the structure and operation of the imperial state. There were four such codes: the Ōmi Codes of 668, the Kiyomihara Codes of 689, the Taihō Codes of 702, and the Yōrō Codes of 718. Of these, only the Yōrō Codes are extant.

THE RITSURYŌ MILITARY

At the dawn of the seventh century, most of Japan was ruled by a confederation of great houses, among which one—the royal, or Yamato—house stood as primus inter pares. Some of these houses were entirely dependent for their position on the Yamato; the majority, however, had their own geographic bases of power. The role of the royal court—and of the Yamato sovereign—was little more than to serve as a vehicle for cooperation among the great houses in matters of "national" concern.[5]

In the administration of lands and people outside the immediate vicinity of the court, the great houses were very nearly autonomous. In theory, their authority came from the court: prominent regional chieftains who had come to terms with the Yamato regime were empowered by the court as Provincial Patriarchs, or *kuni no miyatsuko*. In practice, kuni no miyatsuko appointments were permanent and hereditary, and provincial patriarchs ruled their territories as virtually independent chiefs.[6]

Over the course of the seventh century, this polity gave way bit by bit to a centralized imperial regime. The changeover began in earnest after the sixth month of 645, when a radical clique led by the future Emperor Tenji seized power by hacking their chief political opponents to pieces with swords and spears in the midst of a court ceremony. In the wake of this spectacular coup d'état, Tenji and his supporters introduced a series of Chinese-inspired centralizing measures collectively known as the Taika Reforms, after the calendar era in which they were launched. During the next several decades, the great regional families were gradually stripped of their independent bases and converted to true officials of the state through a judicious combination of cajolery, cooptation, and coercion. The Yamato sovereign became the emperor of Japan, the transcendent repository of all political authority.

The reformers were aided in their efforts by widespread Japanese apprehension over the growing might of T'ang China, which had been engaged since the 630's in one of the greatest military expansions in Chinese history. By the 630's, the Japanese were driven by T'ang forces from their long-established foothold on the Korean peninsula and the threat of a Chinese invasion of the Japanese archipelago itself seemed very real. The fear these events engendered served to mute opposition and promote support for state-strengthening reforms, as central and provincial noble houses set aside their differences in the face of a common enemy.[7]

Under the circumstances, it should be no surprise that the centralization and restructuring of the military was a major element of the state-reformation process. The Yamato "state army" had formerly been knit together from the private forces of the *kuni no miyatsuko*, who led them into battle under the banner of the Yamato sovereign. This can be seen clearly in the makeup of a force sent to the Korean peninsula in 591. Overall command of the army was held jointly by five of the greatest of the noble houses, while the individual divisions were led by the heads of lesser noble families. A similar invasion force eleven years later was centered on a single general, a prince of the royal house, but the army was still a heterogeneous patchwork of troops belonging to various noble houses.[8]

By the close of the seventh century, the whole of the state's military resources came to be subsumed under the direct control of the Yamato king cum emperor. The resulting system is distinguished from its predecessor mainly in terms of principle and formal structure, rather than function or personnel: the same peasant cultivators continued to be conscripted as soldiers and the same regional noble class continued to serve as officers. But there was an important difference, for under the new system, direct conscription by the state—as supervised by the imperial court—replaced private conscription through the medium of the provincial patriarchs. This transformation of the army parallels the transformation of the rule in the hinterlands into a centrally administered imperium. Neither conversion occurred at a stroke; in both cases, officerships and titles tended to be created first and then later empowered little by little—often empowered in fact only years after authority had been granted on paper.[9]

The most important steps in the creation of the imperial military system were taken during the reigns of Emperor Tenmu and his wife-successor, Jitō (that is, between 672 and 697). There are two major reasons for this timing, the first being that the functioning of the ritsuryō military institutions was heavily dependent on the existence of a number of other components of the imperial state structure, many of which did not appear until the final quarter of the seventh century. The second is that Tenmu had come to power literally on horseback, using the private forces of disaffected members of the provincial nobility to seize the throne in the Jinshin civil war of 672. Not wishing to see anyone else duplicate his success, he wanted to draw the reins of all of the country's military resources firmly into imperial hands.[10]

The extent to which Tenmu equated a strong army with a strong state structure is reflected in a decree he issued in 684:

> In a government, military matters are the essential thing. All civil and military officials should therefore sedulously practice the use of arms and of riding on horseback. Be careful to provide an adequate supply of horses, weapons, and articles of personal costume. Those who have horses shall be made cavalry soldiers,

those who have none shall be infantry soldiers. Both shall receive training. Let no obstacle be thrown in the way of their assembling for this purpose.[11]

By 685, Tenmu was able to take the momentous step of outlawing the private possession of large-scale weapons and of the kinds of things, horns, fifes, drums, flags, and the like, that were used to organize and direct troops on the battlefield. But to put a true state military into operation, the court needed to have the ability to conscript soldiers directly. That is, it needed sufficient knowledge of and control over its subjects to be able to call them to service directly, without going through the provincial patriarchs. This condition could not be met until the central government possessed accurate population registers. In 689, Jitō directed provincial governors to draw up "records of the population." She further ordered that the soldiers in each province "be divided into four groups, one of which was to be designated [in rotation] for training in the military arts." The first regular census records date from the following year.[12]

By 690, then, all of the groundwork for the ritsuryō military structure had been laid. The new system—as described in the following pages—must therefore have been launched sometime between that date and 702, when the Taihō ritsuryō codes were promulgated.*

THE PROVINCIAL REGIMENTS

The post-Taika reformers designed the imperial military around two fundamental principles: central control and direc-

---

*The "ritsuryō codes" on which I base my description of the imperial military establishment are, of course, the Yōrō Codes, which were not written until 718. But the Yōrō statutes dealing with the military are thought to be nearly identical to those of the Taihō Codes. For a detailed examination of this point, see Noda, *Ritsuryō kokka*, pp. 1–43.

tion of all military affairs, and public conscription, whereby military service was viewed as a basic duty to the state incumbent on all subjects.

The ritsuryō codes reserved for the emperor and his officials authority for all but the most minor uses of troops, ordering, for example, that "when twenty or more soldiers were to be mobilized, an imperial writ must first be obtained." The overall peacetime administration of the state's armed forces was conducted by the Ministry of Military Affairs (hyōbushō) and the five offices under it. Its responsibilities included the supervision of military officers; the administration of troop registers, armories, pastures, war-horses, public and private pack animals, boats, fortifications, signal fires, and postal roads; the oversight of the manufacture of weapons; the collation of military communications from the provinces; and the calculation of overall troop strength and the balance of forces in the various provinces. All of these functions were handled at the provincial level by the provincial governor and his staff, who also conducted annual inspections of weapons, boats, livestock, and the like and forwarded the information collected to the hyōbushō for collation.[13]

All free male subjects between the ages of twenty and fifty-nine other than the nobility and those who "suffered from long-term illness or were otherwise unfit for military duty" were liable for induction as soldiers, or heishi.* While in theory one was liable for conscription until the age of sixty, in practice heishi were generally quite young—usually in their early twenties—a practice that probably reflected a desire to keep the state's fighting force as young and healthy as possible.[14] En-

---

*Ryō no gige, p. 192. Slaves were excluded, as were all sons and grandsons of holders of the fifth court rank or higher and the designated heirs (chakushi) of persons between the eighth and sixth ranks.

listments in any case appear to have been fairly short, with draftees continually rotated in and out of service.

THE NATURE OF HEISHI SERVICE

A man conscripted as a soldier was joining an organization more akin to a modern national guard than a standing army. Upon selection, he was immediately assigned to the provincial regiment (*gundan*) based nearest his home, and his name was recorded on a special roster made out in duplicate. One copy of the roster was retained in the office of the provincial governor; the other was forwarded to the Ministry of Military Affairs in the capital.[15]

Once assigned and registered as soldiers, most men were returned to their homes and fields. The provincial copy of the regimental roster was then used as a master list from which troops were selected for any of three types of duty, in exchange for which they were exempted from all other corvée imposts.[16]

The first obligation of imperial soldiers was watch duty (*ban*) within their own provinces. Here they drilled in tactics and the use of weapons; guarded the provincial government headquarters, provincial armories, and rice storehouses; maintained and repaired these armories, storehouses, and the items stored in them; apprehended criminals; and performed other related functions.*

The amount of time a soldier was required to spend each year on duty in his province is not specified by the Yōrō Codes. But an imperial edict from 704 ordered that the heishi of each province be divided into ten watches of ten days each, and that

---

* *Ryō no gige*, pp. 184–85, 193, 195, 198, 303–4. In the provinces of Ise, Minō, and Echizen, they also manned the barriers that guarded the approaches to the capital. And in the northern frontier provinces, they guarded and maintained the stockades that protected Japanese settlers.

time on duty be equitably distributed among all troops.[17] Thus in a normal year (354 or 355 days, according to the lunar calendar in use at the time), there would have been thirty-five or thirty-six rotations of watch. All ten watches would have served three shifts each year, and half the watches would have served a fourth.[18] According to this reckoning, heishi served an average of thirty-five days on duty in their provinces each year.

This is actually rather light duty when one recalls that normal corvée obligations (from which soldiers were exempted) totaled sixty days a year. The probable reason for this leniency is that heishi were required to furnish a great deal of their personal food and equipment. Each was to provide six *to* (about 114 liters) of dried rice and two *shō* (3.6 liters) of salt, to be placed in the provincial armory and reissued when the regiment was mobilized for war. Each man was held responsible for replacing his own ration of rice and salt in the event that it became unfit for consumption. Individual soldiers were also required to provide a bow, bow case, and bowstring, fifty arrows, a quiver, a long sword, a short sword, a whetstone, a rain hat, a bag for carrying rice, a canteen, a bag for carrying salt, a pair of leggings, and a pair of straw sandals. All these items were to be brought with them whenever they reported for duty. In addition, each group of ten men was to furnish a tent, two copper trays, two small pots, a hoe, a grass scythe, an axe, a hatchet, a chisel, two sickles, and a pair of metal tongs; and each group of fifty soldiers was to provide a flint, a bundle of tinder grass, and a handsaw. These items were all inspected in the tenth month of every year by provincial officials; soldiers were required to make up for goods lost or damaged—except during wartime—out of their own pockets.[19]

In addition to serving in watches in their own provinces, heishi were rotated into service as guards in the capital or on the frontier. All soldiers on the regimental rosters were, moreover, liable for mobilization for major military campaigns in or out of the country. (These two kinds of tours of duty will be discussed in detail below.) In exchange for service of this sort, troops were excused from watch duties on returning to their provinces. Newly returned capital guards were given one year off, and frontier guards three; campaign soldiers were credited for the time actually served.[20]

THE STRUCTURE OF THE PROVINCIAL REGIMENTS

The gundan were administrative organizations, not tactical formations. For this reason, they did not need to be of uniform size, and in fact they ranged from fewer than 500 men to as many as 1,000. Ordinarily, one regiment was established in each province.[21]

The fundamental tactical unit was the *tai*, or company, composed of fifty men. Tai were classified as either cavalry (*kitai*) or infantry (*hotai*), and mixing the two types of troops within a single company was strictly forbidden. Each company was divided into ten-man campfires (*ka*) and five-man squads (*go*). The former was an administrative grouping—the number of men who shared a tent. The latter was tactical—*go* fought together around a single shield. On the battlefield, each company was also organized into two lines of five squads each.[22]

In keeping with the doctrine of centralized, civilian control, the general administration and supervision of a province's military resources were the direct responsibility of the provincial governor. He was assisted in this task by four types of specialist military officers. Each regiment was overseen by one or more colonels (*ki* or *gunki*). In gundan of 600 men or more, two gunki were posted, one called the *daiki* (colonel) and the other the *shōki* (lieutenant colonel). Regiments of 1,000 men were assigned one colonel and two lieutenant colonels. In each gundan, there were also one or two clerks (*shuchō*); two to five *kyōi*, or warrant officers first class (one for every 200 men); five to ten *rosochi*, or warrant officers second class (one for every 100 men); and ten to twenty *taishō*, or warrant officers third class (one per 50-man company).[23] Figure 1 shows the organization of a gundan of 600–1,000 men.

Warrant officers were men of unusual "skill with the bow and horse" selected from among the eligible commoners not currently in harness as soldiers. Clerks were chosen from this same class, for their "skills in writing and arithmetic." Colonels and lieutenant colonels were of a different mold. They were "men of the province who held rank (up to and including the sixth rank) but no office, men who held military merit rank [*kun'i*], and/or other subjects of martial skill" appointed by the provincial governor.* Like the governor and other provincial officials—but unlike any other provincial military officers— colonels and lieutenant colonels were assigned personal body-guards.[24]

*The court rank system, created by the ritsuryō codes, was used to classify both the central and the provincial nobility. A man's rank determined his status, his eligibility for government posts, and his place in the complex protocol of official and social events. There were nine main ranks, beginning with the Initial rank and continuing upward from the eighth to the first. The first, second, and third ranks were subdivided into senior and junior grades; the senior fourth through junior eighth ranks were further divided into upper and lower categories; there were also four Initial ranks, Greater Initial Rank–Upper Grade, Greater Initial Rank–Lower Grade, Lesser Initial Rank–Upper Grade, and Lesser Initial Rank–Lower Grade. The term "military merit rank" is explained in Chapter 3.

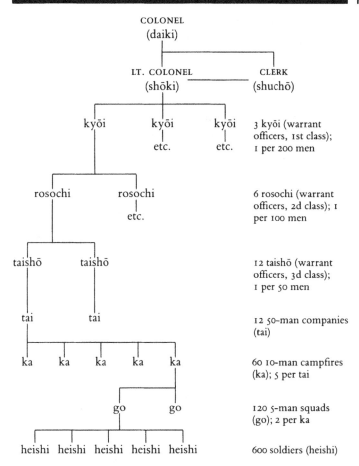

COLONEL
(daiki)

LT. COLONEL   CLERK
(shōki)   (shuchō)

kyōi   kyōi   kyōi   3 kyōi (warrant
            etc.   etc.   officers, 1st class);
                                    1 per 200 men

rosochi   rosochi   6 rosochi (warrant
             etc.   officers, 2d class); 1
                                    per 100 men

taishō   taishō   12 taishō (warrant
                                    officers, 3d class);
                                    1 per 50 men

tai   tai   12 50-man companies
                                    (tai)

ka   ka   ka   ka   ka   60 10-man campfires
                                    (ka); 5 per tai

           go   go   120 5-man squads
                                    (go); 2 per ka

heishi heishi heishi heishi heishi 600 soldiers (heishi)

FIGURE I. Idealized organization of a 600-man regiment. Data from
Ryō no gige, pp. 183, 185.

An examination of the names of those identified in the
sources as gunki reveals that they were usually drawn from the
same socioeconomic class as the district officials (gunji), that
is, from those houses that had formerly been provincial patriarchs. The two posts (gunji and gunki) appear, in fact, to have

carried roughly equal prestige and status. But they were clearly distinguished. No district official ever held simultaneous appointment as a colonel or a lieutenant colonel. And gunki, unlike district officials, could on occasion be rotated to provinces outside their own. This division is of considerable importance, for prior to the Taika Reforms, general political control and military authority had been united at the local level. The imperial state called on precisely the same elements of the population as its predecessor had for soldiers, military officers, and local administrators, but under the new polity, military and civil powers were separated at the grass-roots level. Thus the authority of regional chieftains was fragmented and brought more closely under central control.[25]

Some scholars have argued that gunki were administrative officials rather than true military officers who actually led troops in battle. Proponents of this view point out that no source unequivocally shows a gunki in action on any battlefield, and that no gunki was ever awarded military merit rank.[26] Nevertheless, the Yōrō Codes include martial skill as one of the qualifications for appointment as gunki and prescribe specific functions for colonels in the ranks of campaign armies. It is difficult to fathom what men required by statute to "train with horse and bow" might have been doing in armies if not leading troops, or when they might have "inspected the battle ranks" if they were not field officers as well as administrators.[27]

THE FRONTIER GARRISONS

The regiments were the mainstay of the imperial state's military in the provinces, but they were supplemented in the frontier regions by special types of garrisons. In the southwest—the continental frontier—these were called *sakimori* (literally, "defenders of the edge"). In the northeast—the *emishi* frontier—they were called *chinpei* ("pacification soldiers").* The difference in nomenclature may reflect the differing natures of the two frontiers. By the late seventh century, the southwest was for the most part an established border, along which the court was content to simply hold the line against foreign incursions. The northeast, however, was an advancing frontier, behind which the court was expanding its control into "foreign"-held lands. (See Fig. 2 for a map of the country in ca. 700.)

Sakimori were the older of the two kinds of garrisons. The *Nihon shoki* claims that they were established in the immediate aftermath of the Taika coup d'état. Though this is unlikely, it *is* plausible that the sakimori system began in 664, when fear of an imminent Chinese invasion led the court to order that "sakimori and beacon fires be placed on the islands of Tsushima and Iki, and in the provinces of Tsukushi [Kyushu]."[28] The southwestern frontier garrisons were, in any case, an integral part of the military institutions described by the ritsuryō codes. Chinpei, however, do not appear in the codes. They were established later, as the court stepped up its efforts to extend its control over the northeastern part of Honshu. The first specific reference to chinpei dates from 737, but some scholars believe they were in place a decade or so earlier.[29]

The extent of the southwestern frontier along which sakimori were posted is not made clear by the Yōrō Codes and has

---

*The emishi, also called the *ezo* or *ebisu*, were a tribal people who once inhabited much of eastern Japan. Although of similar racial stock to the Yamato Japanese, they differed in language and custom, and fiercely resisted the court's efforts to extend its authority into their homeland. See Kudō, "Kodai emishi"; and Itō Haruyuki, "7–8 seiki emishi shakai." For an in-depth study of the southwestern frontier, see Batten, "State and Frontier."

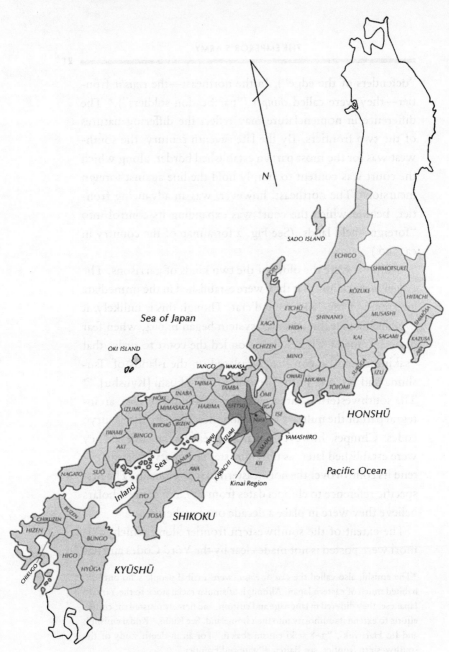

FIGURE 2. The Japanese state in the early 8th century. Adapted from
J. R. Piggott, "Tōdaiji and the Nara Imperium," Ph.D.
dissertation, Stanford University, 1987.

become a matter of considerable debate. At the heart of the controversy is a 730 reference in the *Shoku nihongi* to "sakimori of the various provinces." Some historians have taken the phrase to mean sakimori *sent from* the various provinces and assert that frontier garrisons were found only in Kyushu, Iki, and Tsushima. Others argue that the passage means that sakimori were posted in the Japan Sea coastal provinces of Honshu as well. As we have seen, however, the *Nihon shoki*'s first credible mention of sakimori places them only in Kyushu, Tsushima, and Iki. There are no examples in any source of sakimori stationed in other areas. Moreover, the Yōrō Codes' only references to officials who supervise the frontier garrisons have to do with three posts attached to the *dazaifu*, a supraprovincial government office with jurisdiction over Kyushu, Iki, and Tsushima. Thus it seems unlikely that sakimori garrisons were ever installed anywhere other than these three islands in the southwest.[30]

As noted earlier, service in the southwestern frontier garrisons was one of three types of active duty incumbent on ritsuryō soldiers. In principle, heishi from any province were liable to be called for tours in the borderlands, but in practice, recruitment seems to have been entirely from the *bandō* region of eastern Japan—that is, from the provinces of Sagami, Musashi, Kazusa, Shimōsa, Hitachi, Kōzuke, Shimotsuke, and Awa. There are no examples of sakimori being dispatched from anywhere else. This preference for eastern soldiers probably stems from the fact that this region was famous for producing fighting men of unusual skill and courage. Precedent may have played a role as well, since the region appears to have served as a military base for the Yamato royal house in the preritsuryō era.[31]

The tour of duty for sakimori was three years, excluding

travel time to and from the frontier. Soldiers whose parents or grandparents were old or infirm—and would not otherwise have anyone to care for them—or who had a father, son, brother, grandfather, or grandson currently serving, were excused from garrison duty. Sakimori who so desired were allowed to bring families, slaves, and/or livestock with them to their posts.[32]

On the frontier, sakimori stood duty nine days on and one day off. When not actually fighting or training, they were put to work cultivating paddies or dry fields assigned to them. The tools and oxen necessary to work the fields were provided by the government, with the harvests regarded as rations issued rather than as the soldiers' private property.[33]

The operation of the chinpei system is considerably less well understood than that of the sakimori. For while the Yōrō Codes offer a thoroughgoing description of sakimori, in the case of chinpei, we have only a dozen or so scattered references from which to piece together a coherent picture of these garrisons during the eighth century. We know that by the middle of the seventh century the court had begun establishing stockades in its northeastern frontier region. These outposts served both as places of protection for Japanese settlers in the region and as general administrative headquarters. The Yōrō Codes provided that the stockades be manned and maintained by troops from the provincial regiments, supplemented when necessary by local residents called for corvée service.[34]

Beginning around the third decade of the eighth century, the court augmented its northeastern military with the creation of a special "Pacification Headquarters" (chinjō, later called the chinjufu) in Mutsu and of an additional armed force modeled on the sakimori. These new troops, the chinpei, can be identified in Mutsu as early as 724, but for reasons unknown they did not appear in neighboring provinces until 759. Like the sakimori, the chinpei were recruited from other provinces, presumably from within the regiments. Only two sources identify specific provinces as suppliers of chinpei. The first notes the dispatch of contingents from Sagami, Musashi, Kōzuke, and Shimotsuke; the second refers to chinpei from Sagami. This has led to a general belief among Japanese historians that chinpei, like sakimori, came mainly from the bandō. We do not know the duration of tours of duty in the northeastern frontier garrisons, but evidence suggests they were long, probably the same three-year term as the sakimori's. Chinpei were, for example, permitted to bring their families with them to their duty stations.[35]

From the middle of the eighth century, the court, apparently concerned over the growing expense of transporting soldiers between their home provinces and the frontier garrisons, gradually abridged the garrison system, substituting chinpei and sakimori of local origin for those recruited in the bandō. It is interesting to note that while the dazaifu in the southwest tended to balk at this policy, the provincial governments in the northeast appear to have actively promoted it. In any event, by the early ninth century, frontier garrisons in both the northeast and the southwest were manned entirely by troops recruited locally.[36]

RITSURYŌ EXPEDITIONARY FORCES

The ritsuryō system did not provide for a standing army for large-scale offensive or defensive campaigns. In time of war, a temporary expeditionary force was knit together from temporarily mobilized provincial regiments under staff officers holding temporary commissions. At the close of the campaign, the commissions of the officers expired, the army was dissolved, and the troops were returned to their homes.

As we have seen, any mobilization of more than twenty troops could be undertaken only by imperial edict. The normal procedures for the promulgation of such edicts were quite involved and required the concurrence of the Council of State (*daijōkan*). This meant that a decision to go to war entailed a broad consensus among the entire ruling class. The issue would first be discussed by various deliberative bodies and decided on by the Council of State, whereupon an imperial edict was petitioned for and an order to fight issued in the emperor's name. The Ministry of Military Affairs would then be directed to calculate and report on the number of troops available for mobilization, the number appropriate for the current campaign, and the provincial regiments most suitable for mobilization. Based on this report, the Council of State would issue preparation and mobilization instructions to individual provinces as necessary.[37]

The expeditionary force would be composed of one to three armies, or *gun*, each numbering between 3,000 and 12,000 men. Each army was commanded by a *shōgun* (general), who was assisted by varying numbers of lieutenant generals (*fukushōgun*), major generals (*gunken*), brigadier generals (*gunsō*), and majors (*rokuji*), depending on the size of the army. When three such armies were assembled, an officer known as a *taishōgun* (field marshal) was designated to command the entire expeditionary force. As a symbol of his commission, the taishōgun was given a ceremonial sword, or *settō* (literally, "scepter sword"). Field marshals, generals, and their subordinates were all nobles holding other (civil) posts in the central government who were given temporary commissions, not career military officers. Shōgun, for example, were usually courtiers of the third or fourth court rank, who held offices such as *chūnagon* (Middle Counselor) or *sangi* (Consultant).[38]

The provincial contingents that made up the expeditionary force were led to and from the area of assembly by provincial officials and assigned to an appropriate army. The escorting official was then relieved of responsibility for the regiment for the duration of the campaign.

Each army was divided into battalions, or *jin*. The makeup of these battalions is not described in the Yōrō Codes, but one statute directs that, in the aftermath of a battle, the name, home province, district, company, *and regiment* of each soldier deserving of merit be recorded, battalion by battalion. This could indicate that each battalion contained several regiments, but probably does not, since a regiment could be composed of as many as 1,000 men and an entire army of as few as 3,000. More likely than not, the battalions comprised varying numbers of companies from one or more regiments, rather than several whole regiments. They were, in other words, simply the wartime tactical equivalent of the regiments, which were peacetime administrative structures.[39]

CENTRAL MILITARY INSTITUTIONS: THE FIVE GUARDS

Defense and the maintenance of order in the capital were the purview of five protection agencies collectively known as the *goefu*, or Five Guards: the *emonfu*, the left and right *ejifu*, and the left and right *hyōefu*. To these units fell the responsibility of guarding the gates to the palace and the imperial residence, escorting imperial processions, serving as honor guards at court ceremonies and celebrations, and policing the streets of the capital.*

The manpower for the goefu came from two dissimilar sources. Troops (*hyōe*) for the left and right hyōefu were drawn from among the provincial and lower central nobility; the two ejifu and the emonfu were staffed by soldiers (called *eji*) from the provincial regiments, serving in rotation at court.⁴⁰ In numbers, eji were the dominant military force in the capital.†

The emonfu also had 200 troops called *kadobe* and thirty called *mononobe*. Drawn from among the residents of the capital and of Yamashiro, Yamato, Ise, and Kii provinces, these were vestiges of the pre-Taika era, when they had been private troops used to guard the entrances to the royal "palace" under the direction of the Ōtomo and Saeki clans. Under the ritsuryō system, the kadobe's sole function was to guard the outer gates of the palace, and the mononobe's to administer punishments.⁴¹

The length of eji tours of duty is of some interest. For while the ritsuryō codes specified a term of one year (for which the soldier, following his return from the capital, was given one year off from duty in his home province), all other evidence indicates that in practice eji served much longer terms. In 722,

---

Ryō no gige, pp. 56–57. There were five other agencies involved with military affairs in and around Nara: the left and right Bureaus of the Stables, responsible for the training and care of the court's horses; and the left, right, and inner Armories, responsible for the administration of the court's weapons (ibid., pp. 57–58).

†The Yōrō Codes left the numbers of eji to be assigned to the various guard units unspecified. The numbers were adjusted from time to time, but eji generally appear to have accounted for two-thirds or more of the capital guardsmen (*Ryō no gige*, pp. 56–57; *Shoku nihongi*, 701/8/26, 718/5/27, 741/5/11; *Nihon kōki*, 805/12/7; *Ruijū sandaikyaku*, 1: 184–85; 808/7/20 daijōkan chō).

the directors (*kami*) of the two ejifu complained that the tours of duty imposed on eji were so long that men "returned to their villages with hair become white." Eji tours were thereupon shortened to three years. Later sources speak of rewards for eji who had served for twenty or thirty years. Clearly, eji were serving much longer than the one year theoretically required of them. Hashimoto Yū attributes these inflated tours of duty to government efforts to simplify administration and minimize the problem of training green troops.[42]

Newly assigned eji were led to the capital by designated officials from their home provinces. Once there, they were turned over to the Ministry of Military Affairs, which first verified the numbers of the arrivals and then conducted an inspection to ensure that each man had brought with him the prescribed weapons and equipment. Following this, the eji were divided between the left and right ejifu and the emonfu. They served in one-day-on, one-day-off rotations of watch, but were required to be on continuous call for emergencies. Even on their "days off," they were required to drill in military arts until noon and were not allowed to venture more than thirty *ri* (about 14 km) from their quarters without special permission.[43]

The troops who manned the left and right hyōefu were a very different breed of fighting man from the eji. The latter were simply peasants serving out a part of their corvée obligations; the former were government officials, men who had driven in their first pitons for a long ascent toward high court rank and position. Hyōe were appointed by their provincial governors from among the "sons and younger brothers" of district officials (gunji) and from among the sons of holders of the sixth to the eighth court ranks. They were tested annually for military and other skills, and were eligible for promotion to higher civil or military posts.[44]

Pedigree in the Five Guards was reflected in chores, for it was the hyōe, not the eji, who protected the immediate persons of the emperor and his household.[45] The hyōefu guarded the innermost gates to the imperial palace; the emonfu and ejifu stood watch at the outer and middle gates. And in imperial processions, the hyōefu was assigned to travel directly before and after the emperor's Phoenix Cart, while the ejifu defended the perimeters of the entourage.* This division of responsibilities between the eji and the hyōe is of no little significance; it attests to a fundamental skepticism on the part of the ritsuryō architects about the quality and reliability of the peasant conscripts, who filled out most of the uniforms in the new imperial military system. The draftees provided essential numbers for the central military institutions—which, in the late seventh and eighth centuries, were required to defend and police capitals of ever-expanding scale. But for the most critical tasks, the imperial house and its supporters felt better served by the juniormost members of their own class than by peasants of involuntary employ and uncertain dedication.[46] Increasing reliance on the martial skills of the lower nobility and other provincial elites in parallel with a diminishing use of troops conscripted from the ordinary peasantry is a dominant theme in the evolution of Japanese military institutions between the eighth and tenth centuries. It is material to note that the same psychology and concerns that underwrote this devel-

---

* *Ryō no shūge*, p. 673; *Ritsu*, p. 27. The palace, or *daidairi*, was enclosed within three sets of walls. Under the Yōrō Codes, the gates on the outermost wall were called the *gūjōmon*, those on the middle wall the *gūmon*, and those on the inner wall, closest to the emperor, the *kōmon*. The Taihō Codes apparently called these the *gaimon*, *chūmon*, and *naimon*.

opment were present from the outset of the ritsuryō military system.

The foregoing has been, in a sense, an extended prologue to the story I will relate in the subsequent pages of this volume. In the chapters that follow, I will trace and explain what is perhaps best termed the metamorphosis of the imperial military corpus; for, as we shall discover, while the form changed dramatically, the essence was never really lost. In order to understand its transformation, we need to appreciate three fundamental points about the imperial military system. First, it did not feature a large standing army. The core of the system, the provincial regiments, was a militia, not garrisons. The majority of the troops registered within this militia spent most of their year tilling their own fields. They were called up in rotation for peacetime police, guard, and frontier garrison functions, and for the assembly of a wartime army. It is precisely the adoption of this sort of militia-based system that made it possible for a state at the level of development of Japan at the turn of the eighth century to muster very large-scale fighting forces when necessary without utterly destroying its economic and agricultural base. Second, control of the state's military resources and the authority to exercise martial force were the exclusive prerogative of the emperor and his court. Third, military service was a duty incumbent on all able-bodied adult male subjects, which meant that the imperial military comprised a complex of units manned mainly by peasant draftees. Yet provincial elites were by no means excluded from military functions. They served as officers for the provincial regiments, as hyōe in the capital, and in several other capacities as well. The privately developed martial talents of this group were a vital and integral element of the imperial military system.

By bearing these characteristics firmly in mind, we are now in a position to assess the changes to the imperial military institutions that occurred during the eighth century. The first and third points (the lack of a standing army and the mixed background of the soldiery) are central to comprehending why the changes were necessary, and to grasping why and how they took the form they did. The second point (imperial control) is material to the contention that I will develop in the next chapter: that the changes of the eighth century represent adjustments to—not the abandonment of—the state's military apparatus.

2

PEASANTS AND PROFESSIONALS

Raw in the fields, the rude militia swarms,
Mouths without hands, maintained at vast expense,
In peace a charge, in war a weak defense.
JOHN DRYDEN

All soldiers run away, madam.
THE DUKE OF WELLINGTON

My description in the preceding chapter of the military system established during the late seventh century betrays a bit of historiographical sleight-of-hand. I have depicted the components of the system in vignette, artificially divorcing them from the ongoing modifications that defined them. In so doing, I have merely painted an image of a child at rest; and no such still image can reveal much of the character, the dynamics of its subject. Much less can one conclude from a portrait of a child at three why he shows no interest in athletics at eleven.

Yet this is precisely the trap into which many scholars have fallen. By conceptualizing the ritsuryō military as a static edifice that either stood or did not stand, they have been led to view the emendations of the eighth century as halfhearted attempts to stuff bricks back into a collapsing wall.[1]

A careful examination of the history of the imperial military system, however, reveals a long, consistent pattern of modifications. Amendments began within months of the promulgation of the Taihō Codes and continued well into the thirteenth century. Throughout this process, the court was tinkering with its military institutions, not turning its back on them. As I shall demonstrate in the following pages, the proximate motivation for each particular change varied, but each served the common purpose of advancing the overall efficiency of the system.

SHORTCOMINGS OF THE IMPERIAL MILITARY

The institutions of the imperial military system were carefully adapted from those of T'ang China to meet Japanese needs. At the same time, however, they were the product of all-too-often-conflicting exigencies and thus incorporated a number of rather unhappy compromises. The original foibles of the system were, moreover, exacerbated by changing conditions: the needs and priorities of the Japanese state in the mid-eighth century were not the same as those in the late seventh.

One of the worst difficulties the government faced was enforcing its conscription laws. Under the ritsuryō polity, military conscription was simply one component of the state's tax requirements; induction rosters were compiled from the same population registers that were used to levy all other forms of tax.[2] For this reason, the peasants' efforts to evade any of these taxes served to place them beyond the reach of the conscription authorities as well.

Peasant flight to avoid taxes can be seen in the sources as early as 709 and had become a problem of epidemic proportions by the middle of the eighth century. In like manner, complaints of desertion and lackluster performance by military conscripts had already begun to surface in the early 700's; by 780, the situation was bad enough to bring officials to complain that "to send [these draftees] to fight would be to throw them away." Military reforms during the eighth and subsequent centuries are therefore closely analogous to the government's reshaping of its general tax structure and tax-collection mechanisms during the same period.[3]

Cavalry and Military Technology

Far more important than the reluctance of subjects to serve in the military, however, were the fundamental tactical limitations of the ritsuryō armies. The problem was that the premier military technology of the era was cavalry—specifically, mounted archery—whereas the imperial military, by virtue of its having been constructed around peasant conscripts, was predominantly an infantry force.

The origin of mounted warfare in Japan is a point of scholarly contention. On one side of the debate are those who see the genesis of the Yamato polity in an invasion by horse-borne conquerors from the continent. This invasion is variously said to have occurred in the mid- to late third century or in the late fourth to early fifth century. Other scholars dismiss the possibility of such an invasion and argue that the Japanese learned the techniques of warfare on horseback from their opponents during the excursions into Korea that began in the fifth century.[4]

There is, in any case, little doubt that cavalry was a central element of armies on the continent, or that equestrian culture was widespread in Japan by at least the late fifth century. One notes, for example, that the majority of the armored *haniwa*

FIGURE 3. Left: *Haniwa* figurine wearing *keikō*-style armor. Right:
Artist's recreation of *keikō*. Reprinted from Sasama,
Nihon kōchū-bugu jiten, pp. 2, 6.

figurines discovered in eastern Japan are clad in a style of armor
called *keikō* or *kakeyoroi* (literally, "hanging armor," probably
because it was suspended from one's shoulders). Made from
iron or leather platelets strung together in strips, it was the fa-
vored type of armor among the horsemen of the continent.
The strips were assembled in overlapping rows to form a long-
skirted jacket that closed in the front or on the side. To this
were added a helmet with a wide, sweeping tail to cover the
neck, and shoulder pieces, gauntlets, and leg armor (see Fig.
3). Enclosing the entire body this way afforded great protection, but the outfit was also terribly heavy. It was clearly armor
for horse-borne, not infantry, warfare.[5]

In any event, by the late seventh century, cavalry had clearly come into its own in Japan. It was cavalry, not infantry, that proved to be the decisive element when Emperor Tenmu swept to victory in the Jinshin War of 672–73.[6] Cavalry continued to be a key factor in the fighting that accompanied later civil conflicts as well; horsemen carried the day for the court in Fujiwara Hirotsugu's rebellion in 740 and in the revolt of Fujiwara Nakamaro in 764.[7]

The value of cavalry certainly did not escape the notice of the Japanese court at the time the ritsuryō codes were written. This can be seen in the numerous exhortations in the codes for soldiers to train with "bow and horse," in the requirements that regimental officers and hyōe be skilled in mounted archery, and in the fact that special contingents assembled as shows of force for ceremonies attendant on the arrival of foreign emissaries were invariably cavalry. Nevertheless, the ritsuryō armies were predominantly infantry forces.[8] This infantry-heavy balance was partly a matter of design and partly a matter of necessity.

The imperial military was contrived to meet two major threats: invasion from the continent and challenges to imperial house and/or central court prerogatives from the regional nobility. Large-scale, direct conscription of the peasantry was an important part of the answer to both dangers.

To neutralize threats from domestic sources and ensure that no one would ever repeat Tenmu's capture of the throne by force, the court needed to take direct control of whatever military resources might be available to would-be emperors. We have seen how the ritsuryō codes subordinated the former provincial patriarchs in the military chain of command to centrally appointed provincial governors, and divorced military from political authority at the district level. As a corollary to this, the state needed to minimize the ability of potential rivals to raise forces outside the system. The surest way to do so was to corner the market on military manpower. If the court could create loyalist armies of daunting volume, and if all or most of the bodies that could be drawn off to serve as soldiers were already incorporated into the state's military machine, the door to military challenges to the imperial polity could be effectively closed. This is precisely what the ritsuryō military statutes did, mandating that one of every three free fit men be carried on the military rosters.* An army of imposing numbers was also, of course, exactly what was needed to cope with the anticipated invasion from T'ang China. But the court was opting for size at the expense of the elite technology of the age, choosing a force composed primarily of infantry rather than cavalry.[9]

*But there is evidence to suggest that this mandate was not followed in practice. An imperial edict of 732, for example (quoted in *Shoku nihongi*, 732/8/22), ordered that troop strength in several provinces be brought up to "the full, one man for every *four* [emphasis added] specified by the *[ritsu]ryō* codes." This discrepancy has led Japanese scholars to a long and generally inconclusive search for the true conscription formula. In 1959, Ishio Yoshihisa added further confusion to the question when his examination of three early-8th-century population registers led him to conclude that conscription was based not on the number of adult males per province, but on the number of legal households (*ko*): one heishi, he asserted, was drawn from each household (Ishio's "one household, one heishi" thesis has provoked vigorous criticism and equally vigorous defense, but, even if correct, it does not explain the discrepancy between the one-in-three ratio given in the ritsuryō codes and the one-in-four ratio cited in the 732 edict. A comparative analysis of all extant population registers from this period, moreover, reveals that none of these three formulas was consistently employed (Yamanouchi, "Ritsuryō gundan ni kansuru," pp. 38–40). Perhaps the most reasonable explanation of all is Muraoka Kaoru's suggestion that the numbers of heishi conscripted from a given area varied with the total number needed at any given time. That is, the guidelines established by the ritsuryō codes notwithstanding, no fixed ratio or formula for troop conscription was ever followed in practice ("Enryaku 11 nen," p. 35).

The state did try to maintain as large a cavalry force as possible, but the effort ran afoul of two major logistical difficulties. In the first place, there was the considerable expense of raising, training, and keeping so large a stable of horses. In the second, fighting from horseback was an extraordinarily complex skill to master, one that required years of training and practice. It was simply impossible to produce first-rate cavalrymen out of short-term, peasant conscripts. These problems were addressed by drawing cavalry troops from among only those who already possessed the necessary skills, and by making the care of the state's war-horses the responsibility of private parties.

In early Japan, cavalrymen were born, not made. The ritsuryō codes provided that all new recruits "be assigned to companies and squads. Those skilled with bow and horse were to be placed in cavalry companies; the remainder were to be placed in infantry companies."[10] The government expended minimal effort training ordinary conscripts as horsemen, preferring instead to rely on the talents of those who had acquired skills in mounted archery before their induction.* In similar fashion, the codes directed that, of the horses received as tax or tribute, or raised in state-owned pastures, "all those suitable for riding be attached to the regiments. These were to be assigned to the care of soldiers from those regiments whose families were wealthy and able to care for the animals." Horses so assigned were to be looked after and brought along at times of

---

*One exception to this practice was the soldiers serving in the capital as eji; another was a 724 order (quoted in *Shoku nihongi*, 724/4/14) to train 30,000 men from nine provinces in eastern Japan to fight with horse and bow. To come up with such numbers, the authorities would clearly have had to draw the majority of the would-be cavalrymen from among the infantry.

mobilization. Animals that died (except under unavoidable circumstances) were to be replaced by the family that was caring for them.[11]

The effects of these policies were twofold. They meant, first of all, that only a small portion of the imperial armies could be cavalry. They also meant that the cavalry would be composed solely of the scions of the elite elements of provincial society. For if the prerequisite for becoming a cavalryman was skill with "the horse and bow" before induction, cavalrymen could have come only from backgrounds in which they could acquire this skill privately; that is, only from families that possessed horses. The practice of keeping horses did not spread beyond the provincial nobility and the very top tiers of the peasantry until the middle years of the Heian period.[12] Thus, in military as well as economic and social status, this segment of the rural population was set apart from the rest, and was accorded a monopoly among the emperor's subjects over the elite military technology of the day.

All of this is not to say that the ritsuryō armies were utterly incompetent fighting forces. At the outset, at least, the infantry companies were well equipped, well trained, and supported by an effective artillery. The training conducted for imperial soldiers has been amply discussed by Japanese scholars but, owing to the paucity of sources, remains poorly understood. Nevertheless, it is clear that troops serving duty in the provinces were required to drill during each watch, while those serving in the capital as eji spent every other morning training with "bow and horse, sword and spear, ōyumi [see below] or sling." In the provinces, this training was supervised jointly by the regimental colonel(s) and the provincial governor or assistant governor. In the capital, it was conducted by the ejifu or emonfu officers in charge of each watch. Each sol-

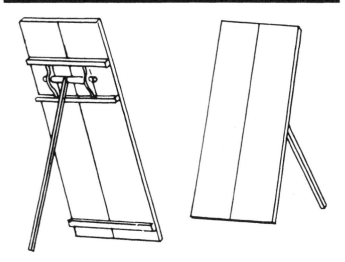

FIGURE 4. Japanese shield. Reprinted from Sasama, *Nihon kōchū-bugu jiten*, p. 426.

dier in the regiments carried a bow and quiver, fifty arrows, a pair of swords, and an assortment of support equipment. In addition, each five-man squad fought behind a shield.[13]

Shields were used in Japan from ancient times and continued to be employed into the Kamakura period and beyond. But as the illustration in Figure 4 shows, they were far different from the handheld shields most familiar to Western readers. Rather, they were large wooden barriers, approximately eye level in height and about the width of a man's shoulders, used as a sort of portable wall. The best were constructed from a single board, but most were made from two or even four planks. They were made to stand by means of a pole, or foot, which fitted into the back and could be folded against the shield for carrying—in advance or retreat—or for storage.[14]

By far the most important weapon of the imperial armies was the artillery piece called the ōyumi. "Among the weapons

of this court," wrote the tenth-century courtier Miyoshi Kiyotsura, "the ōyumi is god. . . . The old tales tell us how the Regent Jingū had it made [following] a wondrous inspiration."[15]
The unlikelihood of such a venerable origin notwithstanding,
the device was clearly in service in Japan by the time of the
Jinshin War and remained so at least until the early tenth century. In the provincial regiments, two soldiers from each fifty-
man company were designated as ōyumi operators, and these
twenty to forty or so men were divided equally between the
various watches. The weapon was also used by the Five Guards
in the capital.[16]

The form of the ōyumi is not actually known, since no
drawings or detailed descriptions of the Japanese version survive. The same character (read *nu* in Chinese) was used in
China to name several types of crossbow, but the Japanese
weapon does not seem to have been the same as any of these.[17]
A late-seventh-century source, which informs us that "the
ōyumi were lined up and fired at random; the arrows fell like
rain," suggests that it may have been a kind of multiple arrow
launcher.[18] (For one artist's conception, see Fig. 5.) Kiyotsura
referred to the ōyumi as a primarily defensive weapon, but it
must in any case have been formidable. A petition to the court
from Mutsu province declared that "when ōyumi are brought
into the fighting, even tens of thousands of barbarians cannot
bear up to the arrows of one machine. The savages stand in awe
of [its power]."[19]

As redoubtable a weapon as the ōyumi seems to have been,
it was also a very complex machine to operate. This in fact appears to have been its undoing. Between 814 and 901, the court
received requests for ōyumi instructors from a full seventeen
provinces. All had the same complaint: regrettably, the weapons in their armories were going to waste because no one knew

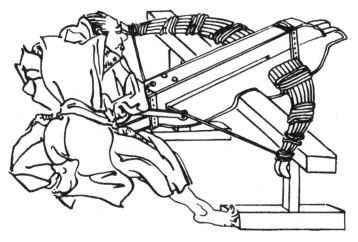

FIGURE 5. Artist's conception of an ōyumi. Reprinted from Sasama, *Nihon kōchū-bugu jiten*, p. 392.

how to use them.[20] In his memorial of 914, Miyoshi Kiyotsura went further, complaining of the incompetence of even the teachers:

> At the time of their appointments, those named do not yet even know of the existence of the weapon called the ōyumi, still less how to use the springs and bowstrings. Although the realm is now at peace and we fear nothing from any direction, we must each day be cautious, never forgetting danger. For, however unlikely, what if there should come invading neighbors who challenge us with death? The weapon has become empty nostalgia; who can use it [in our defense]?[21]

Diminishing Returns on the Provincial Regiments

The ritsuryō planners had done a competent job of playing the hand they had been dealt; the military institutions they created were adequate to the task set before them at the turn of the eighth century, when they were designed. But by the middle of that century, the political climate both domestically and abroad had changed enough to render the provincial regiments anachronistic and superfluous in most of the country.

The Chinese invasion the Japanese had so feared never materialized. The real threat, if indeed the danger was ever real, was probably over by the late 670's, when the kingdom of Silla forced the T'ang out of the Korean peninsula and checked its eastward expansion. Midway through the eighth century, a rebellion by a Turkish general named An Lu-shan shook the T'ang dynasty to its foundations and made it abundantly clear to the Japanese that the specter of Chinese ships appearing over their horizon had faded.[22] The threat of challenges to the central polity from the regional nobility also dwindled rapidly in the decades after the Jinshin War. By the mid-eighth century the former provincial patriarchs had accepted the imperial state structure as the arena in which they would compete for power and influence.

The relaxation of these two threats reduced the necessity of a large army. The need to garrison the southwestern frontier did not vanish, of course, nor did the problem posed by the emishi in the northeast. Nevertheless, the military demands of the interior provinces—the vast majority of the country— were quickly pared down to the capture of criminals and similar police functions. For this, the unwieldy, artillery-backed infantry units based on the provincial regiments were neither necessary nor well suited. Small, highly mobile squads that could be assembled with a minimum of delay and sent out to pursue raiding bandits were far more appropriate to the task at hand. It was accordingly on the development of units of this nature that the court now began to focus its attention.

Meanwhile, the diminishing military need for the gundan promoted the misuse of the regiments by their officers and by provincial officials. As early as 704, one finds admonitions that soldiers were "not to be used for purposes other than those specified by statute." A 753 Council of State edict complained that provincial officials "violate the law and use troops for private labor. Soldiers throw away the bow and arrow and attend the plow. Henceforth violators shall be relieved of office and made ineligible for future posts."[23] Complaints of this nature were repeated with some frequency in the ensuing half-century.

The state responded to the various shortcomings outlined above with a series of adjustments, amendments, and general reforms of its military institutions that continued into the medieval era. The nature of this process in later centuries will be taken up in due course; here we will confine ourselves to the developments of the eighth century.

We have seen that the bulk of the manpower for the imperial military was drawn from the general peasantry. But we have also seen that the ritsuryō codes presupposed the private cultivation of martial skills by provincial elites and the lower elements of the central nobility. It was these groups that were moved to center stage by the military reforms of the 700's.

THE PASSING OF THE PROVINCIAL REGIMENTS

The first major adjustment to the provincial military system occurred in 719, when the numbers of regiments, officers, and soldiers were reduced nationwide, and eliminated entirely in the provinces of Awaji, Wakasa, and Shima. The generalized cutbacks may have been, as Yamanouchi Kunio believes, a move by a sympathetic government to soften the tax burden of the peasantry or, as Nakata Katsumi has suggested, simply a readjustment to bring military rosters into more realistic line with population size. But the out-and-out abolition of the three regiments appears to have been a matter of administrative efficiency. All three of the provinces in which gundan were dropped were tiny. A 729 tax register for Shima reveals only 932 adult males in the entire province—807 if one excludes temple and shrine servants. This means that the gundan in Shima would have consisted of between 200 and 270 men, at best half the size of the smallest regiments anticipated by the Yōrō Codes. The time and effort involved in training and administering such tiny units probably outweighed whatever military value they might have had, inducing the government to trim them away as unneeded fat.[24]

In 739, the court discontinued the operation of gundan in all but the frontier provinces and those that contained the barriers protecting the approaches to the capital. Some scholars have interpreted this as a direct sequel to the 719 abrogations, but this view does not adequately explain why the regiments were revived only seven years later, in 746. The discontinuation was, in point of fact, intended from the first to be a temporary measure: in the words of the 739 edict implementing it, heishi inductions and service were simply to be terminated "for a while" (shibaraku). The reason for the hiatus lies in the smallpox epidemic that began in Kyushu in 735 and swept across the country over the next eight or nine years. With the disease claiming the lives of up to 70 percent of the peasants in some areas, the court was forced to curtail military conscription in all but the most strategically vital regions. The regiments were not abolished and later restored; they were simply suspended for the duration of a crisis.[25]

Nevertheless, the court's dissatisfaction with the gundan appears to have been acute by the 780's. In the third month of 780, the government grumbled that most of its soldiers were unfit for service and ordered that "those already conscripted who so desire should be released, and the weak returned to their farms." In their stead, "wealthy commoners skilled with the bow and horse" were to be sought out and inducted. In 783, the court made a similar complaint and directed that future conscription be centered on "the sons of those with rank but without posts and the sons and younger brothers of the idle rich." A 788 order similarly demanded that induction efforts concentrate on men with cavalry skills and/or combat experience.[26]

In 792, the government at length arrived at the conclusion that in most of the country the gundan system had become more trouble than it was worth:

> The soldiers exist for emergencies, yet in recent years provincial officials and regimental officers have used them unreasonably, thus wasting public funds and showing themselves to be evil officials. . . . Henceforth, the regiments shall be abolished in the capital region and the provinces of the seven circuits, thereby eliminating an onerous burden.* However, Mutsu, Dewa, Sado, and the provinces under the jurisdiction of the dazaifu are strategic areas wherein defensive preparations must not be lacking. Heishi shall continue in these places as of old.[27]

In 802, Nagato was added to the list of "strategic areas" and a regiment revived there, but for most of the country, the gundan system had been done away with once and for all in 792.[28]

These developments took place against a background of near-continuous warfare with the emishi in the northeast. The emishi had been an annoyance to the Yamato court ever since its inception. But the court had bided its time in trying to extend its authority into northeastern Japan, confining itself at

---

*The ritsuryō codes grouped the provinces into the Capital Region (or *kinai*) and seven circuits (*dō* or *michi*): the Tōkaidō, Tōsandō, Hokurikudō, San'indō, San'yōdō, Nankaidō, and Saikaidō.

first to providing a haven for colonists who had pushed the ritsuryō state's borders into emishi homelands. Settlers, or *kinohe*,
were protected by a series of stockades, or *ki*, into which
they could retreat in times of trouble. This more or less
passive approach was dropped around 730, when the court's
policy toward the northeast turned from one of enforced col-
onization to one of military occupation, centered on the newly
created chinpei. In 737, Ōno no Azumabito led a large and generally unsuccessful suppression effort into Mutsu. From this
time forward, violent confrontations with the emishi became
more frequent, as the court's objective shifted from simple ab-
sorption to military conquest and subjugation.[29]

In 774, the court committed itself—albeit with some internal opposition—to a policy of "pacification" that would take
more than three decades to complete. Two days after this policy was adopted, emishi attacked Momonō stockade in Mutsu, and
Ōtomo Surugamaro was placed in charge of catching them.
The struggle quickly grew to include the emishi of Dewa as
well. The campaign was temporarily halted in 778, but on
New Year's Day in 780, emishi attacked and burned peasant
homes in Nagaoka. The government responded by establishing an additional stockade near the Iji district. This in turn
sparked a revolt by the emishi leader Iji no Azumaro in which
one of the Japanese commanders was killed, and an important
stockade captured. The army sent against them was a dismal
failure and broke up in 781 with the court not even sure if Iji
was still alive. An army sent out in 788 also met with a mis-
erable defeat—including the loss of over 1,000 men—at the
hands of another emishi leader, Aterui. The next expedition,
in 789, was an abysmal failure as well. In 794 and 801, enormous campaigns, involving some 100,000 and 40,000 troops,

respectively, were undertaken. Details on these are scant, but the last, led by Sakanoue Tamuramaro and resulting in the surrender of Aterui, was declared a success, bringing this stage of the court's northeastern frontier policy to a close. Henceforth, the emishi were considered pacified, although small-scale rebellions continued to break out from time to time into the tenth century.[30]

That the court should have chosen to abolish most of its provincial regiments while in the middle of prosecuting a war says much about the problems it was encountering with the regimental system and about the nature of the war itself. There is nothing to indicate that the court perceived its actions in 792 as in any way weakening or curtailing its military machine. On the contrary, the regiments were eliminated in the interest of increasing the overall strength and efficiency of the state's military forces, much as a boxer will trim excess weight before a match.[31] In this context, it is important to keep in mind that both the gundan and the chinpei were retained in Dewa and Mutsu, where the fighting was taking place. In the interior provinces, however, the regiments had simply become more of a liability than an asset.

As the complaints from all quarters indicate, soldiers in much of the country were not receiving the kind of training they were supposed to get and were in fact being misappropriated as slave labor by provincial officials and regimental officers. The gundan were, in other words, of little value as sources of troops and were instead abetting corruption among government officials. The pattern of the edicts on the regiments issuing from the court during the 780's, moreover, indicates that the government had reached the conclusion that it was more efficient—and probably cheaper as well—to rely on the privately acquired military skills of the provincial elite than to continue to attempt to conscript and train the peasantry at large.

The nature of the fighting in Dewa and Mutsu made this policy even more attractive to the court. The emishi were superlative mounted archers. As one source put it, "Horse-and-bow warfare is learned from birth by the barbarians. Ten of our subjects cannot equal one of them."[32] The court armies were, as we have seen, predominantly a mixture of light and heavy infantry and light artillery, fighting with swords, and with bow and arrow and ōyumi from behind portable wooden shields.

In principle, the government forces should have enjoyed a distinct advantage over their opponents on the battlefield. Generally speaking, an archer on foot has much the better of it in combat with a bowman on horseback. He has the benefits of a stable platform and the ability to give his full attention to his shooting, allowing him both a higher rate of fire and greater accuracy. He can also, as the Japanese did, shoot from behind a standing shield, protected from his adversary's arrows. The horseman, on the other hand, must divide his attention between operating his weapon and controlling his mount, cannot employ a shield (since both hands are already occupied), and must shoot from a moving, bouncing platform. The fundamental battlefield superiority of the imperial armies over the emishi is, in fact, confirmed by the very source we heard before singing the praises of the emishi's skills in mounted archery: "yet when ōyumi are brought into the fighting, even tens of thousands of barbarians cannot bear up to the arrows of one machine."[33]

As long, therefore, as the court's objectives in the northeast were confined to injecting Japanese settlers into the region and to defending those settlements, the ritsuryō armies were more than up to the job. But when, in the late eighth century, the court adopted a policy of thoroughgoing "pacification," the situation changed. Since the Japanese were now attempting to control not just bits of territory but the (hostile) population residing on and around them as well, their opponents could mount a very troublesome resistance simply by adopting hit-and-run guerrilla tactics.

This is precisely what the emishi did, forcing the Japanese to grapple with a classic problem in military strategy. A large body of troops was still required to occupy and defend conquered lands. But no army, no matter how large, can be everywhere at once. The strength of the raiding strategy the emishi adopted lay in the ability of small, highly mobile bands to refuse combat with an otherwise more powerful opponent—to strike in areas where the enemy's forces were weak or nonexistent and then to flee before troops could be brought up to counterattack. To wage a successful campaign against an enemy of this sort, the court would have required both a large infantry force to garrison wide areas against the emishi and a skillful cavalry to pursue raiders and conduct search-and-destroy operations.

There is evidence to indicate that the court had been experimenting with cavalry forces outside the normal gundan structure for some time. The *Shoku nihongi* describes part of the anti-emishi campaign army of 737, for example, as consisting of "196 cavalrymen, 499 chinpei, and 5,000 heishi." The 196 cavalrymen distinguished here from the rest of the heishi were part of a force of 1,000 horsemen raised by the provinces of Hitachi, Kazusa, Shimōsa, Musashi, and Kōzuke. In 740 (a year *after* the provincial regiments had been suspended), "400 cavalrymen from the east and west" were mobilized. And a

780 order to officials in Kyushu directed that "when enemy
ships arrive at our coast, . . . heishi and their officers, and
peasants skilled with horse and bow, should be formed into
companies" and sent out to meet the invaders.[34]

Beyond the fact that the horsemen referred to in these and
similar sources were clearly not ordinary heishi, there is little
that can be said about them with certainty. It is not clear how
often or by what mechanism such cavalry contingents were assembled, although the numbers involved preclude the likelihood that they were as yet a major component of the state's
military. Nor does it appear that they represented an additional
military institution. The circumstances of their use and creation vary too greatly for that; in all likelihood they were simply
ad hoc creations and experiments.

The eighth century did, however, witness the birth of one
addendum to the imperial military, at least part of which involved cavalry. I refer to the well-known but poorly understood institution of kondei.

KONDEI

One week after the Council of State abolished the provincial
regiments, it issued an edict establishing a nationwide system
of kondei, or "stalwart youth," to be selected from among the
"sons and younger brothers" of district officials.[35] The close
timing of the two edicts and a reference in the second to the
dissolution of the gundan have led scholars to conclude that
kondei were intended as a replacement for the regiments in all
manner of military affairs. This view, pioneered by Nishioka
Toranosuke in 1928, long remained the accepted explanation
for historians on both sides of the Pacific. According to Nishioka, the court's objective in implementing the kondei system
in 792 was to replace the troublesome and inefficient regiments

Kondei Unit Strength by Province, 792

20 men: Izumi	30 men:	60 men: Tōtomi
	Wakaba	
30 men:	Yamato	100 men:
Aki	Yamashiro	Echigo
Awa		Echizen
(Kantō)	50 men:	Harima
Awa	Bingo	Ise
(Shikoku)	Bitchū	Izumo
Awaji	Bizen	Kazusa
Iga	Etchū	Kōzuke
Iwami	Hōki	Mino
Izu	Inaba	Sagami
Kai	Iyo	Shimotsuke
Kawachi	Mimasaka	Shinano
Kii	Nagato	
Mikawa	Nōtō	150 men: Musashi,[a]
Oki	Owari	Shimōsa
Settsu	Sanuki	
Suo	Suruga	200 men: Hitachi,
Tango	Tajima	Ōmi
Tōsa	Tanba	

SOURCE: *Ruijū sandaikyaku*, 2: 558–59.
[a]The 105 in the document is probably a typographical error.

with a more elite military drawn from among the same segment of the population that had been serving as officers and
cavalrymen within them: the provincial gentry.[36] Though this
was indeed the objective behind the 792 military reforms, kondei were not the new fighting force the court had in mind.

The numbers of kondei specified for each province alone
render Nishioka's hypothesis unlikely. The 792 directive provided for only 3,200 men nationwide (see the accompanying
table). Kondei unit strength in most provinces was between
thirty and sixty men, and even the largest contingents—in
Ōmi and Hitachi—had only 200. In contrast, several later
sources call for provinces to raise forces of 1,000 men or more
for various military tasks.[37] Moreover, the kondei of each
province were required to serve a maximum of four fifteen-

day watches a year. This means that the total number of "stalwart youths" on duty in a province at any one time was between five and thirty-four, hardly a formidable fighting force. There are virtually no examples in any source of kondei performing generalized police functions or serving in combat. The single exception occurred in 857, when the governor of Ōmi was specifically ordered to use kondei to help man the two new barriers that were to be erected at Ōishi and Ryūge (a barrier had existed at Ōsaka since the seventh century).[38]

The most likely thing, then, is that the kondei units established in 792 were intended to perform exactly those duties with which the document charges them: to guard "the armories, bell storehouses, and government headquarters" of the provinces in which they were formed. This is in fact the view now held by most Japanese scholars.[39] It is even questionable to what extent the kondei represented an elite military organization. The Council of State's edict specified that they be drawn from the families of district officials. And yet five years later, in 797, the court found it necessary to order that provinces cease recruiting ordinary peasants as kondei. In 804 and again in 810 it reversed this decision, directing that peasants be used to fill out kondei ranks whenever necessary.[40]

Moreover, 792 did not mark the nascency of kondei in Japan. The first appearance of the term in a Japanese source is a *Nihon shoki* entry for 642, in which we learn that a number of "kondei" were ordered to wrestle for the amusement of visitors from the Korean kingdom of Paekche. The term appears again in the *Nihon shoki* in 663, when the king of Paekche ordered his kondei to execute, and pickle the head of, a general he suspected of treason; and then again when the same monarch reported to his court that Omi Ihohara no Kimi would soon be arriving from Japan at the head of 10,000 kondei.

None of these examples suggest that "kondei" at this time referred to anything beyond its literal meaning of "stalwart youth."[41]

But an auxiliary military corps known as kondei was established—or added to—in 733, when a court decree dictated that "300 heishi shall be made kondei." This force may well have been established at least a decade earlier; a series of documents from Ōmi province indicates that one Otomo Kibimaro served as a kondei between 725 and 734. It is difficult to judge exactly what this organization was. The documents cited above make it clear that though at least some of these men were simply regimental soldiers (heishi) serving special duty, others were from provincial elite families. Some or all of these kondei appear to have been cavalry. And they would seem to have been more stalwart than youthful: Kibimaro, the only individual we can identify as a kondei during this period, was thirty-five when he entered the service and forty-four when he left it. We also know that kondei existed countrywide. A 734 edict directed that kondei "of the various circuits" be excused from paying half their rice (densō) and miscellaneous labor (zōyō) taxes. Beyond this, we know only that the institution was short-lived. It was terminated in "the Tōkai, Tōsan, San'in, San'yō, and Saikai circuits" in 738.[42]

In 762, the kondei were revived on a limited basis. "In the four provinces of Ise, Ōmi, Mino, and Echizen, sons and younger brothers of district officials and the [elite] peasantry, between the ages of twenty and forty and skilled in the use of horse and bow," were to be selected to serve. In accord with the 734 precedent, the new kondei were to be excused half their rice and miscellaneous labor taxes. This incarnation of the kondei appears in one, and only one, source. Thus, as with their predecessors, we know nothing about their function, or even their numbers. What we do know is that these units were intended to be an elite cavalry of some description, and that they must have fallen under the supervision of the provincial governor, in the same manner as the gundan, since we are told that annual reports on kondei were carried to the hyōbushō by the same envoys who carried the annual status reports of the provincial government to the Council of State.[43]

In any event, whatever hopes the government had for the kondei system that was activated nationwide in 792, the new forces did not function well for long. In a little over half a century, in fact, the quality of the troops had declined to the point where the Council of State lamented:

> When there is peace, we must not forget danger; when order prevails, chaos should not be forgotten. Such are the most profound teachings of the ancients. . . . Currently those who serve as kondei lack ability. They are called teeth and claws in vain, being no different from the defenses of the praying mantis. Why do they no longer train? How shall they ward off sudden enemies? If one walks ten paces, one finds fragrant grasses; in one hundred fortresses are there no soldiers of spirit?[44]

Be that as it may, the kondei were not abolished; they continued to function as a component of the provincial government office until at least the end of the Heian period.[45]

THE EMERGENCE OF THE SIX GUARDS

In the capital, the emonfu and the two ejifu were beleaguered by the same problems with their peasant conscripts as plagued the provincial regiments. More important, the Five Guards system as a whole began to warp and buckle under another sort of pressure.

It has often been assumed that at least the early years of the imperial state were characterized by a court in which the emperor held transcendent power and authority and the great noble houses served him as obedient bureaucrats. But though there is no disputing the political authority of the ritsuryō emperor, his political power was circumscribed. Many of the same great houses that had dominated the Yamato court during the first half of the seventh century continued to dominate the imperial government throughout the eighth. And the ritsuryō codes themselves placed a number of practical checks on the emperor's ability to exercise his authority arbitrarily. The result was a political milieu in which the emperor remained largely the primus inter pares figure he had been in the pre-Taika era. Political power during the eighth and ninth centuries was, as Bruce Batten has observed, extremely fluid, with control of the court tending to swirl back and forth between the emperor and other elements of the aristocracy.[46]

Political competition at court between the imperial house and the other great noble houses, then, was intense during the eighth century. And in this struggle, control of martial resources of one sort or another could be an important asset. In a political arena in which attempts at assassination or coups were not infrequent, private soldiers were needed to protect the persons as well as the status of the top courtiers and their heirs. The great families, accordingly, began to assemble private military forces and to press for control of state military resources. This development is reflected in the recurring references in the amnesty edicts of the day to the crime of stockpiling weapons.[47]

Changes to the military system in the capital began in the first decade of the eighth century, propelled by the pressure placed on the system by the political dynamics of the court. As the century progressed, courtier houses vied with one another to recruit men of martial talent into the ranks of their household service and to staff the officerships of the central military units with their own kinsmen or clients. An imperial edict of 728, for example, complained of difficulty in assembling men of military skill for service at court because of the large number who had been drawn off for private service by the aristocracy.[48] Within this atmosphere, the state's central military institutions began to bend and transform.

One of the most critical points of contention in court politics was the matter of imperial succession. Under the ritsuryō codes, this was ostensibly a private concern of the imperial house—the designation of an heir was supposed to be left entirely to the discretion of the reigning monarch. But in most instances, descent lines were thoroughly entangled by the partisan interests of the other noble houses in the candidacy of one prince or another. The result was a political atmosphere charged with plots and treachery, one in which the physical elimination of an opposing candidate or his spokesmen was often viewed as more efficacious than simple debate.

In this dangerous situation, the Five Guards were of little value to an emperor, for they were the military forces of the state as a corporate whole, not the personal military of the sovereign. Effective control of this public military was a function of the same factors, the same political competition, that determined political power at court in general. The goefu were reliable in intracourt disputes only insofar as the emperor could count on the support of their officers—or rather on the support of the family or clique to which those officers belonged.[49]

Acutely aware of its own vulnerability, the imperial house responded to this danger by creating new military organizations outside the goefu—its own Praetorian Guards. The intention in each instance was to establish forces dependent on and loyal to the ruler who fashioned them. The long-term effect was the complete reorganization of the state's central military institutions.

The Establishment of the Chūefu

In 707, just four days after her accession, the Empress Genmei formed a new corps of fighting men, which she called the *jutō toneri ryō*.[50] Its purpose was to protect and ensure the succession of her grandson Prince Obito, the future Emperor Shōmu. The background to this move is a bit complicated.

The illustrious Emperor Tenmu had died in 686, leaving the throne to his son Prince Kusakabe. When Kusakabe died abruptly in 689, his mother, who had been acting as regent since Tenmu's death, ascended the throne as Empress Jitō, in order to preserve the succession for Kusakabe's eight-year-old son, Prince Karu.* As soon as Karu came of age, Jitō abdicated in his favor, and in 697 he became Emperor Monmu. He reigned for only ten years. At the time of Monmu's death, *his* son, the crown prince Obito, was only seven years old, and so Monmu's mother assumed the throne as Genmei in order to hold it for him.

The accessions of Monmu and Genmei, and the selection of Obito as crown prince, had all met with considerable opposition at court.[51] This put Genmei and her grandson in a precarious position. Jitō and Kusakabe had been able to trade on the immediate legacy of the unusually powerful Tenmu to ensure their position; Monmu had had the backing and protection of a living former sovereign (Jitō). But Monmu's untimely death

---

*Karu was both grandson and nephew to Jitō, who was a daughter of Tenmu's brother Tenchi. It is not clear why Jitō waited three years before enthroning Kusakabe or formally taking the throne for herself. She may have done so in imitation of the Chinese custom of observing a three-year mourning period following the death of an emperor.

had left Genmei and Obito to fend for themselves. Genmei understandably felt an acute need for additional protection for her crown prince. Her answer was the creation of the jutō toneri ryō.

To man her new unit, Genmei selected troops, called *azuma toneri*, of similar background to the hyōe of the left and right hyōefu; that is, scions of the provincial elite and lower central nobility. To command it, she turned to her most natural political allies at court, the Fujiwara family. Obito was the grandson of Fujiwara Fubito by his daughter Miyako. This family connection was, in fact, one of the reasons for the opposition to him. The crown prince's ties to the Fujiwara were made even stronger in 716, when he married another of Fubito's daughters, Kōmyō. The Fujiwara thus shared with Genmei a strong desire to see Obito elevated to the throne.

Genmei had added reason to choose the Fujiwara for her commanders, namely, to change the balance of military ascendancy at court. At the time, the Fujiwara had virtually no influence within the goefu. Until the 730's, the top posts in the Five Guards were monopolized by old military houses like the Saeki and the Ōtomo. If that was her goal, the plan succeeded famously. The Fujiwara were to dominate the jutō toneri ryō for the next hundred years; all but two of the first twenty-two men to command the unit were Fujiwara.[52]

In 724, Obito became Emperor Shōmu. Four years later, in 728, the jutō toneri ryō was reorganized and renamed the *chūefu*. The new unit was a qualitative departure from the ritsuryō Five Guards. To begin with, in place of the titles of *kami*, *suke*, *jō*, and *sakan* (director, assistant director, secretary, and clerk) used for the officers of the Five Guards and most other ritsuryō offices, the chūefu staff were styled *taishō*, *chūjō*, *shōshō*, *shōken*, and *shōsō* (grand general, middle general, lesser general, captain, and lieutenant). Plainly, these titles were based on the nomenclature applied to the general staff for expeditionary armies; they were probably selected to underline the new organization's military prowess. The ranks stipulated for those who held the posts were all a step or two higher than those specified in the Yōrō Codes for the equivalent posts in the other guard units. This most likely reflects Shōmu's desire to tip the military balance at court away from the goefu.[53]

In any event, the transformation of the jutō toneri ryō to the chūefu converted it from a private corps of imperial guards to a public military unit, equivalent to, albeit slightly higher in status than, the units of the Five Guards. By the late 730's, its duties appear to have become essentially similar to those of the left and right hyōefu: to guard the persons of the emperor and his household and to patrol the palace and the streets of the capital.[54]

The Establishment of the Kon'efu

During the 720's and 730's, the court was dominated by Fujiwara Fubito's sons, Muchimaro, Fusasaki, Umakai, and Maro. The situation changed abruptly in 737, however, when all four succumbed to an epidemic of smallpox that was sweeping the country.[55] The breach was filled by an anti-Fujiwara clique led by Tachibana Moroe.

The following year, Shōmu named his daughter by Fujiwara Kōmyō, Princess Abe, crown princess. This choice of successor was vehemently opposed by the Tachibana clique, which was not eager to see another Fujiwara sovereign ascend the throne. Abe's designation, moreover, represented a sharp break with precedent. Up to now, female monarchs had always succeeded sons or husbands; no emperor had ever before named a daughter to succeed him. The opposition to Abe rallied around her ten-year-old half-brother Prince Asaka.[56] Asaka's candidacy came to an unceremonious end in 744, when he was suddenly stricken with leg pains and died the same day.* But opposition to Abe did not end there; in fact it remained strong even after her eventual accession as Empress Kōken. A year later, it was Shōmu himself who fell mysteriously and gravely ill. Seeing the specter of his own death looming before him while his designated heir was opposed by a powerful clique, he sought to protect his daughter and her succession by creating a new version of the same institution his grandmother had established to protect his own accession. In 746, he gathered a force of armed bodyguards, which he named the *jutō toneri*.[57]

This unit bore no direct relationship its nominal predecessors, but the reuse of the name plainly indicates that the jutō toneri were intended for a similar purpose. This point is reinforced by the wording of an edict Shōmu is thought to have given Abe when he ceded the throne to her in 749: "We gave swords to men from the east and had them serve, in order that they might protect your person."[58] The number of jutō toneri in 746 is unknown, but ten years later there were 400 of them. Initially, they appear to have answered directly to Shōmu, but following his death in 756, the supervision of the group passed to the chūefu, although the troops themselves remained distinct.[59]

In 758, Empress Kōken (Abe) abdicated in favor of Emperor Junnin. But she remained politically active.† She soon found

---

*Historians have long speculated that Asaka may have been the victim of a Fujiwara assassination.

†It was not unusual for abdicated sovereigns to retain a measure of political influence. Kōken, however, was exceptional in the degree to which she attempted to control the court. She treated the reigning emperor, Junnin, as a

herself at odds with Fujiwara Nakamaro, son of Muchimaro and an erstwhile supporter of Junnin, who had quickly moved to manipulate the new emperor to his own advantage.[60] Nakamaro had been serving as Grand General of the chūefu since Kōken's accession in 749, a post that, the *Shoku nihongi* informs us, "gave him sole grasp of the important military affairs of state."[61] It was probably to offset Nakamaro's power that Kōken contrived in 759 to make the jutō toneri independent of the chūefu by shifting them to a new unit with its own independent staff of officers. She called the new organization the *jutōe*. Five years later, Kōken discovered Nakamaro plotting against her with Junnin and maneuvered him into a revolt. The fighting in this short-lived rebellion was largely between the Nakamaro-dominated chūefu and the Kōken-controlled jutōe. In the aftermath, Kōken exiled Junnin to the province of Awaji and reascended the throne as Empress Shōtoku.[62]

In 765, about six months after Nakamaro's ill-fated rebellion, Shōtoku reorganized the jutōe and renamed it the *kon'efu*, giving the new corps a set of officers of similar nomenclature to, but of slightly higher court rank than, those of the chūefu. At about this same time, she also established a third extra-codal guard organization, called the *gaiefu*, with officers of the same title and rank as those of the chūefu. Her intention was plainly to offset the organization that Nakamaro had dominated for so long. Her choice of names for the new units is probably significant in this regard. The "*chū*" ("inside" or "middle") of the chūefu was most likely originally meant to signify the inside

---

virtual puppet and, when this proved difficult, had him deposed; eventually, she took the throne for herself (in 764) as Shōtoku. The potential power that the Japanese political system made available to retired monarchs was not fully realized until the late eleventh century, when former emperors became the dominant figures at court. On this phenomenon, see Hurst, *Insei*.

of the palace; the chūefu was to be the "inner-most guards," as opposed to the original Five Guards. Shōtoku now flanked it with the near (*kon*) and outer (*gai*)*efu*.[63]

There were now eight distinct guard units in the capital: the left and right ejifu, the left and right hyōefu, the emonfu, the chūefu, the kon'efu, and the gaiefu. This was obviously more military than was needed, and over the next several decades the court streamlined the system (the twists and turns by which this was accomplished are illustrated in Fig. 6).

In 772, the gaiefu was eliminated, and its troops divided among the kon'efu, chūefu, and the two hyōefu. During the first decade of the ninth century, the court began to trim away the excess manpower in the capital. In 805, 270 men were cut from the emonfu and the two ejifu; an additional 200 eji were cut in 808. That same year, the two hyōefu, the kon'efu, and the chūefu were also reduced by 100 men each.[64]

The institutions were also redone. In 807, the court noted that the functions of the chūefu and the kon'efu had become so nearly identical that the differing nomenclature no longer made sense. The two units were recast as the left and right kon'efu. Similarly, in 808, the functions of the emonfu were acknowledged to overlap with those of the ejifu, and it was merged into those two units. In 811, however, the name emonfu was revived, and the two ejifu were thenceforth known as the left and right emonfu. The new system became known as the *rokuefu*, or Six Guards, and continued without major formal change until the modern era.[65]

THE EXPANDING MILITARY ROLE OF ELITES

The ritsuryō polity severely circumscribed the opportunities for government service available to scions of provincial elites. The only administrative offices open to the members of this

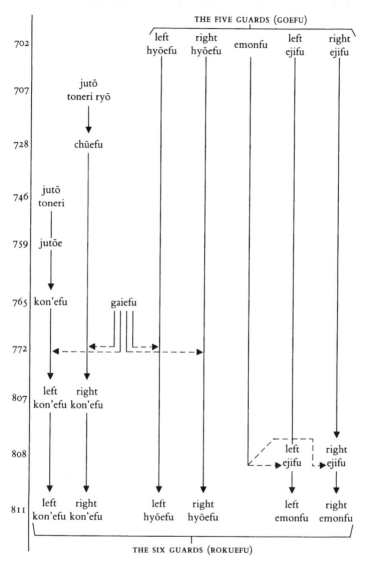

FIGURE 6. Evolution of central military institutions, 700–811.
Adapted from Sasayama, *Kodai kokka*, p. 127.

class were those of district official (gunji) and some very minor functions in the provincial office.* But there were still a few avenues for personal advancement open to an ambitious young gentleman unable to obtain a gunji post. One of these was the cultivation of military skills. As we have seen, young men of martial ability were eligible for appointment as officers within the provincial regiments or for service at court as hyōe.

The *kun'i*, or merit rank, system was another means by which those with martial talent could advance themselves. Originating with the Taihō Codes (702), the system allowed for promotion in rank as a reward for meritorious performance in battle. The kun'i (designated as first through twelfth *tō*) were parallel to the senior third through the junior eighth ranks of the normal civil hierarchy.[66] Following a military campaign, the performance of each soldier was assessed, on the basis of which he was awarded points (*ten*). The relationship between performance and points varied from campaign to campaign. "Points," explains the *Ryō no gige*, "have no fixed meaning; for example, in one year's campaign, the taking of ten heads may constitute a point, while in another year's fighting, five heads may make a point."[67]

Earning a prescribed number of points brought with it promotion in rank; the battlefield thus offered a soldier more than one means of getting ahead. The higher one climbed in the sys-

---

*See Morita, *Zuryō*, pp. 32–34. Provincial nobles were legally handicapped even by the system of court ranks. For those holding the sixth through the Initial rank, a distinction was made between Inner and Outer versions—that is, between rankholders belonging to the central versus the provincial nobility. This last point is discussed in detail by Kawahara, "Ritsuryō ikaisei," pp. 11–15. Kawahara argues, however, that the distinction was largely symbolic, superfluous to its purpose, and never rigidly enforced. Locals, he believes, were clearly seen as locals with or without the additional label "Outer" attached to their ranks.

tem, the more points were needed for promotion.[68] Though points in excess of what one needed for promotion could not be accumulated from campaign to campaign, they could be passed on to a parent or child. This clause applied even to soldiers who had received their commendations posthumously. Men of the fifth rank or higher who had no living parent or child were awarded two *chō* (about five acres) of paddy land for each extra point earned.*

The system was no empty legal fiction. The *Shoku nihongi* lists at least one example of ascent to the first merit rank, at least eleven instances of varying numbers of men being awarded second, at least nine examples of promotions to the third, fifteen cases of advancement to the fourth, and forty-four instances of men upgraded to the fifth through the twelfth ranks.

A third door that could be opened by military skill was service in the households of the top central nobility. The ritsuryō codes provided that high-ranking courtiers and imperial princes be assigned servants and attendants called *chōnai* or *shijin*. These attendants were selected from among the sons of nobles of middle and lower rank, and were appointed to their posts by the Ministry of Ceremonials (*shikibushō*). Duly recognized public officials, they were accorded public salaries and were subject to annual evaluation and promotion like the run-of-the-mill officials. At the same time, their relationship with the head of the household they served was more private than public; their masters had considerable say in their selection and appear to have paid for their service in part out of their own pockets.[69]

Ryō no gige, pp. 191–92. This land was classified as *shiden* (awarded fields) rather than *kōden* (merit fields) and therefore reverted to the state on the death of the recipient.

Semiprivate attendants such as chōnai or shijin were often used to guard courtier homes. We have seen that nobles were pursuing men of martial ability for these posts by the early 700's. This trend accelerated from the late eighth century onward.

The amendments to the regimental system during the eighth century, and the creation of the jutō toneri ryō, chūefu, jutōe, gaiefu, and kon'efu, greatly amplified the role of elites in the military establishment. Opportunities to parlay martial skills into career advancement were enhanced considerably. The heyday of the monk Dōkyō, Japan's Rasputin, was an especially fertile time. The violent upheavals that surrounded Dōkyō's regime (ca. 754–70) produced a situation in which military ability could bring spectacular jumps in rank, across gaps that could not otherwise have been bridged in a lifetime. Ishimura Ishitate, for example, who slew Fujiwara Nakamaro, was raised in a single step from Greater Initial Rank, Lower Grade—the third-lowest position in the hierarchy—to Junior Fifth Rank, Lower Grade—admitting him to the middle tier of the court aristocracy.[70] To be sure, upward mobility on this scale did not last long after Dōkyō's fall from power, but opportunities for the martially talented continued to grow steadily into the medieval era.

In the course of a little over a century, the battery of military institutions laid down in the ritsuryō codes were signally transformed. A courtier of 702 examining an organizational chart for the state's military system of 815 would surely have puzzled over what had become of the provincial regiments and the Five Guards, but he would not have been astonished by the answers. For the ritsuryō military system had not collapsed or been abandoned; it had simply evolved. It had evolved, moreover, in a steady, consistent pattern, and as I will demonstrate in Chapter 4, while the mechanics of the state's military apparatus changed radically, the principles that underlay it remained viable until the onset of Japan's medieval age.

The pivotal feature of this transformation was the state's increasing reliance on the martial skills of the provincial elite and lower central nobility, and the diminishing use of troops conscripted from the ordinary peasantry. The engine that drove it was the court's desire for maximum efficiency in its military institutions. In the provinces, the regiments were first augmented with special cavalry corps and then discontinued entirely, in favor of a more flexible system (which is the subject of Chapter 4); in the capital, the Five Guards were superseded by more dependable units manned by nobles and gentry.

Even in the early 700's, the state structure made the acquisition of martial skills an attractive path to personal advancement for provincial and low-ranking central aristocrats. The military system that unfolded over the eighth century paved this path and added lanes to it, making military abilities an increasingly traversable route to success. An important effect of this trend, one that was to have profound consequences in subsequent centuries, was to encourage the private cultivation of military skills. In the next chapter, I will explore the long-term repercussions of this development as I examine the emergence of private bands and networks of professional fighting men.

3

WARRIORS AND WARBANDS

Generally, the management of many is the same as the management of a few. It is a matter of organization.
SUN TZU, *THE ART OF WAR*

Fidelity gained by bribes is overcome by bribes.
SENECA, *AGAMEMNON*

The profession of arms is as old in Japan as the earliest forms of statecraft. The regional chieftains whose confederation produced the Yamato polity of the late sixth century and eventually the imperial state of the late seventh were military as well as religious and political leaders. Indeed, the foundation mythology of the imperial house is rife with images of weaponry and tales of combat.

Around the turn of the eighth century, the architects of the ritsuryō polity created an elaborate battery of military institutions centered on the principle of public conscription and training. Yet, as we have seen, the private cultivation of martial skills did not disappear. Quite the contrary, it was actively encouraged and exploited by both government military policy and the premier noble houses of the court.

A hundred years later, much of the ritsuryō military apparatus was dismantled as the state shifted to reliance on the privately acquired martial skills of provincial elites and members of the lower echelons of the court nobility. This policy was continued and refined over the course of the next four centuries. At the same time, the state itself was becoming privatized. A growing identity developed between hereditary status and government officeholding, and bit by bit certain key government functions came to be performed through essentially private channels. Correspondingly, public and private rights and responsibilities became increasingly hard to separate.[1]

Within this milieu, incentives toward private arms-bearing received new impetus and resulted in the emergence of an order of professional mercenaries. An early-eleventh-century text describes the archetypical member of this order:

> The husband of his second daughter is the greatest warrior in the land. He is highly skilled in the conduct of battles, night attacks, archery duels on horseback, and ambushes; in shining for deer;* and in all forms of mounted and standing archery competition, including *kasagake, yabusame, yatsumato, sanzaku,* and *tahasami.*[2] He is, moreover, heavenly gifted in the arts of donning armor, bearing bow and arrow, taking up his spear, and using a sword; in flying banners and setting up shields; and in directing companies and leading troops. A fierce and courageous man of great martial skill, he is known to emerge victorious from every battle site; he has yet to know the shame of submission to an enemy. He has the archery skill of Yang Yu and bears

---

*"Shining for deer" translates *tomoshi,* a style of hunting at night in which torches were used to locate deer. The eyes of a deer are highly reflective and appear to glow in the dark when struck by even small amounts of light (this same phenomenon can be observed today when driving at night past deer by the side of the road), making them easy targets for hunters equipped with torches (or flashlights), who need only shoot at the glowing eyes.

his quiver like the Crow Breaker.* Truly he can be said to be a match for a thousand men. I do not know his surname, but he is called Gen. His given name is said to be Kuntōji.[3]

It was the focus on the profession of arms as a means to personal success by sizable segments of the provincial elite and of the middle and lower central aristocracy that created and defined the Heian warrior order. Yet in the private acquisition of martial skills as such, Heian fighting men differed only in degree from their Nara predecessors. Of far greater consequence to the nature of the military and police system that developed during Heian times—and to the course of Japanese history—was the predilection of Heian warriors to arrange themselves into bands and networks. This greatly increased the efficiency of the services that the state or a private employer could draw on, because the responsibility for mustering and organizing the forces necessary to carry out an assignment could simply be delegated to warrior leaders, who could in turn delegate much of the responsibility to their own subordinates.

THE NEW HEIAN STATE

Over the course of the Heian period, profound changes occurred in the fundamental relationship between the central court and the provinces. While the provinces were not, as has often been suggested, simply left to their own devices, the mechanisms by which they were kept bound to the center changed considerably.[4]

---

*Yang Yu-chi was a famous archer of the state of Ch'u during China's Warring States period (403 B.C.–221 B.C.). "Crow Breaker" appears to refer to Yi I, an archer during the reign of the legendary Chinese emperor Yao in the third millennium B.C. According to a famous tale, Yi saved the world by shooting down nine of ten suns that suddenly appeared in the sky together one day and were setting fire to crops and trees. The nine extra suns turned out to be crows, whence Yi's nickname.

In the public sphere, this transformation revolved around changes in the tax system. The tax structure established in the late seventh century had been erected on the premise that all peasants were created equal; accordingly, taxes, in the form of labor, rice, and handicraft goods, were levied on a per capita basis.* But the theory behind the system failed to account for differences in individual ability: some peasants proved to be better—or luckier—farmers than others. Some were able to exploit the system successfully and make sustained profits year after year; others found themselves incapable of making ends meet, let alone meeting their tax obligations. The result, by the late eighth century, was a growing class stratification among the peasantry. Some grew wealthy, while others were forced to abscond or become dependent in some form on their more successful neighbors. A gap was developing between the structure of provincial society as envisioned by the ritsuryō authors and the reality in the countryside. As the gap widened, tax collection through the procedures set down in the ritsuryō codes became increasingly difficult. Bit by bit, the court became aware of this difficulty and took steps to address it.

Between the eighth and tenth centuries, the court gradually came to view the extraction of tax revenue more as a problem between the central and provincial governments than as one between the capital and the peasant population.[5] The tax system was therefore amended so that demands for revenues would be made of provincial governments rather than of peasants directly. The theory of direct individual responsibility for

---

*Strictly speaking, the ritsuryō tax system did not treat all peasants as undifferentiated equals. Minors, the elderly, women, and slaves were all treated slightly differently from free, adult males in terms of both legal obligations and privileges. A detailed discussion of the tax system appears in D. R. Morris, "Peasant Economy," pp. 42–106.

paying taxes did not change, but the court recognized that pressuring individual delinquents usually just resulted in their absconding. Henceforth, tax quotas were set by province, and provincial officials were made accountable for seeing that they were met. The means by which taxes were actually collected was left largely up to the officials responsible for payment. These officials, in turn, delegated most of the burden to local elites, who were charged with assembling the tax revenues due from specific locales in which they had influence. The lead in this direction appears to have been taken by the local elites, but with the state's tacit approval. That they were ready and able to take on this task should not be surprising, since these changes gave them a greatly expanded role in government administration within their bailiwicks and, along with this, new ways to increase their personal wealth and power. As Dana Morris observes, the new tax structure proved lucrative to both provincial officials and local tax managers, who quickly learned to collect revenues beyond their assigned quotas and pocket the surplus.[6]

Even as the state was redefining the nature of this fundamental aspect of the relationship between its central and provincial organs of government, the great houses and religious institutions in the capital were making concerted efforts to create and expand private sources of revenue and influence outside the official government structure. The efforts of court figures to advance their private interests in the hinterlands became a persistent source of trouble for provincial residents and officials from the 830's onward.[7]

"Temples, shrines, princes, and officials," we are told, were "behaving like peasants,"

contesting over peasant paddy fields and stealing movable property. They did not follow the orders of the provincial governor;

they ignored district officials. They invaded provinces and districts and used their prestige and influence to pressure [residents and officials]. They did not distinguish right from wrong. Because of this, paddies and fields were laid to waste; property became empty of value.

    . . .

In matters of paddy fields, homes, and property, these temples, shrines, and great houses did not go through the provincial governor [as the law required] but issued private house edicts directly to district officials and functionaries within the provincial government offices. . . . Moreover, they sent their messengers, who led followers through the provinces, causing major disturbances to peasant household activity and to provincial government business.[8]

Provincial governors, for their part, showed a marked inclination to regard their provinces as simple revenue-producing resources and became increasingly indifferent to the needs and welfare of residents. The fact that most provincial governors were able to amass sizable landholdings and build impressive homes attests that these were particularly lucrative posts. A reasonable estimate suggests that a typical governor was able to skim off about 10 percent of the total production of his province, an enormous sum for an individual.[9]

Problems with gubernatorial abuses of authority began to appear in the mid-ninth century. The extent of the problem can be imagined when one considers that during the whole of the century, only forty-four provincial governors were officially designated "Good Officials" (ryōshi). This is less than 3 percent of the 1,500-odd appointees who served over this time span; and even those who earned the appellation appear to have done so less often by positive activities than by simply not doing anything outstandingly wicked. Nor was the problem short-lived. Between the late tenth and early eleventh centuries, the court received a steady stream of petitions from provincial residents demanding the impeachment of rapacious governors.[10]

The most famous of these is one filed in 988 by the "district officials and peasants" of Owari province. The document accused the governor, Fujiwara Motonaga, of tax fraud, extortion, nepotism, murder, and a host of other greater and lesser crimes. He was said to have collected nearly three times the prescribed amount of taxes, often beginning his collection efforts as much as four months ahead of the traditional schedule and using agents who stole even the furnishings from the lodgings provided for them as they made their rounds. His relatives and followers, it was charged, were allowed to seize land throughout the province and operate it as private, tax-exempt holdings. They also "commandeered" horses and cattle from provincial residents and then sold them back several days later for three to five times their fair price.[11]

The situation that was developing from the ninth century onward, then, was in essence a competition for wealth and influence in the provinces between three groups: provincial-resident elites; provincial governors; and the "temples, shrines, princes, and officials" of the court. Of the multitude of stratagems pursued by the parties to this competition, two are of significance to the present study. First, all three sides were discovering and learning to exploit the value of vertical alliances between the groups. And second, certain elements within each of the groups were also learning the value of using military force in the competition. The second strategy provided an additional stimulus, over and above that created by state military policy, for the cultivation of private skills-at-arms. The first created the framework within which the private military networks of the middle and late Heian period could develop.

THE FORMATION OF VERTICAL FACTIONS

A cardinal feature of political activity at all levels of the Heian polity was what Cornelius Kiley has termed "consociation between persons of disparate status." Heian society was rigidly stratified. Functionally unbridgeable gulfs of station separated the top tier of court aristocrats (*kugyō*), the lower and middle-level central nobles who served as provincial governors, and the rural elite. For each stratum in this hierarchy there were reserved certain rights of access to specific types of government posts, rights over land, and forms of income. The rights and privileges of each stratum were sealed from below, as well as from above. That is, scions of the top court families were as effectively barred from assuming district and local government posts as provincial elites were from becoming top court officials. This formed a basis for vertical cooperation between members of different strata because neither party could effectively challenge the prerogatives of the other. Social disparity during the Heian period contributed to the solidarity of vertical factions, because each member of the alliance could aid the others in obtaining rewards for which he himself was ineligible.[12]

Thus the confrontation in the provinces that was developing between provincial governors, the great houses and religious institutions of the capital, and provincial elites resembled a competition among a butcher, a tanner, and a dairyman for the products of the same herd of cattle. The interests of each could often put them in conflict—the same cow cannot, for example, provide both milk and meat at the same time—but they could also be mutually supportive—the same cow *can* readily be used for both meat and leather.

The members of all three groups found vertical alliances

with members of one or both of the other groups useful in forestalling rivals and horizontal competition within their own strata, and in offsetting the advantages of adversaries from other strata.

Alliances of this sort were probably most thoroughly institutionalized at the top, that is, between lofty aristocrats and elites of the provincial governor level. This phenomenon has been discussed in some detail by G. Cameron Hurst. Heian court society, he observes, was dominated by a small number of high-ranking nobles who were heads of powerful familial interest groups. These familial interest groups developed out of the system of semiprivate household officials, established by the ritsuryō codes, that I discussed in the previous chapter. Men of the provincial governor class, that is, courtiers of the fourth and fifth court ranks, would attach themselves to powerful nobles by becoming members of their household staffs. In exchange for the performance of miscellaneous personal services by the lower-ranked noble, the kugyō would in effect become the man's patron and would sponsor his advancement at court.

The system worked to the advantage of both. It permitted top courtiers to exploit both the administrative talent and the private wealth of provincial governors in the administration of their private affairs, and it assured provincial governors of continued appointment to lucrative posts. The patron–client relationship, then, was rooted in mutual need; the need of the kugyō for administrative help within their households, and the need of lower-ranking courtiers for kugyō to sponsor their interests. The accepted manner for would-be clients to enter the service of a patron was to call on him at his residence and request an audience (*kenzan*). The junior figure would then present his name placard (*myōbu*) and pledge to render loyal service to the patron, whom he referred to as lord or master (*nushi* or *shujin*). For his part, the new patron was henceforth obliged to look after the needs of his client, normally by sponsoring his career at court.[13]

Alliances were also developing between senior court figures and provincial elites. By the late ninth century, the latter were clearly learning to use their connections—real or pretended—with the former to gain greater autonomy from the provincial government. A petition from Settsu, for example, complained: "Natives and drifters claim to be housemen of princes and government officials. They do not fear the authority of the governor and do not obey the injunctions of district officials."[14] Thirty years later, the Council of State observed that "evildoers claimed to be housemen of princes and government officials and behaved violently, refusing to obey the governments of provinces and districts."[15]

During the eleventh and twelfth centuries, linkups between rural magnates and powerful central nobles became centered on the practice of land commendation. A great deal has been written on this exceedingly complex phenomenon and to do the topic justice would take us much too far afield from the central issues of this study. Briefly, it was a process by which provincial elites contrived to convert certain special rights they possessed over an ostensibly public piece of land into a private domain by negotiating to have the land declared a private estate (*shōen*) of a powerful court figure. Once this had been accomplished, the local magnate's rights over the land would be confirmed by the estate owner, not the government, and the taxes that had hitherto been forwarded to the government via the provincial governor would now go to the estate owner.[16]

A third type of alliance was a more purely local one—the private connections that linked provincial officials and the residents of the provinces to which they were appointed. During the Heian period, governors and assistant governors found that they could use the power and perquisites of their offices, and the strength of their court connections, to establish landed bases in their provinces of appointment and to continue to exploit the resources of these provinces even after their terms of office expired. As early as 797, one finds central government complaints of problems caused in the hinterlands by "officials who have finished their terms of office and by sons and younger brothers of princes and court officials." Such figures, we are told, were "settling down in their [former] areas of jurisdiction. They hindered agriculture, gathered up the peasantry like fishermen gathering fish, and constructed plans for their own evil gains." This trend was clearly both widespread and enduring. The court issued repeated prohibitions against it in 797, 842, 855, 884, 891, and 895, in areas as far apart as Kyushu and Kazusa.[17]

The practice of elements of the central nobility "settling down" in the provinces is a well-known phenomenon of the Heian period, but expressed in these terms, the concept is a bit misleading, for few central aristocrats actually abandoned life in the capital for a provincial existence. Typical exurban provincial officials concluded marriage and other alliances with local figures and held packages of lands scattered about the countryside, which provided them with income. At the same time, they maintained extensive contact with political affairs in Heian-kyō and nearly always maintained homes there, to which they shipped most of the profits from their rural enterprises. Some individuals and branches of families became more thoroughly committed to a provincial existence than others, but most were still careful to keep their ties to the capital alive. They could not afford to do otherwise, for to cut oneself off completely from the court was to cut oneself off from the source of gubernatorial appointments and thereby end all hope of maintaining one's social and political position. To provincial governors and their families, Heian-kyō was the source of the human and physical resources that made their provincial business activities possible, as well as the marketplace for the goods they brought from the country. By the same token, they used their provincial activities to reinforce their foothold within the political and official world of the capital.[18]

An often-cited example of this type of existence is the case of Fujiwara Kuromaro and his descendants, who "settled" in the province of Kazusa on Kurihara Estate. Kuromaro established a private pasture on this piece of land, probably in the late 770's, when he was serving as governor of Kazusa. He passed it on to his son, Harutsugu, who lived on the estate and was apparently buried there. In addition to his activities in Kazusa, Harutsugu was active in Hitachi, serving as assistant governor there and marrying the daughter of a local magnate. Harutsugu's son Yoshinao served in Kazusa as assistant governor and as acting assistant governor, and held provincial official posts in several other provinces as well. But through all this, Kuromaro and his heirs remained firmly part of the world of the capital. Harutsugu served as deputy director of the Office of Central Affairs (*nakatsukasa no shō*). Yoshinao also held a number of central court posts and was known to have been "a resident of the capital" and "a close retainer of Emperor Montoku."[19]

PRIVATE LURES TO PRIVATE ARMS

We saw earlier that during the eighth century a major inducement to the private development of skills-at-arms among provincial elites was the possibility of parlaying such abilities into personal advancement through official and semiofficial channels. This sort of incentive waxed appreciably during the Heian period. But from the ninth century onward, certain martially adept provincial residents were also learning that service to the court was not the only use to which their skills could be put. A significant element was turning to outlawry either in addition to or as an alternative to public service. From around the turn of the ninth century, there was a steady stream of government complaints about troubles caused by armed bands of marauders: bandits and pirates.[20] These outlaws "burned people's homes and used weapons to rob" and "strode about the villages opposing government officials and intimidating the poor," "interfering with government business" and "harming public morals." They also conducted regular raids on government tax shipments, stealing not only the tax goods themselves but also the horses and boats used to transport them. "For a single, worn-out packhorse, they would take a peasant's life."[21] By the middle of the ninth century, the problem had become endemic. "Warnings and admonitions pile up," railed a Council of State edict, "yet we hear that the activities of bandits do not cease, they become worse. All who travel by land or sea lament the damages they cause."[22]

Provincial residents were not the only ones employing physical force outside the law in the countryside. Government communications also speak of "men of power and influence" or "government officials and their housemen . . . forcibly impressing men and horses passing through [certain provinces], causing much suffering for the people." Throughout the ninth and tenth centuries, "agents of temples, shrines, government officials, and great families . . . formed bands and blocked packhorses on the road, . . . led followers near the ports to rob tax shipment boats," and engaged in "the forced confiscation of boats, carts, horses, and men."[23]

Provincial officials, compelled by a need to defend themselves and their prerogatives against this sort of outlawry and armed tax resistance, as well as by simple greed—the desire to expand their take from their provinces by all means fair or foul—also began to add a private martial component to their authority. "True and righteous government," admonished an eleventh-century set of instructions to governors, "has no need of warriors. Yet the hearts of men are like those of wolves. In times of crisis, warriors must be employed." Governors were therefore enjoined to include a few "warriors of ability" among the personal entourages that accompanied them to their provinces of appointment. This practice appears to have been thoroughly institutionalized by the end of the tenth century.[24]

Gubernatorial military retainers (usually referred to as *rōtō*, *jūsha*, or *rōjū*) were normally recruited in the capital and traveled with their master to his new post.* They were drawn from several different sources. Some were young members of the

---

*The use of the terms rōtō, jūsha, and rōjū was not restricted to the military followers of provincial governors. "Jūsha" was a generic term for "retainer" or "follower" and was used to describe all manner of men in service to kugyō and other central nobles. "Rōtō" and "rōjū" appear to have been essentially interchangeable and were used in two overlapping contexts. They were applied to the higher-ranking retainers in a provincial governor's entourage, men who served as general functionaries in the provincial government, not just as soldiers (*Shin sarugakki*, p. 148). They were also used to refer more generally to military followers of all sorts, including even those of men who were themselves rōtō of governors (*Dainihon shiryō*, series 1, 2: 641, 898/12/13 Isei kugyō chokushi zōrei; *Nihon kiryaku*, 989/11/23; *Chūyūki*, 1092/5/23; *Konjaku monogatari shū*, 25.6). On rōtō as nonmilitary figures, see Batten, "State and Frontier," pp. 79–81.

governor's own household, for whom service as a rōtō was a step toward a career in government. For others, being a governor's retainer was in itself a career. Some served a single man over the course of several appointments to different provinces, while others moved from governor to governor.[25]

Noble-sounding rhetoric notwithstanding, rōtō appear in the sources far more often as private thugs than as servants of the public good. In fact the same document that offered the elevated raison d'être quoted above also contained repeated cautions to governors to keep their retainers under control.[26] The activities of the armed followers of provincial governors are dramatically and hyperbolically described in the petition of Owari district officials and peasants cited earlier. These agents, we are told, would "enter the domain and torture the population":

> For the sake of their own honor and reputations they willfully pluck out people's eyes. Arriving at people's homes, they do not dismount but enter on horseback. Mounted retainers and followers tear down wooden screens from homes and carry off tax goods. Those who dare to protest this injustice are meted out punishment. Only those who offer bribes are spared. . . . The relatives and retainers [of Governor Fujiwara Motonaga] are no different from barbarians. They are like wild wolves. They butcher human meat and use this as ornaments for their bodies. They rob things from the people and take these to their homes in the capital. There is not one thing that meets their eyes that they fancy but do not take.[27]

In addition to what appears to have been a near-universal practice for career provincial officials to employ military followers, a significant number of these officials cultivated their own martial skills. In a well-known document from the middle tenth century, the province of Suruga requested permission for

provincial and district officials to arm themselves. The petition
cites the murders of a district official and a governor's deputy
(*mokudai*) two years earlier as a result of "private grudges and
resistance to tax collection," and notes that Kai, Shinano, and
other provinces had requested and received similar permission
a decade or more earlier. But provincial officials had been
training in military arts for well over a century before the Suruga petition. Fujiwara Yoshinao (whom we met earlier) is an
example. He is described in his obituary as "an aficionado of
the martial arts, surpassing other men in his strength of arms."
Another is Fun'ya Makio (died 887 at the age of seventy-eight),
who served as a provincial official in six different provinces.
He is described as a man of "courage and power" and as "a
superlative mounted archer," who "did not like reading books
but studied the horse and bow." An even earlier example is Fujiwara Masao, who died at the age of forty-five in 811. A governor of Bizen and assistant governor of Ōmi, Masao was
known as "a man of surpassing courage and high skill in the
martial arts."[28] Obituaries from the first half of the ninth century indicate that men like Yoshinao, Makio, and Masao were
by no means unusual.[29]

Fighting ability would unquestionably have been useful to
provincial officials in winning the respect of, or intimidating,
armed residents of their provinces. In this regard, it could
serve some of the same purposes as the employment of warrior
rōtō. But martial talents could also strengthen a provincial official's position at court—and thereby speed the advance of his
career.

In the first place, an officership in one of the Six Guards or
in the later established Office of Imperial Police (*kebiishi-chō*)
was one of the more attractive posts open to young nobles at
the lower end of the rank scale. For many would-be governors,

in fact, such posts became the first step into state service, and a sizable percentage held a number of appointments to military/police organizations during their careers. Fujiwara Yoshinao is a case in point. Yoshinao was the third generation in his family to serve as a provincial official. He was born in 817, the great-grandson of Fujiwara Muchimaro, the founder of the southern branch (*nanke*) of the Fujiwara clan. Little is known of his early career, but at the age of thirty-three, he was appointed Acting Captain (*gon no shōken*) of the right kon'efu. Four years later, he became Acting Senior Secretary (*gon no daijō*) of Yamato, while still retaining his kon'efu post. In 855, he was promoted to Junior Fifth Rank, Lower Grade, became Lesser General (*shōshō*) of the right kon'efu, and was appointed to the assistant governorship of Yamato. The following year, he became assistant governor of Kazusa. About this same time, owing to his post in the kon'efu, he became an Imperial Private Secretary (*kurōdo*) and a close retainer of Emperor Montoku. In 859, he was named Lesser General of the left kon'efu and acting assistant governor of Kazusa. He resigned the latter post the next spring and became acting assistant governor of Ōmi. In the winter of 860, he was raised to Junior Fifth Rank, Upper Grade, and in 866 he was raised again, to Senior Fifth Rank, Lower Grade. He was promoted again in 869 to Junior Fourth Rank, Lower Grade, and made Acting Middle General (*gon no chūjō*) of the left kon'efu. In 875, he was promoted a final time to Junior Fourth Rank, Upper Grade, and named director (*kami*) of the right hyōefu and governor of Sagami. He died in 877 at the age of sixty.[30]

But a post in the capital military or police agencies was not the only way—or even the best way—for a man with military skills to accelerate his official career. Of even greater importance were the back doors—entrance into the private service of important court figures—that could be opened in this manner.

The political atmosphere of the court during the Heian period was such that the sponsorship and patronage of powerful courtiers were vital to any young man who hoped to succeed. At the same time, the upper nobility had, as we have seen, been collecting men of military talent to serve as bodyguards and private troops since the early 700's.* An important confluence of interests thus existed between a top courtier in search of private muscle and a young noble with martial skills in search of a patron. It is hardly surprising that a number of would-be governors should have recognized this fact and moved to exploit it. Both Fun'ya Makio and Fujiwara Masao, in fact, started out this way. Makio began his career as a military retainer (*tachihaki toneri*) of Prince Michiyasu (the future Emperor Montoku) and later served in the right hyōefu and the left kon'efu, in addition to his provincial appointments. Masao was "a close retainer of Emperor Heijō," who accompanied the sovereign on processions in and out of the capital "bearing bow and sword."[31]

Increasingly, military service at court and service as a provincial official became parallel and mutually supportive careers for certain Heian nobles. The result was the appearance of figures like Minamoto Mitsunaka (912–97),

> a warrior without peer in this world, as a consequence of which he earned the trust of the emperor and was employed for important tasks by ministers, great nobles, and the people of the world. . . . For long years he served at the court and as the governor of various provinces. His might and influence were with-

---

*The right of the topmost courtiers to maintain fighting men in their household service even enjoyed some degree of official recognition. Periodic state edicts appeared from the early 700's granting such figures specific permission to employ as many as 100 "sword-bearing attendants" (*tachihaki shinin* or *jutō shinin*). See, among others, *Shoku nihongi*, 720/3/12, 721/3/25, 759/11/30, 762/5/28, 764/9/16.

out equal. . . . He had many sons, all of whom were experts in
the way of the warrior.[32]

THE EMERGENCE OF WARRIORS AT COURT

As the statement about Mitsunaka's sons implies, by the middle of the tenth century, skill at arms within the court was
coming to be identified with certain families, not just individuals. This development was in keeping with a generalized
trend during the middle and late Heian period for central aristocratic houses to become hereditarily identified with certain
occupations and posts.[33] Possession of military skills and service in public or private military offices did not by any means
become the exclusive property of any of these families—even
within the capital—but references in the literature of the period to men who, "although not [themselves] of warrior
houses," were "of fierce courage and masters of the way of the
bow and arrow" suggest a growing public equation of this
profession with certain specific houses.[34]

Mitsunaka belonged to a branch of the Seiwa Genji; the
other lineages most often identified as warrior houses were an
offshoot of the Fujiwara referred to by historians as the Hide-
sato-*ryū*, or bandō Fujiwara, and a few branches of the Kammu
Heishi.* Collectively, the scions of these houses formed what
Japanese scholars have dubbed the *miyako no musha*, or "warriors of the capital."

The *miyako no musha* were men of the provincial governor
class—men of the fourth or fifth court rank—who used the

*The term Genji is derived from the Sino-Japanese reading of the surname
Minamoto. The Seiwa Genji, then, were the Minamoto line that claimed descent from Emperor Seiwa (r. 858–76). "Hidesato-*ryū*" means "the line to
which Hidesato belonged" (i.e., the lineage of Fujiwara Hidesato). The bandō
region was the provincial base of this Fujiwara line. Similarly, "Heishi" is a
sino-Japanese reading of the surname Taira. The Kammu Heishi were the
branches of the Taira descended from Emperor Kammu (r. 781–806).

profession of arms as a vehicle for more general career advancement. That is, they sought the patronage of the higher nobility and recognition by the state by serving as bodyguards and police in—and also outside—the capital. They were, to borrow a phrase from Jeffrey Mass, "bridging figures," men who maintained close economic and personal ties in both the capital and the provinces, but who resided primarily in the capital and who looked chiefly to the central court for their livelihoods. It is mainly this central direction of their career emphasis, rather than pedigree or residence as such, by which "warriors of the capital" can be distinguished from "provincial warriors." In any event, the *miyako no musha* were not nearly so few as the limited number of surnames might suggest, since there were a good many competing houses within each clan.[35]

The term Seiwa Genji actually refers not to one lineage group but to many. Emperor Seiwa had nineteen sons, the descendants of nine of whom bore the surname Minamoto. The lines of most interest to military historians claim descent from Seiwa's sixth son, Prince Sadazumi, through his son Tsunemoto, who fathered nine sons, at least three of whom became warriors of some reputation. The most important of these was his eldest son, Mitsunaka, whom I introduced above. It is of Mitsunaka and the progeny of his three eldest sons, Yorimitsu, Yorichika, and Yorinobu, that historians generally speak when they refer to the Seiwa Genji.[36]

The warrior Fujiwara were a branch of the Northern (*hokke*) Fujiwara (the same line from which the Regent's House, or *sekkanke*, emerged), descended from Fujiwara Uona (721–83). Uona was a major court figure (he rose to Senior Second Rank and held the post of Minister of the Left), but none of his sons climbed higher than the fifth rank. It was his fourth son, Fujinari, who became the ancestor of the warrior branch of the clan. Fujinari, a career provincial official, established a base for himself and his descendants in Shimotsuke and married the daughter of a resident of that province. His eldest son, Toyozawa, also married a local woman, as did Toyozawa's son Murao. Although some medieval texts, such as the *Azuma kagami*, make claims of military service to the state for Toyozawa, Murao's eldest son, Hidesato, was the first scion of his family who can be identified as a warrior in contemporary sources.[37]

The Kammu Heishi can be divided into four main lineages, the descendants of four different princes. The warrior line began with Kammu's eldest son, Katsurahara, through his son Takami and grandson Takamochi. Takamochi was presented with the Taira surname in 889 and appointed assistant governor of Kazusa. According to tradition, he was given both the appointment and the name as a reward for his activities in suppressing an attempted court coup during the reign of Emperor Uda (r. 887–97). Although there is good reason to doubt the accuracy of this story, the fact that Takamochi's descendants believed in—or created—such a venerable military tradition for their house is significant. In any event, Takamochi had eight sons. All established bases for themselves and served as provincial officials in various locations in eastern Japan. The descendants of four continued to obtain posts in provincial and central government offices and developed formidable reputations as military servants for the court for several generations. The others appear to have committed themselves to a more thoroughly provincial existence within a generation or two. The most successful of the four warrior lines were the descendants of Takamochi's first son, Kunika (also called Yoshimochi), particularly those of Kunika's eldest son, Sadamori.[38]

Scions of the bandō Fujiwara can be identified as martial ser-

vants of the upper nobility and/or as holders of central court
military posts down to the end of the Heian period. But they
never achieved the sort of sustained prominence at court that
the Minamoto and Taira did. Hidesato and his progeny enjoyed their greatest measure of success as provincial, not capital, military figures. The most spectacular example here is
Hidesato's great-great-great-grandson Tsunekiyo and his
heirs, who, on the strength of marriage ties to powerful northern warrior houses, managed to establish what came near to
being an autonomous kingdom in Mutsu province from the
late eleventh century to the late twelfth.* Other bandō Fujiwara laid down deep roots throughout the north and east.
Some of the most illustrious warrior houses of medieval Japan
claim descent from Hidesato, notably, the Satō, the Ōtomo,
the Mutō, the Iga, the Matsuda, the Oyama, the Shimokabe,
and the Sano.[39]

From the late tenth to the early twelfth century, warriors of
Minamoto descent dominated the military world of the capital
owing to a combination of martial prowess and a hereditary
client relationship with the Fujiwara regents.† In 995, for ex-

*Tsunekiyo married a daughter of Abe Yoritoki, Minamoto Yoriyoshi's op-
ponent in the so-called "Former Nine Years' War" of 1055–62. Both Tsunekiyo and Yoritoki were killed during the conflict, and in the aftermath, Tsunekiyo's widow married the son of Kiyowara Takenori, one of Yoriyoshi's most
important allies. As a reward for his services, Takenori was given most of the
property interests formerly held by the defeated Yoritoki. Added to his own
lands, this made him a truly formidable power in northern Japan. But not so
formidable as Tsunekiyo's son Kiyohira, who inherited most of Takenori's
holdings, was to become. Kiyohira turned his inheritance into an empire that
endured until 1189, when it was destroyed, along with his great-grandson Ya-
suhira, by Minamoto Yoritomo. For more on Kiyohira and his "empire," see
Takahashi Tomio, *Hiraizumi*.
†The alliance between the Fujiwara regents (sekkanke) and the Seiwa Genji is
thought to date to 969, when Mitsunaka helped Fujiwara Morotada eliminate
his chief court rival, Minamoto Takaakira. Morotada's success in this affair

ample, three of the four warriors summoned by Middle Counselor (*chūnagon*) Fujiwara Akimitsu to apprehend robbers in
the capital and surrounding mountains were Minamoto (Yorinobu, his brother Yorichika, and his uncle Mitsumasa). Until
the early 1100's, it was usually men of the Minamoto surname
to whom the court turned for martial service.[40]

The military preeminence of the Genji peaked during the
mid-eleventh century with the careers of Yoriyoshi (995–1082)
and his son Yoshiie (1041–1108). Yoriyoshi, we are told,
"loved martial valor and many submitted to him. So great
were the deeds and majesty of Yoriyoshi that rebels all became
as slaves to him. He loved his warriors and enjoyed bestowing
things upon them. The greater part of those of the way of the
horse and bow east of Ōsaka became his followers."[41] Yoshiie
was an even more colorful figure. To his contemporaries and
to subsequent generations of Japanese warriors, he was
"Hachiman Tarō" Yoshiie—the First Born of Hachiman, the
deity of war. "Yoshiie was of surpassing courage, he shot arrows from horseback like a god. . . . With his great arrow-
heads, he shot down enemy leaders again and again, never
loosing an arrow in vain, always hitting his mark. Like the
thunder, he rushed; like the wind, he flew. He was divine valor,
alive in this world."[42] Yoshiie's prestige was so high, in fact,
that he became the object of the sort of land commendation
normally reserved for much higher-ranking nobles, a practice
that the government found it necessary to forbid.[43]

But Minamoto fortunes waned considerably during the next
few generations, prompting one contemporary observer to
moralize that "the late Yoshiie was an outstanding warrior, but

(known to historians as the Anna Incident, after the calendar era in which it
occurred) left him virtually unchallenged at court. The ensuing patron-client
bond between the two houses endured for several generations.

he took many innocent lives, and these sins have been visited on his posterity."[44] During the late 1090's, Taira Masamori, the head of a theretofore relatively minor branch of the Kammu Heishi, managed to establish for himself and his family a similar patron-client relationship with successive retired emperors (*in*) as existed between the Minamoto and the Fujiwara Regent's House.* By the second decade of the twelfth century, the strength of this new alliance and Masamori's martial prowess had brought the Taira to full parity of prestige with the Minamoto at court. This situation was to endure until the 1150's, when the events of the Hōgen and Heiji incidents all but destroyed the Seiwa Genji and set the stage for first Taira Kiyomori's brief domination of the court and then Minamoto Yoritomo's revolt in 1180.[45]

HEIAN PRIVATE MILITARY NETWORKS

The warrior alliances of the Heian period are commonly referred to by Japanese historians as *bushidan* (literally, "warrior groups"). But for several reasons, I find it advisable to avoid the use of the term. To begin with, it is a historiographical, not a historical term, one that first came into use during the 1930's. Contemporary sources speak of *ikusa* (translated by William R. Wilson as "warbands") in the context of the battlefield and make no references at all to organizations as such in other contexts. Instead they use a variety of terms on the order of "follower," "retainer," "minion," and "henchman." Presumably, each of these expressions initially designated a specific type of relationship, but in most cases any distinctions they drew ap-

---

*This alliance is thought to date from 1097, when Masamori commended several parcels of land in Isei to Roku-jō-in, one of many chapels through which the *in* controlled his land proprietorships. Further details on this relationship and its development can be found in Mass, *Warrior Government*, pp. 15–30.

pear to have been lost rather quickly. In any event, the precise meanings of this terminology need not concern us here. The point at issue is that it was necessary for historians to invent an umbrella term—bushidan—to refer to the panoply of private military organizations that appeared in Heian Japan because no contemporary equivalent ever existed.[46]

During the Heian period, private martial entourages were assembled by retired emperors and top courtiers, by monastic institutions, by career provincial officials, and by provincial residents of many levels of status. Though all such organizations shared an obvious similarity of purpose, and warrior groupings at various levels were knit together into networks of alliances, both the networks and their component groups varied considerably in scale, complexity, and cohesiveness from place to place and from time to time. For this reason, historians attempting to generalize about Heian private military organizations must be careful not to lose sight of the fact that they are dealing with a variety of interactive, but diverse entities, a point that is all too easily obscured by the application of jargon like "bushidan."

Many of the organizations I have mentioned would not, of course, fall under bushidan rubric as the term is normally used, which points to a third problem: that the word can be unnecessarily restrictive just as readily as it can be deceptively inclusive. For a number of Japanese scholars, "bushidan" has connotations that go considerably beyond assemblages of private military forces. The existence of a bushidan, they argue, presupposes certain specific types of socioeconomic relationships between its members. Yasuda Motohisa, for instance, defines "bushidan" as "a certain type of combat-oriented authority organization in which a hierarchical structure can be discerned and which takes as its core the consanguineous unions of the *zaichi ryōshu* class, who would become the masters of medieval society."[47]

A key point for Yasuda is the term *zaichi ryōshu* ("on-site proprietor"), which he contrasts with *shieiden ryōshu* ("proprietors operating private fields"). The distinction between the two terms is complex, but turns on the degree of the provincial resident proprietor's direct involvement in the agricultural process. Shieiden ryōshu, according to Yasuda, were not true bushi and did not lead true bushidan; zaichi ryōshu were and did. Accordingly, he places the military organizations of some mid-tenth-century warriors outside the definitional bounds of bushidan while at the same time allowing that other warbands of the same period better fit the construct.[48]

Yasuda's views are in step with those of a significant segment of the Japanese historical community. But the fine distinctions he makes between older and newer types of warriors and private military assemblages appear unnecessary and even artificial in the context of the present study. Insofar as they relate to the emergence of a state military and police system centered on the use of privately developed, privately controlled martial resources—that is, to the central focus of this study—the similarities of tenth-century warbands to each other and to those of eleventh- and twelfth-century provincial warriors seem more significant than the differences.[49]

The Genesis of Warrior Networks

A historian trying to determine how and when private military networks began to appear in Japan is in much the same situation as a small boy trying to figure out how his mother produced his new baby sister: he knows what things were like before, and he can see the results of the birth, but he can only reason and speculate on what actually took place in between.

Early literary accounts of warriors like the *Konjaku monogatari shū* and the *Shōmonki* make it clear that by the early tenth century, Japanese fighting men had assembled networks of private forces, and that the government was already exploiting these organizations for its military and police needs. And there is evidence that this phenomenon might have begun by the late eighth century. A document from 780 concerned with coastal defense in Kyushu, for example, directed that "when enemy ships arrive at our coast, local men shall take their warrior followers [*zuishin no tsuwamono*], provision them, gallop to the area of danger, and fight to the death."[50]

But the earliest sustained indication of private military organizations in the provinces is the steady flow during the ninth century of government complaints about the depredations of bands of marauders. Armed robbery was by no means a new occurrence in Japan in the ninth century, to be sure.[51] But beginning in 798, court edicts begin to make specific references to bandit bands (*guntō*), rather than simply to robbers (*tōzoku*), suggesting that the government viewed them as a qualitatively different phenomenon.[52]

These bands were not all identical. Some were made up of *emishi* now living under Japanese rule; others, as we have seen, were alliances of provincial elites.[53] The bands that received the greatest amount of government attention, however, were those that formed around men with strong ties to the central court:

> One now hears of provincial officials whose terms have expired and sons and grandsons of princes and court officials forming bands and living in gangs. Such bands aid each other in the performance of evil. They pander to provincial officials and bully the peasants. They disturb cultivation and rob production. They are as worms burrowing deep into the public good.[54]

The degree to which armed bands of this sort were the institutional forerunners of the private military organizations of the mid-tenth century is difficult to judge. The ninth-century sources refer to a generalized problem and give few details about these early gangs. Nevertheless, circumstantial evidence—in particular, the fact that the warbands mentioned in tenth-, eleventh-, and twelfth-century sources and the "gangs" of the ninth century were organized around similar types of figures—does suggest that the later organizations were related to the earlier ones. The outlaw bands of the ninth century probably represented an early reflection of the same insights and considerations that produced the fighting organizations of later Heian warriors. It would have taken only a small leap of imagination for martially adept provincial elites and central nobles to realize that many of the objectives behind militarization could be more efficiently accomplished through the creation of bands of armed men than through the simple cultivation of individual skills. They would seem to have begun to act on this realization by the middle of the ninth century.

Reports of bandit and pirate activity continued throughout the Heian period. But generalized complaints about the existence of armed bands formed around elites tapered off sharply after the turn of the tenth century.[55] Presumably this reflects two developments: first, that such bands had become so prevalent by now that the court had given up on eliminating them entirely and was concentrating instead on controlling those that committed specific crimes; and second, that the state was learning that private military organizations could be useful—that they could be coopted for its own military and police needs.

The Structure of Heian Warrior Networks

Most private military organizations during the Heian period were patchwork assemblages of several types of forces. Leading warriors in both the provinces and the capital maintained relatively small, core bands of fighting men who were at their more or less constant disposal. Manpower to staff these martial entourages could be drawn from a variety of sources. Some troops were simply hired mercenaries; others were sons or close relatives of the organization's leader; still others were conscripted from among the residents and cultivators of lands over which the leader exercised some degree of control. But the most interesting—and most important—means by which private martial networks were formed was through alliances of various sorts between warrior leaders of different levels. This technique made it possible for warriors to assemble forces many times the size of their core organizations. Thus we find that while one prominent tenth-century figure's personal military band was only around 400 men, he was able to ride into battle "leading several thousand warriors," each themselves "leading followers as numerous as the clouds."[56]

The incentive to build or belong to military organizations of larger and larger scale was a natural consequence of the same factors that induced men to take up arms or create martial bands in the first place. The most obvious way for a warrior to augment his personal corps of followers was to go into partnership with his peers, but this idea was far less practical than it sounds. Throughout Japanese history, horizontal cooperation between coequals has tended to be an ephemeral phenomenon. The corollary to the principles encouraging the vertical factions that became so ubiquitous during Heian times was that the interests of men of similar station were generally at odds with each other. This tended to exercise a divisive influence, rendering lateral alliances unstable and therefore difficult to maintain for long periods.[57]

Warrior leagues that were in essence alliances between co-equals did come into existence during the Heian period, most notably in the southern part of Musashi,[58] but the predominant organizational pattern for warrior cooperation was hierarchical, centering on a figure of transcendent status.

In the provinces, the figures who emerged as the heads of private military networks of noteworthy scale were, broadly speaking, of two main types of pedigree: men from the central court houses that had established bases in the provinces; and men from families that traced their descent back to old provincial patriarchs or to other longtime provincial elites. The genealogies of medieval warrior houses suggest a preponderance of the former group—in particular men descended from cadet branches of capital warrior houses, like the Hidesato-ryū Fujiwara, the Seiwa Genji, and the Kammu Heishi. But the reliability of such genealogies is open to some question, and in practice the scions of both groups intermarried and interacted so thoroughly as to become functionally indistinguishable. A large percentage of families that should probably be included in the second group appear instead in the genealogies of the first, owing to marriage, master-retainer, or other ties.[59]

In any case, the prestige and status accorded to figures who could claim noble descent by one means or another enabled them to serve as rallying points for alliances between provincial warriors. Peer rivalries could be readily subsumed and transcended in warrior networks that were centered on men of overarching status. The structures of the outlaw bands discussed above make it clear that this phenomenon was already occurring by the middle of the ninth century. By the middle of the tenth, the process had advanced to the point where the most powerful provincial warrior leaders could terrorize whole regions and, if the numbers given in the sources are to be believed, could bring thousands of fighting men to this enterprise.[60]

Yet no matter how powerful these warrior leaders were in and around their provincial bases, and regardless of how formidable their military assemblages, they were still dependent on connections with the court to maintain their political and economic positions.[61] This need became the occasion for another type of warrior alliance, between major provincial warrior leaders and the most prominent of the central warrior nobility.

Miyako no musha were not, of course, the only central court figures with whom provincial warriors established ties. Taira Masakado, for instance, is known to have maintained a relationship of some sort with Fujiwara Tadahira, the imperial Regent (*sesshō* and *kampaku*) from 936 to 949.[62] But for many of them, capital warriors were an attractive and logical bridge to the court. First of all, the *miyako no musha*'s sometime presence in the provinces made them accessible in a way that higher-ranked courtiers were not. Second, and more important, both the *miyako no musha* and their provincial clients were warriors. Sharing as they did common skills and a common ethic, it is hardly surprising that warriors in the countryside should have been drawn to men they could look up to as illustrious practitioners of their own vocation.[63]

Like their provincial counterparts, warriors in the capital had core organizations of armed retainers who lived and operated with them in the capital and traveled with them to provincial posts. But the sources also indicate that by the early eleventh century, *miyako no musha* were, in addition, establishing alliances with prominent warriors in or near the areas to which they were posted as governors.[64] Such arrangements worked to the advantage of both parties. For provincial warriors, they were a means by which to gain a connection to the court and could provide entrance into the patron-client network of a senior court figure. Connections of this sort served to raise the prestige, military and otherwise, of provincial warriors; to aid them in obtaining or maintaining posts in local government or on private estates; and generally to advance their ability to compete with local rivals. For the *miyako no musha*, the alliances greatly expanded their efficiency as martial servants of the state—or the top nobility—when they operated in the provinces.* Minamoto Yorinobu is a good example. Thanks to his alliance with Taira Tadatsune, he was able to settle a rebellion by Tadatsune without firing a shot—after earlier pacification efforts by others had failed miserably. And through another alliance, with Taira Koremoto, he appears to have more than doubled the military forces that he could bring to bear in Koremoto's home province of Hitachi.[65]

Cases in Point: The Ashikaga, Kazusa, and Miura

Detailed information on specific warrior networks during the Heian period is extremely scarce, and the memberships of these organizations difficult to reconstruct. Diaries and other kinds of contemporary documents with explicit descriptions of military organizations are rare indeed. Our best sources of

*On the other hand, as in all alliances, the parties tended to become embroiled in each other's quarrels. In 1091, for example, Minamoto Yoshiie and his younger brother Yoshitsuna were drawn into a dispute over land rights in Kawachi between two of their retainers, Fujiwara Sanekiyo and Kiyowara Norikiyo. The incident threatened to escalate into a major battle in the capital city between Yoshiie and Yoshitsuna, but the *in* was able to defuse it (*Hyakurenshō*, 1091/6/12).

information, consequently, are the accounts of the warbands active in the Gempei War of the 1180's in medieval histories and literary works such as the *Azuma kagami*, the *Heike monogatari*, and the *Gempei seisuiki*. Used with caution and in combination with the fragmentary information that can be culled from other sources, these texts provide a number of useful illustrations of and insights into the nature of late Heian warrior groupings.[66]

The first case I will consider is that of Ashikaga Toshitsuna (d. 1181), a resident of Shimotsuke province and a descendant of Fujiwara Hidesato. Japanese historians refer to Toshitsuna's house as the Tōshō, or Fujiwara-line, Ashikaga, in order to distinguish it from the better-known Genshō, or Minamoto-line, Ashikaga, from whom the Ashikaga shōguns of the Muromachi age (1338–1573) later derived.

As we have seen, Hidesato's ancestors had been establishing bases in Shimotsuke and marrying into local families since the early ninth century. The surname Ashikaga was derived from Ashikaga District in southwest Shimotsuke, where Toshitsuna's ancestors appear to have settled some time during the mid- to late eleventh century. It was Toshitsuna's great-grandfather Nariyuki who first adopted the family name.[67]

By the 1180's, the Ashikaga had established themselves across southwestern Shimotsuke and the southeastern tip of Kōzuke and had become a major military power in the region. Thus Toshitsuna's son Tadatsuna was able to ride into battle on the side of the Taira (Heike) in 1184 at the head of "more than 300 horsemen." This contingent included the heads of Ashikaga cadet and collateral houses in Shimotsuke and neighboring Kōzuke, as well as a number of unrelated rōtō, who held lands adjacent to those of Toshitsuna and Tadatsuna, along the border between Shimotsuke and Kōzuke.[68]

Toshitsuna and his line faced intense competition in their own backyard from their Minamoto-descended namesakes, who had established themselves in Ashikaga during the first half of the twelfth century, when Minamoto Yoshikuni (d. 1155) won legal recognition for special tax and administrative privileges over land that he had newly opened—or reopened—for cultivation in the district. His second son, Yoshiyasu, was the progenitor of the Genshō Ashikaga. Toshitsuna also competed fiercely with his cousin Oyama Tomomasa, of south-central Shimotsuke. It was in large part these local rivalries that prompted Toshitsuna to stand with the Taira against Minamoto Yoritomo and his coalition in the 1180's, a decision that proved to be his undoing.[69]

Toshitsuna had good reason to align himself with the Heike. Among other things, the Taira had been instrumental in helping him maintain his position on his lands. In 1142, most or all of Ashikaga District had been converted to a private estate and commended to the Anrakuji, a holding of the retired emperor Toba.[70] During the late 1160's, Minamoto Yoshikuni's eldest son, Nitta Yoshishige, succeeded, "through the treacherous act of a certain woman" and adroit legal maneuvering, in wresting Toshitsuna's managerial post away from him. Toshitsuna had thereupon turned for help to Taira Shigemori, who was able to arrange to have him reinstated.[71]

But gratitude was not Toshitsuna's only motive for supporting the Taira. Equally important was the fact that all three of his bitterest competitors—Ashikaga Yoshikane (Yoshiyasu's first son), Nitta Yoshishige, and Oyama Tomomasa—had ranged themselves more or less on the Minamoto side. The *Azuma kagami*, which describes Toshitsuna and Tomomasa as "two tigers in a single province," is quite specific in its assertion that Toshitsuna perceived the campaign against Yoritomo and his supporters as an opportunity to crush his Oyama kinsman.[72]

An incident recounted in one version of the *Heike monogatari* reveals a great deal about Toshitsuna's wartime objectives, and about his standing *vis-à-vis* his own warrior followers. The passage relates that in return for Ashikaga Tadatsuna's outstanding performance in the Battle of Uji (fought on the twenty-sixth day of the fifth month of 1180), Taira Kiyomori offered him any reward he desired. Tadatsuna asked that his father, Toshitsuna, be named assistant governor of Kōzuke and manager of Nitta Estate.[73] The Kōzuke office would have been a formidable public buttress for Toshitsuna's domination of other warrior houses in Kōzuke.* Similarly, Nitta Estate was the base of Toshitsuna's rival, Yoshishige; to have taken the managerial rights of this area away from him would have been a serious blow to Nitta power.

Kiyomori readily acceded to Tadatsuna's request, but no sooner had he issued an order to this effect than the other members of the Ashikaga military network—in particular the "sixteen collateral houses"—complained that Tadatsuna's success at Uji had been due as much to their support as to his own efforts, and that therefore any reward forthcoming ought by all rights to be shared. The posts Tadatsuna had asked for could not, of course, be shared out, and Kiyomori was of no mind to offend the warriors who made up Tadatsuna's warband and risk their defection to Yoritomo. Accordingly, he withdrew his order on the same day that he had issued it.[74]

---

*During the Heian period, the governorships of the provinces of Hitachi, Kōzuke, and Kazusa were traditionally given as sinecures to imperial princes, who inevitably remained in the capital. To serve as assistant governor of one of these provinces was therefore tantamount to being governor. On this point, see Takeuchi, *Bushi no tōjō*, p. 14.

The glow of the Uji victory did not last long. Toshitsuna—and the house of Ashikaga itself—came to an inglorious end the following year (1181), when Kiryū Rokurō, an erstwhile rōtō, murdered his master and presented his head to Yoritomo, in the hope of being accepted as a Minamoto vassal. Yoritomo, however, observing that he could hardly trust a man who had shown himself to be so treacherous as to slay his own lord, promptly had Rokurō executed instead.[75] The fates of Tadatsuna, his brother Yasutsuna, and their sons are not known. Perhaps they went into hiding; in any case, they disappear from the sources at this time. The managerial post of Ashikaga Estate appears to have then passed into the hands of (Genshō) Ashikaga Yoshikane, who subsequently bequeathed it to his own progeny.

The case of Kazusa Hirotsune (d. 1181), a prominent warrior of the Chiba (or Boso) Peninsula, contrasts with that of Toshitsuna on several counts. First, while Toshitsuna's legal authority in and around his base of operations was limited to his rights as manager of Ashikaga Estate, Hirotsune enjoyed provincewide, public authority as acting assistant governor of Kazusa. Second, unlike Toshitsuna, who was locked into a bitter struggle for preeminence with his neighbors and relatives, Hirotsune had no dangerous rivals in or immediately around his homelands and maintained a very cooperative relationship with his powerful cousins the Chiba of Shimōsa. Third, and probably owing in large measure to the first two facts, Hirotsune was able to draw troops from virtually the whole of Kazusa province and from parts of Shimōsa as well, whereas Toshitsuna's military network was confined to a fairly restricted geographic area in and around southwestern Shimotsuke.

Hirotsune's ancestors were a provincial offshoot of the Kammu Heishi, descended from Prince Takamochi's sixth son, Yoshifumi, who established a base in Sōma District in Shimōsa in the tenth century. In the early eleventh century, Yoshifumi's grandson Tadatsune deepened his family's roots in the peninsula, but still maintained a residence in the capital.[76]

Tadatsune is best remembered for his insurrection of the late 1020's, an unusually destructive affair that devastated much of Shimōsa, Kazusa, and Awa.[77] This uprising first became a matter of concern to the imperial court in early 1028, when Tadatsune attacked the provincial government office (*kokuga*) in Awa and murdered the governor. The court, after some delay, responded by commissioning Taira Naokata to apprehend him. Tadatsune, however, was not to be easily taken. For the next two years he ran rampant up and down the Chiba Peninsula, until an utterly exasperated court sacked Naokata and replaced him with Minamoto Yorinobu in late 1030. Yorinobu proved to be a wise choice, for he was able to take advantage of a patron-client relationship with Tadatsune dating back some twenty-five years to, as he later put it, "capture the rebel as I sat," "without pulling a bow, without loosing an arrow, without concern, and without attacking."[78]

Following Tadatsune's surrender and subsequent death from illness en route to the capital, the exhausted court elected not to continue efforts to hunt down his sons, Tsunemasa and Tsunechika (who had not formally surrendered with their father), in the interests of sparing peninsular residents the further hardships that would surely have resulted from a renewed chastisement campaign.* The two brothers were allowed to

---

*In 1031, the governor of Shimōsa reported widespread starvation in his province—even his own wife and daughter had perished in the famine (*Shōyūki*, 1031/4/3). Things were still in a sorry state three years later, according to the

return to their homes, and forsaking the dual, capital-and-country existence of their father and his forebears for a thoroughly provincialized life-style, they began rebuilding the power and influence of their family in the region. Tsunemasa's grandson Tsuneharu (also called Tsunetoki) is considered the founder of the Kazusa house.

The private military organization commanded by Hirotsune, Tsuneharu's grandson, was of staggering scale. In the eleventh month of 1180, he is said to have reported to Minamoto Yoritomo near the Sumida River at the head of some 20,000 horsemen. Various sources for the Gempei War show that Hirotsune's army included men from four estates and seven districts in Kazusa, as well as from three estates and one district in Shimōsa.[79]

The most important asset that Hirotsune could manipulate to tie this sprawling martial network together was the acting assistant governorship of Kazusa, a post held for at least the two generations before him, by Tsuneharu and his son Tsunezumi. But the fact that he was able to raise troops from Shimōsa and from private estates in Kazusa in addition to those drawn from public lands in Kazusa, as well as the fact that he was able to assemble this enormous and far-flung force to support Yoritomo—legally a rebel against the state—clearly shows that he had more at his disposal than just his public authority.[80]

The Kazusa's ties to the Seiwa Genji dated back to the 1140's,

governor of Kazusa. Although the region was at last showing signs of recovery, the suppression effort had left unparalleled devastation in its wake. Because Kazusa had been the home of Tadatsune, and because of the exactions of "the warriors of various provinces" involved in trying to hunt him down, "not even dust remained." Of the more than 22,980 chō of paddy land in the province, only 18 had been left in production in the immediate aftermath of the fighting. (*Sakeiki*, 1034/10/24.)

when Hirotsune's father, Tsunezumi, turned to Minamoto Yoshitomo for help in wresting an estate in Shimōsa from his cousin Chiba Tsunetane.[81] Hirotsune's own affiliation with the Minamoto was ensured in 1179, when Taira Kiyomori managed to have one of his own retainers, Fujiwara Tadakiyo, installed as assistant governor of Kazusa. This action, which threatened Hirotsune's authority within the province, effectively drove him into Yoritomo's camp.

Unfortunately, from Yoritomo's viewpoint, a powerful ally like Hirotsune was as much a liability as an asset. A chieftain who commanded most of the warrior population of an entire province and who had no nearby enemies that could be manipulated to keep him off balance was not easily dominated. At length, Yoritomo concluded that his all-too-independent supporter could never be converted into an appropriately docile subordinate, and, in 1183, he elected to have him assassinated. Although he later pardoned, and restored the lands of, most of Hirotsune's relatives and followers, Yoritomo was careful not to allow any of them to step into Hirotsune's boots and reconstitute the military organization he had controlled.[82]

Our third, and final, case is that of Miura Yoshiaki (1093–1181) and his son Yoshizumi (1127–1200) of Sagami province. There are many surviving genealogies for the Miura, who became one of the major warrior houses of medieval Japan. All of them trace the family's descent from the Kammu Heishi, but there is little other agreement among them until the late eleventh century. All are products of later medieval scholarship and, in point of fact, none is without serious flaws. This raises the distinct possibility that Yoshiaki's real pedigree traces back to the old provincial aristocracy—the provincial patriarch class—and that one of his ancestors simply assumed the Taira surname on the strength of marriage or other ties to the Heishi. In any event, the family was clearly identifying itself as a Taira offshoot by the late eleventh century; if the Miura's claim to Heishi blood was a fabrication, it dates back at least this far.[83] Yoshiaki's most famous ancestor was Tametsugu, who fought with Minamoto (Hachiman Tarō) Yoshiie when Yoshiie took the field in Mutsu in the Latter Three Years' War of 1083–87. This campaign, one of the most celebrated events of Heian military history, began as a conflict between two kinsmen, Kiyowara Sanehira and Iehira, into which Yoshiie, at the time serving as governor of Mutsu, was drawn following an appeal from Sanehira. Iehira, reinforced by his uncle Takehira, took refuge in his stronghold, Kanezawa Stockade. Yoshiie began preparations for a siege of the stockade and, in the meantime, reported to the imperial court that the Kiyowara were in rebellion against the state and asked for authorization to proceed against them. But the court, suspecting that Yoshiie's motives were more personal than public, refused to sanction the campaign. Undaunted, Yoshiie invested and eventually took Kanezawa Stockade anyway and then made a second application to the court, this time for rewards for himself and his men. The court, however, stood firm in its refusal to endorse the action, forcing a frustrated Yoshiie to reward his troops from his own pocket.*

---

*The name Latter Three Years' War was coined in juxtaposition to the Former Nine Years' War, the campaign fought in Mutsu in 1055–62 by Yoshiie's father, Yoriyoshi, against long-time troublemaker Abe Yoritoki and his son Sadatō. This action, unlike Yoshiie's two decades later, had been undertaken at the behest of the court. Studies of both wars abound. Excellent capsule histories can be found in Yasuda, *Senran*, pp. 30–35; and Takayanagi and Suzuki, *Nihon kassenshi*, pp. 35–46. A more in-depth but very accessible treatment is Shōji's *Henkyō no sōran*. An English-language discussion of the Former Nine Years' War appears in H. McCullough, "Tale of Mutsu."

According to an incident related in a literary account of the campaign, during one battle Miura Tametsugu found himself fighting alongside a fellow Sagami resident, Kamakura Gongorō Kagemasa. Kagemasa, a spirited sixteen-year-old warrior of impressive pedigree, took an arrow in his right eye. Before collapsing, however, he managed to shoot down the archer who had wounded him. Seeing his distress, Tametsugu rushed to his side and attempted to remove the arrow. When this proved difficult, he placed his foot against his friend's face for leverage and successfully withdrew the shaft. Far from being grateful, Kagemasa sprang to his feet and tried to stab Tametsugu to death with his sword, growling to his would-be benefactor that to be shot and killed by arrows was a natural fate for a warrior, but to have one's face trod upon by the booted foot of another was an insult that no man should have to endure.[84]

Dramatics aside, this episode does show that the Miura had established an alliance with the Seiwa Genji by the 1080's, a relationship that appears to have been continued more or less without interruption through the middle of the thirteenth century. Yoshiaki and his father, Yoshitsugu (a son of Tametsugu), are named as part of a force of rōtō of Minamoto Yoshitomo that invaded an estate belonging to the Ise Grand Shrine in 1145. Yoshiaki and Yoshizumi continued to serve the Minamoto during the Gempei War.[85]

The Miura warband during that conflict appears to have consisted mainly of Yoshiaki's sons, grandsons, and in-laws. In the eighth month of 1180, fresh from a major victory over Hatakeyama Shigetada of Musashi in the Battle of Yui-no-ura, Yoshiaki and Yoshizumi found themselves besieged in their stockade at Kinugasa in Sagami. Badly outnumbered, Yoshizumi managed to escape with most of his troops to Awa, but Yoshiaki perished in the fighting. Yoshizumi persisted in his support of Yoritomo, who later rewarded him with appointment as Military Governor (*shugo*) of Sagami.[86]

Yoshiaki's power in and around Sagami appears to have been based on two main components. First, he held an important position in the on-site provincial government (*zaichō*). The Miura thus had public authority behind them, an asset that made them preeminent among the warrior houses in Sagami.[87] Second, he was the manager of Miura Estate, which covered most of the part of southeastern Sagami known as the Miura Peninsula. This promontory, which extends southward from the present-day city of Yokohama into Tokyo Bay, occupies an extremely strategic position along the Kantō coastline. Miura Estate sat directly on the original *tōkaidō* route, which ran from the Sagami provincial office across Miura to the bay, then picked up again at Awa, to run on through Kazusa, Shimōsa, Hitachi, and points north. The route was changed during the mid-Nara period to include Musashi, so that it now ran from Sagami to Musashi to Shimōsa, but the old route remained a major transport artery.[88]

The combination of the location of his homelands and his position in the provincial government enabled Yoshiaki to extend his influence throughout the Miura Peninsula, upwards into central Sagami, and eastward across Tokyo Bay into Awa, Kazusa, and Shimōsa.* It may also have enabled his family to develop into a naval power.

*Yoshiaki maintained ties with houses from several of the other provinces around Tokyo Bay. His son Yoshizumi, for example, was married to a daughter of Itō Sukechika of Izu, and one of his daughters was married to Kanada Yoritsugu of Kazusa. (Yoritsugu is a particularly interesting figure: a younger brother of Kazusa Hirotsune and son-in-law of Yoshiaki, he appears to have been affiliated with the military organizations of both warrior leaders.) Yoshizumi, moreover, was able to serve as a "guide to the province and districts" of Awa for Yoritomo and his entourage in 1180, suggesting that the Miura

Seaborne warfare would have been a natural field for the Miura to exploit, strategically located as they were along the sea-lanes between the provinces of the bandō. Moreover, the regulation of boats, boathands, and shipping was the responsibility of the provincial government. It surely would not have been difficult for the Miura, as the dominant power in the Sagami provincial office, to have reserved this sphere of governance for themselves, as part of their "miscellaneous duties." In any case, the *Azuma kagami* depicts the Miura and their forces escaping by sea to Awa after the fall of Kinugasa Stockade, and numerous sources note that Yoshiaki's eldest son, Yoshimune, had been killed in 1163 in an attack on a stockade in Awa. These military operations would not have been possible had the Miura not possessed the ability to conscript boats and crews. The Miura's control of naval resources in southeastern Sagami would also explain the otherwise mysterious failure of the Hatakeyama, Ōta, and other forces that had besieged them at Kinugasa to pursue them into Awa. That is, it was simply a question of access to vessels and boathands.[89]

COHESION IN HEIAN WARRIOR ORGANIZATIONS

Some scholars see this alliance-building process as analogous to the land-commendation process by which estates (shōen) were created.[90] Indeed, there were some similarities between the two phenomena, but there was also at least one major difference, for unlike commendation arrangements, bondings between warriors were not supported by written contracts. Commendation instruments exist in abundance, but one searches in vain for a single document formalizing a military

maintained a firm foothold in that province as well. (*Azuma kagami*, 1180/9/3, 10/19; Enkyōbon *Heike monogatari*, quoted in Noguchi, *Bandō bushidan*, p. 158n.)

alliance prior to the agreements issued by Minamoto Yoritomo in the 1180's.[91]

The absence of legal paperwork regulating Heian warrior alliances reflects the amorphous nature of the lord-vassal relationship during the period. Formal arrangements under which specific benefices were given in return for defined services did not develop until much later in Japanese history. The exchange of obligations that accompanied warrior partnerships during Heian was far less palpable, the nature, extent, and duration of these obligations much less precise, than in medieval times. Accordingly, the warbands of this era tended to be rather nebulous and short-lived entities. On occasion, illustrious warriors like Minamoto Yoshiie and Yoshitomo were able to construct martial networks that extended across several provinces, but until Yoritomo, no one was successful at creating a regionwide organization that survived the death of its founder.[92] It is no coincidence that the first truly enduring warrior organization—the *gokenin* system devised by Yoritomo and his successors—was also the first vassalage network to receive the sanctions of law and documentation.

Some historians have pointed to kinship ties—real or fictive—as the glue that held Heian military alliances together. And indeed, circumstantial evidence does support this conclusion. Most telling in this regard are the descriptions in Kamakura period texts of the warbands active in the Gempei War. As the case studies above indicate, a significant number of these organizations were clearly composed largely of cadet and collateral houses of single lineage groups. This perception has been reinforced by the predilection of Japanese scholars to discuss Heian warbands in the context of warrior houses, a result of their focus on tracing the origins of Kamakura period and later medieval warrior society. Attention has also been drawn to the use of terms that suggest some form of kinship—*kenin* ("houseman"), *ie no ko* ("child of the house"), and the like— to designate vassals; and to the frequency with which warriors arranged marriages between their offspring or siblings and those of allies, followers, or lords.[93]

There seems little reason to doubt that warriors thoroughly plumbed the possibilities of family connections in the hope of bolstering their ties to other fighting men. But there is at the same time good reason to doubt the efficacy of such efforts. The problem was that, ideology to the contrary, consanguinity was by no means a guarantee of harmony in Heian society. Conflict, indeed out-and-out warfare, between brothers-in-law, cousins, uncles and nephews, and even brothers was a near-constant theme of Heian military history. We see this in dozens of famous and not so famous skirmishes throughout the period.[94]

In practical terms, the cohesion of kinship groups during Heian times tended to devolve to the smallest possible units, that is, to nuclear families. The Minamoto and Taira "clans" that receive so much attention in survey histories—and even the branches of these clans—were, to quote Jeffrey Mass, "mere aggregates of heterogeneous and usually noninteracting units and were not in any sense the sums of their separate parts."[95]

The literature of the period shows that though ties between parent and child were strong, those between siblings were relatively weak, and those between cousins, uncles and nephews, and in-laws weaker still. The father-son relationship is well illustrated, for example, in a story found in the *Konjaku monogatari shū*. It tells how when Taira Koremochi expresses his outrage at the murder of one of his retainers by a servant of his father, Kanetada, his father rebukes him, observing that the

killing had been undertaken to avenge the death of the servant's
father some years earlier at the hands of Koremochi's retainer:

> Killing the enemy of one's parent is sanctioned by the Way of
> Heaven. Since you are an unrelenting warrior, I would have
> thought that one who killed me would have found little peace.
> Yet it seems that I may not even be mourned, if you press me so
> and censure a man who has simply killed his parent's enemy.[96]

In like manner, the *Mutsuwaki* depicts Abe Yoritoki declaring his refusal to hand over his son Sadatō to provincial governor Minamoto Yoriyoshi for judgment: "It is for the sake of
their wives and children that men exist in this world. While
Sadatō is a fool, a father loves his son; he cannot abandon and
forget him. How could I bear it if Sadatō were to be executed?"[97]

Compare these sentiments to the reception Fujiwara Morotō
gets from his brother-in-law in another episode in the *Konjaku
monogatari shū*. In the midst of a feud between Morotō and
Taira Koremochi, Morotō's brother-in-law refuses to admit
him into his home:

> Do not stay here long. I feel that your presence here is extremely
> profitless for me. For an old man to fight over a trivial man at
> this hour is a tremendous waste. It is all the more stupid that in
> my many years of dealing with people, I have astutely avoided
> this sort of thing until now. Kindly leave here at once![98]

Emotional rhetoric aside, there were important institutional
causes for the lack of strong ties within extended families. As
Mass has demonstrated, the laws and customs governing inheritance during the Heian period dictated that the disposal of
family property be at the discretion of the person making the
bequest, with the approval of the authorities—provincial governors or estate owners—who had jurisdiction over the lands

and titles being bequeathed. Wills were probated, and disputes among heirs settled, by these authorities, not by clan or family patriarchs (or matriarchs). Inheritance was, moreover, nearly always lineal (parent to child), not lateral (sibling to sibling). All of which meant that, in legal and economic matters, cousins, and uncles and nephews (or nieces), had little or no meaningful relationship to each other.[99]

One consequence of this kind of inheritance system was that, while siblings usually maintained a fair degree of family unity during the lifetime of their father, the various cadet houses tended to split off following his death and become independent of each other. Each new household head inherited properties and titles of his own, which he would subsequently pass on to his own heirs. Each followed his own career path and maintained his own retinue or private warband. The primary heir's residual rights over the affairs of these cadet houses were minimal at best; consociation between collateral lines did not extend beyond an innocuous consciousness of a shared heritage.[100]

Clearly, then, kinship ties could not have been a determining factor in holding Heian military alliances together. Cadet houses joined, or refused to join, the military networks of more prestigious kinsmen based on the same considerations that might have led them to follow completely unrelated warrior leaders: based, that is, on a communality of interests, not of bloodline.[101]

In the final analysis, the integrity of private military networks during the Heian period was only as strong as the adherents' perceptions that the affiliation worked to their advantage. A warrior could count on the services of his followers only to the extent that he was able to offer them suitably attractive rewards for their attendance—or, conversely, impose suitably daunting sanctions for their refusal. This ability in turn depended on a number of factors. Some of these, such as possession of lands, government posts, or positions in the administrative structures of private estates, were relatively stable and could often even be inherited. Others, such as personal military skills and reputation or connections at court, were more elusive.

In like manner, the rewards offered could take many forms. In many instances, warriors performing services for the state were able to obtain government posts and similar benefits for their followers as well as for themselves. On other occasions, fighting men divided the spoils of successful campaigns with those who served them. In 1006, for example, Minamoto Kunifusa was hired by agents of the Enryakuji to settle by force a dispute with rival temple Tōji over an estate in Owari. Kunifusa attacked and drove out the current manager-officials, placing in their stead one of his own rōtō, Taira Yukinaka. Warriors could also count at times on the offices of powerful masters to run interference between them and the court. A case in point occurred in 1114, when Minamoto Tameyoshi was able to protect one Kinmasa (surname unknown) from both the Imperial Police (kebiishi) and Kinmasa's former master, Taira Shigetoki, for nearly three months after the rōtō had been accused of theft.[102]

Medieval texts like the Heike monogatari and the Azuma kagami, which purport to describe events of the late Heian period, are filled with edifying tales attesting to the fierce loyalty displayed by the warriors of the age. Earlier sources, closer to these events, do give some hints that the fighting men of this time were not entirely oblivious to the concept of fealty as a virtue valuable to and befitting a good warrior; and yet the real effect of this notion on warrior behavior does not appear to

have been very great. In practice, loyalty was based almost entirely on, and severely limited by, a warrior's self-interest. Fighting men of the period were more than ready to desert to another master whenever they thought they might better their situation by doing so.[103]

Heian warrior allegiances were further circumscribed by the multitiered, hierarchical structure of the military networks to which they belonged. Most of the provincial warriors in the organizations of prominent central warrior nobles had organizations of their own, and many of the members of these, in turn, had followers. The loyalties of lower-ranking warriors in this complex hierarchy to those at the top were tenuous at best, being buffered at each interceding level by the allegiances of their higher-ups. One of the best illustrations of this is an incident related in the *Mutsuwaki*:

> At that time, in the government army there was one called Saeki Tsunenori, a man of Sagami province. The General [Minamoto Yoriyoshi] had always treated him generously. When [Yoriyoshi's] army was defeated, Tsunenori had broken free of the rebels surrounding him, but having gotten out, he did not know where the General was. He asked a warrior, who answered:
> "The General is surrounded by the enemy. There are not more than a few horsemen with him. I think he will not escape."
> Tsunenori reflected: "I have already passed thirty years in the service of the General. I am an old retainer, already in my sixtieth year; the General's age approaches seventy. If this be the time of his destruction, can my fate be other than the same? I will follow him to the underworld; this is my will." Wheeling his horse about, he entered the rebel cordon.
> At this, two or three of Tsunenori's followers cried: "Our lord is about to share the General's fate and die honorably. Can we remain alive alone? It is said we are only subvassals, yet we too yearn for honor."
> Together they entered the enemy host. They fought [val-

iantly], killing more than ten of the enemy. And yet [at length]
all perished before their foe.[104]

The fidelity displayed here by Tsunenori and his men is quite
clearly hierarchical, corresponding exactly to the organizational tiers within Yoriyoshi's army. While Tsunenori pro-
claims his allegiance to Yoriyoshi, it is obvious that the concern
of the "subvassals" is for Tsunenori, not Yoriyoshi. *

To some degree, this chapter has been an interruption in my
account of the evolution of the military and police system in
early Japan. It has nevertheless been a purposeful excursus, designed to illuminate some important parts of the background
against which the military procedures of the Heian era were
conceived.

It should be clear from the foregoing discussion that what I
have termed "an order of professional mercenaries" emerged
slowly and steadily from among provincial elites and the lower
tiers of the central nobility over the span of three centuries.
The private acquisition of martial skills among this group was
both presumed and encouraged by court military policies that
began with the establishment of the imperial state; it was accelerated by the political and economic changes that occurred
as Japan entered the Heian era.

To ask precisely when this order can be said to have fully

---

*The loyalty-to-the-death demonstrated here seems at odds with my earlier
assertion that self-interest generally overrode a sense of duty. This incident
might of course simply be an exception to the rule, but an alternative explanation suggests itself. The key lies in the words of Tsunenori's followers, "we
too yearn for honor." Throughout the literature of the period, bushi are depicted as willing to overlook family and personal obligations, the orders of
superiors, even to die, to protect their honor and reputations. By choosing to
die with Yoriyoshi, then, Tsunenori and his men were not totally abandoning
their self-interests; in a very real sense, they were actually furthering them.

emerged, however, is to raise a question whose answer depends more on how one chooses to define the order than on any matters of fact salient to the principal issues of this study. Some scholars have argued that true warriors (bushi) did not appear in Japan until after the mid-tenth century.[105] And yet we have seen that the very same skills of "bow and horse" associated with later Heian warriors were already developing in the early eighth century. From a purely military perspective, moreover, there is little difference to be discerned between the fighting men of the middle tenth century and their immediate predecessors in the early 900's, or between *them* and their predecessors in the mid- to late ninth century. If the military figures of the ninth century were not warriors in the strict sense of the term, they may at least be described as proto-warriors.

By the middle of the ninth century—or perhaps even as early as the late eighth—these proto-warriors formed themselves into privately organized martial bands. By the third decade of the tenth century, private military networks of substantial scale had begun to appear, centered on major provincial warriors. As we shall see in the following chapter, these networks, although initially opposed by the government, filled the gap in the state's military system created with the dismantling of the ritsuryō provincial regiments at the outset of the Heian period. Without the gundan, the court had no formal mechanism by which to conscript troops when it needed them; private military organizations could be coopted to provide such a mechanism.

Nevertheless, warrior networks during Heian lacked strong institutional foundations. The bond between military master and follower was a fragile one. It was not supported by documents or formal contracts, and Heian warrior society as yet lacked even effective moral imperatives commanding loyalty to one's liege or kinsmen. Whatever economic or social pressures there were in that direction could be easily tossed off when circumstances changed.

4

THE CONTRACT CONSTABULARY

*A samurai in service may be said to borrow his master's
authority and also to rob him of it. And similarly his lord
may lend it to him or let him steal it.*

DAIDŌJI YŪZAN, *BUDŌ SHOSHINSHŪ*

*If the king wants to make me constable, he must pay his
soldiers, [for] if they aren't well paid, they won't serve, and
if they go unpaid, they'll pillage.*

BERTRAND DU GUESCLIN

The turn of the ninth century marked the onset of a new era
in Japan, symbolized by the transfer of the imperial court from
the old capital at Heijō, near modern-day Nara, to Heian-kyō.
It was the preface to a new chapter in Japanese military history
as well, for the transition from the Nara to the Heian period
saw much of the ritsuryō military structure discarded; from
the ninth century onward, the court, without a soldiery of its
own, increasingly depended on the members of an emerging
order of professional mercenaries to act as its "teeth and claws"
in military and police affairs. Private warriors were commis-

sioned with new military titles that legitimized their use of personal martial resources on behalf of the state.[1]

None of the important offices of the Heian police and military systems were described in the ritsuryō codes; all were created later in response to specific needs and conditions. Many Western-language treatments of warriors during the Heian period see the ad hoc military titles adopted at this time as contributing factors in the decline of central government authority in the provinces. Given to provincial officials at first on an emergency and temporary basis, titles like ōryōshi ("Envoy to Subdue the Territory"), tsuibushi ("Envoy to Pursue and Capture"), and kebiishi ("Envoy to Investigate Oddities") tended to become permanent as "emergency" situations began to extend over long periods of time. The effect of this development, to continue this line of reasoning, was to make the use of military force—and the possession of military/police titles—increasingly integral to the exercise of provincial administration. Eventually, military titles came to overshadow civil appointments. Martial power thus became the sine qua non of authority in the countryside; the ascendancy of the imperial government was fatally undermined. This line of argument, then, sees the distribution of ōryōshi, tsuibushi, and related titles as constituting an unwilling surrender by the court of its control over an important governmental function—the exercise of military and police powers.[2]

In fact, the reverse seems closer to the truth. These military/police posts were created and modified in order to keep pace with the emerging warrior order. Their evolution reveals a consistent, long-term effort by the central nobility·to keep abreast of developments in the countryside and to use the very source of trouble there—privately organized bands and networks of fighting men—to its own advantage. By and large, the effort was successful. Warriors, no matter how powerful, were never able to disengage themselves completely from control by the center. Until the establishment of the Kamakura shogunate, titles such as ōryōshi and tsuibushi enabled the imperial court to remain the sole source of legitimation for the use of force, as well as for the possession of land.[3]

THE INSTITUTIONAL VACUUM

As we saw in Chapter 2, in 792 the court abolished the provincial regiments that had been the base for most of the military forces created by the ritsuryō codes. Even though the order did not include all the provinces (Mutsu, Dewa, Sado, and the provinces under the jurisdiction of the Dazaifu retained their regiments), this edict effectively spelled the end of generalized peasant conscription in the country. Textbooks and survey histories of the period tend to characterize this action as indicating the collapse of the ritsuryō soldiery and the abandonment of the ideal of a public military. What this view fails to recognize, however, is that the government's edict in 792 was just one step in a continuing series of reforms and modifications directed toward a rationalization of the state's armed forces.

The court abandoned neither the ritsuryō martial institutions nor the notion of the conscripted citizen-soldier in 792. Ritsuryō military organizations operated in the northern and southern frontier regions until the late ninth century, and the government continued to raise troops by conscription, albeit now from a select group of its citizenry rather than from the population at large, through at least the mid-tenth century.[4]

In Chapters 2 and 3, I argued that a pattern of increasing reliance on the martial skills of elites (the upper tiers of rural society and the lower ones of the central nobility) and lessening use of the ordinary peasantry in both the capital and the provinces can be seen from the very inception of the imperial state military system. The gundan were eliminated in the interior provinces in favor of a more select fighting force drawn from the same segment of the population that had been serving as officers and cavalrymen within the regiments and capital guard units: the rural gentry and the lower central aristocracy. This idea is not new to either Japanese or Western scholarship, but its significance has often been overlooked. For the edict of 792 created an institutional vacuum in the military system in all but the frontier provinces. The court had recognized the weaknesses of the earlier system and moved to correct them. But it had identified its best source of military power without working out the kind of organizational framework that would put those forces to the best use.[5] The result was more than a century and a half of groping and experimenting on the part of the central government. Various ideas were tried, only to be modified or abandoned, before the court achieved a workable system during the middle of the tenth century. There were two problems to be solved: how were troops to be called up, and who was to lead them. As the court struggled with these problems, the military system that gradually took shape reflected the emergence of the new Heian warrior order and the court's efforts to keep pace with its evolution.

Some authors have argued for the existence, both before and after 792, of a distinct military conscription mechanism centered on the district officials (gunji). Termed the *jinpei* or *koku heishi* system, this mechanism is said to have existed countrywide in parallel to the gundan system before that system was abolished. According to these authors, the provincial regiments' sole purpose had been to cope with foreign enemies; police functions were left in the hands of district and provincial officials. Thus district officials, under the authority of the provincial governor, maintained their own means of raising fighting men when needed to apprehend criminals, a means distinct from the normal regimental conscription mechanism. After 792, so the argument goes, the jinpei system was simply retained as the only military and police apparatus (outside of the frontier provinces). Morita Tei, a proponent of this theory, characterizes the military of the ninth century as a system based on the recruitment talents of district officials and the conscription authority of the provincial governor. The basic unit of the system, he maintains, was the district (*gun*); troops were called to service on the basis of their irregular corvée (*zōyō*) obligations.[6]

Inviting as this concept is, the assertion that a district official–centered police system existed in tandem with the provincial regiment–centered military apparatus of the eighth century is implausible. The section of the Yōrō Codes that deals with the pursuit and capture of criminals, escaped prisoners, and military deserters *does* assign a part of this responsibility to "the officials in charge of that area" in which the crime occurred or to which the fugitive had fled; and it also authorizes the use of subjects not included on the gundan rosters as troops. But it also makes the clear point that in the ordinary course of things, any forces that might be needed to track down and apprehend felons in the countryside were to be made up of soldiers (heishi) from the provincial regiments. Other peasants could be employed instead of, or in addition to, gundan troops only in emergencies.[7]

Nevertheless, this code provision would not preclude the possibility that something on the order of Morita's jinpei system was instituted after 792 to replace the regiments. And in point of fact, troop mobilization and conscription during the ninth century appear to have been conducted largely as he has described. A few words of caution are in order, however.

There is no question, as we will shortly see, that provincial governors were entrusted with important responsibilities in police and military affairs between the ninth and twelfth centuries. District officials, moreover, were at the grass-roots end of the government's chain of command and were at the top of the hierarchy of the rural elite, the group on which post-792 conscription was centered. Although ninth-century sources provide no clear descriptions of the induction-mobilization process below the provincial level, it is not difficult to suppose that district officials played a major role. In addition, the use of *"ninpu,"* a general term for those eligible for corvée service, in some troop mobilization orders strongly suggests that fighting men were called up on the basis of their corvée obligations.[8]

But it is important to note that the term jinpei, from which Morita has named his system, is by no means the only one used to indicate soldiers during this period; nor does it even appear in most cases. The terms *kanpei*, *gunshi*, and *heishi*, as well as "ninpu," are used in what appears to be precisely the same context. More important, "jinpei" was not a technical term employed to distinguish a certain type of fighting man separate and apart from the soldiers in the provincial regiments, but merely an abbreviation for "ninpu or heishi."[9] Finally, Morita has inferred the existence of a district-based conscription mechanism from a single chronicle entry, dated 883, that speaks of a disturbance in Kazusa and the mobilization of 1,000 "jinpei of the various districts" to deal with it.[10] No other source connects jinpei with the district in this manner. In every other instance, it is stated that province so and so has mobilized, or been directed to mobilize, troops in response to such and such a problem. All of this calls into question the idea that the "jinpei system" represented any sort of formal mechanism worthy of the name. It is more likely that troop mobilization and induction during the ninth century were conducted on an essentially ad hoc basis. Responsibility for mustering fighting men as the need arose rested with provincial governors; the specific means by which this was to be accomplished varied from case to case.

Over time, the recruitment mechanism underwent considerable change, gradually coming to be conducted on a largely private basis. The term jinpei continued to appear in mobilization orders at least as late as the 940's, indicating the continuation of recruitment based on purely public authority. Yet the "Court Army" during the Taira Masakado Rebellion (935–40) drew its fighting strength from private forces. The changeover was not abrupt. Nor was it ever complete; the ideal of public military service remained alive throughout the Heian period.[11]

The increasing tendency for "government" troops to be recruited and mobilized through private chains of command was a result of the growth of private martial networks among professional fighting men. This growth, in turn, both fueled and derived from the state's creation of various new military and police posts through which to harness the warrior leadership.

THE OFFICE OF IMPERIAL POLICE

In the capital, most of the responsibilities connected with law enforcement came to be exercised by an extra-codal agency called the Office of Imperial Police, or *kebiishi-chō*. This organization appears to have originated during the second decade of the ninth century as a special unit within the left and right emonfu. It was detached and given its own administrative apparatus during the 930's, but the connection with the older guard unit remained strong: for most of its history, virtually all kebiishi-chō personnel held concurrent posts in the emonfu.[12]

Like the emonfu from which it derived, the kebiishi-chō was divided into left and right branches, each with its own set of officers and staff. By law, each branch was responsible for half the capital. Later sources give little indication that this jurisdictional division was anything more than a legal fiction, but the administrative distinction between right and left officers can be observed at least as late as 1031.[13]

A surviving fragment of what seems to be a statute dealing with the emonfu from a legal compendium completed in 820 observes that, for each half of the capital, "one officer [kanjin], one sergeant [fushō], and five group chiefs [kachō]" had been designated to take charge of "the investigation of violations of the law."[14] The ranks and titles of these men are not given. A later court history, however, informs us that in 816, one Okiyo Fuminushi was appointed a Senior Secretary (daijō) of the left emonfu and concurrently assigned as a kebiishi. This suggests that the officers mentioned in the 820 statute were ordinarily secretaries, under the directors (kami) and assistant directors (suke) of the emonfu.[15]

During the first hundred years or so of its history, the numbers of personnel attached to the Office of Imperial Police grew steadily. The first "director [bettō] of kebiishi" was named in 834; by 837, the office also had one or more assistant directors (suke; later practice suggests there were probably two, one for the right branch and one for the left). In 858, the number of officers was increased to seven with the addition of a secretary (jō) and a clerk (sakan) to each branch. The *Engi shiki*, a legal compendium completed ca. 927, lists one director, one right and one left assistant director, one right and one left secretary, one right and one left clerk, one right and one left sergeant, and nine left and nine right group chiefs. These numbers were later increased by one additional assistant director and one additional secretary for each branch.[16]

Kebiishi directors were senior court figures—in most cases either Imperial Advisers (*sangi*), Middle Counselors (*chūnagon*), or Acting Middle Counselors (*gon no chūnagon*)—and held simultaneous appointments as directors of one of the emonfu or hyōefu branches. The assistant directorships were filled by middle-level courtiers, men of the fourth or fifth court rank, who served concurrently in equivalent posts in the emonfu. In addition to assisting, and when necessary filling in for, the director in the overall administration of the agency, assistant directors appear to have had primary responsibility for the supervision of personnel. It was, for example, the assistant directors, not the directors, that subordinate officers had to go to for permission to travel outside the capital.[17]

Secretaries and clerks were normally lower-tier central nobles of the sixth court rank and, like the assistant directors, served concomitantly in commensurate positions in the left or right emonfu. In general, the court seems to have preferred to fill both of these posts with scholars with backgrounds in legal studies, but from the mid-tenth century onward, warriors of the *miyako no musha* variety were commonly appointed as secretaries. The inclusion of such professional fighting men in the kebiishi-chō officer corps probably reflects an effort to augment the armed strength of the military police (which had hitherto been derived mainly from the troops of the emonfu), since the warriors brought with them their private martial followers. The cooptation of the bushi for this service appears, however, to have been quite limited during the Heian period. In most instances in which the court found it necessary to use the military resources of warrior leaders within Heian-kyō, it issued special orders to them directly, or more often, via their kugyō patrons.[18]

Sergeants (fushō) functioned as general orderlies for the assistant directors, secretaries, and clerks. Unlike the higher officers, who usually moved on to more lucrative posts after a short stint in the kebiishi-chō, they tended to spend their entire careers in the office and in the emonfu, sometimes holding their posts for twenty or even thirty years. The title kachō, or group chief, was derived from the title of the campfire leaders (katō, or hi no kashira) of the ritsuryō provincial regiments. These men were recruited from among the soldiers who manned the two emonfu. Some were simply assigned as aides to kebiishi-chō officers; others were designated as overseers (kado no osa) or superintendents of records (anju). The latter were, as their translated title implies, a kind of agency librarian in charge of maintaining documents. Overseers were initially used only for the supervision and guarding of prisoners, but their duties were later broadened to include the pursuit and capture of fugitives as well.[19]

One of the most baffling questions about the Office of Imperial Police is why it was created in the first place. This is a true conundrum, one that has stymied generations of historians and that may, in fact, be unanswerable.

The ritsuryō codes did not provide for a single, centralized police agency for the capital. Instead, law enforcement functions were divided, in overlapping jurisdictions, between several organizations and offices. The left and right Offices of the Capital (kyōshiki), responsible for the general governance and administration of the city, and their subordinate east and west

Market Offices, for example, were empowered to "patrol their sphere of jurisdiction" and to "investigate and censure violations of the law." Broad powers to "patrol and investigate within the imperial palace and the capital, and to censure or impeach violations of the law" were also given to the Censorate (*danjōdai*). The Five Guards shared the task of patrolling the capital; the apprehension of fugitives was left mainly to them, though the Censorate and the Offices of the Capital were active in this area as well. Criminal proceedings were conducted, depending on the gravity of the offense and the rank and official residence of the offender, by the Offices of the Capital, the Censorate, the Ministry of Justice (*gyōbushō*), or the Council of State.[20]

Such a complex system must have been awkward and confusing, and cannot have operated very smoothly. This consideration has led a number of scholars to speculate that the kebiishi-chō might have been conceived as a consolidated police force to redress what had come to be seen as a deficiency in the system established by the ritsuryō codes. The need for an organization of this sort, goes the argument, was most acutely felt in the absence of any body that combined the authority for investigating criminal activity with the physical resources necessary to pursue and apprehend felons.[21]

This is an attractive hypothesis—particularly since, as we shall see, the Office of Imperial Police did come to absorb most of the law enforcement functions of the offices and agencies noted above over the course of the Heian period. Unfortunately, early evidence tends to argue against it.

One must, first of all, question whether the kind of omnibus police agency that was wanted, capable of both investigation and apprehension, demanded the creation of an entirely new department. While it is true that neither the Offices of the Capital, the Market Offices, nor the Ministry of Justice had direct command of any troops, and that the Five Guards (and the Six Guards that succeeded them) did not have any authority to conduct investigations, the staff of the Censorate did include a corps of ten *junsatsu danjō*, or Patrolling Censors.[22] To be sure, ten men spread out over the whole of the capital would scarcely have constituted a very formidable police force. But none of the supporters of this theory attempts to explain why the court could not simply have increased the numbers of patrolling censors or given them command over units of *eji* instead of inventing a whole new organization.

A more telling point is the fact that, initially, the kebiishi's authority did not extend to the pursuit and capture of criminals. A document from 820 states that "the duties of the kebiishi are the same as those of the Censorate: to [respond to] special directives and to censor or impeach [violations of the law]."[23] Another document from that same year is a bit more specific about the functions of the new agency, but still fails to mention pursuit or arrest: "The activities of the kebiishi are not only the patrol of the capital and the interrogation of felons, but also the carrying out of special directives."[24] The mission of the kebiishi as it was initially formulated, then, merely duplicated the duties of the Censorate. Consequently, the goal behind the creation of this unit could not have been to establish a more widely empowered police force than had hitherto existed.

All the same, that is what it became. Once the new organization had come into being, the close connection between it and the emonfu—first as a subdepartment of the guard units and later as an agency whose officers held concurrent commissions in them—made it considerably better suited than the Censorate to conduct operations requiring armed force. It took the government more than two decades to recognize this point, but at length it did, and in 839 the Council of State issued a proclamation declaring:

> While the Censorate and the kebiishi have been established separately, their functions—the investigation and censure of reported crimes—are identical. However, when criminals flee or wicked robbers conceal themselves, the mandate of the Censorate does not enable it to pursue and apprehend them. Henceforth, if, in accordance with the investigation of reported crimes, there are persons who must be pursued and captured, the Censorate and the kebiishi shall communicate with each other, and kebiishi shall be dispatched for the pursuit and arrest. Let this be a permanent precedent.[25]

Over the next several decades, the powers of the Office of Imperial Police continued to expand. By the end of the ninth century, the kebiishi-chō had largely supplanted the Censorate and other agencies in matters of law enforcement within the capital: "The duties of the kebiishi," intoned an 895 petition from the director, ". . . include arrest, imprisonment, and interrogation by torture. . . . We have many other functions as well, placing us in charge of investigating persons and crimes and of determining punishments."[26]

Bit by bit, the organization stretched not only the scope of its authority, but also the geographical scope of its operations. The kebiishi-chō had developed originally as a police force for the capital, although, like the Six Guards (and the Five Guards before them), it was on occasion ordered to perform special service just outside the city limits. But it quickly became apparent that something had to be done about the criminals who darted in and out of Heian-kyō. Felons who fled or simply resided beyond jurisdictional lines constituted a common enough problem that in 874 the kebiishi-chō formally petitioned the

Council of State for the right to pursue its investigations in the ports and countryside surrounding the capital city.[27]

By the middle of the tenth century, kebiishi had begun to investigate, or direct the investigation of, complaints of criminal activity or tax evasion throughout the kinai, or Capital Region—the provinces of Yamashiro, Yamato, Kawachi, Settsu, and Izumi.[28] In order to arrest fugitives who were wanted for crimes in the capital, Imperial Police officers could even be sent farther afield. In the fourth month of 1031, for example, Kebiishi Sergeant Kiyowara Kanetoki received information that led him to believe that Mibu Yorihira, a convict who had escaped Kanetoki's charge three months earlier, was hiding out in Iga province.

> Since he was outside the capital [read Kanetoki's report], I contacted the Office of Imperial Police [for instructions]. Several days then elapsed, but on the twelfth day of the fifth month, I received orders directing me to proceed to Yorihira's location in the Ahai district of Iga. When I attempted to apprehend him, Yorihira put up a fight; in the ensuing shooting, he was struck by an arrow and died. . . . I then took his head and now request that the local district official confirm that it has been forwarded to the capital. . . . Although Yorihira was killed in the course of an arrest outside the capital, his whereabouts had already been declared to be within my authority. . . . I therefore request that I be pardoned for his escape and restored to my former position.[29]

This incident illustrates two important points concerning the jurisdiction of the Office of Imperial Police: first, that kebiishi-chō personnel did, on occasion, venture outside the kinai in the pursuit of felons; and second, that the kinai represented the geographical limits of the office's normal sphere of authority. To leave this region required special authorization.[30] Throughout its history, the kebiishi-chō remained a police force for the capital.

But the officers and personnel of the central Office of Imperial Police were not the only figures to be called kebiishi during the Heian period. A second species of kebiishi began to appear in the provinces beginning around the middle of the ninth century.

PROVINCIAL KEBIISHI

The post of provincial kebiishi is something of a phantom in Japan's military historical opera. For while it continued for a long time as a cast member, its appearance on an only dimly lit historical center stage was decidedly brief. Neither the beginning nor the end of this appearance is made clear by any source.

There are two phases to the story of the provincial kebiishi, representing two different periods of time and two different types of officers. During the first, they were provincial officers of the central government. During the second, which continued well into the Kamakura era, the post was completely absorbed by the provincial government, becoming a department (*tokoro*) staffed by locally appointed functionaries (*zaichō kanjin*).* It is impossible to pinpoint when this transition took place, but it appears to have begun during the middle of the tenth century. The outward form of the earlier office is plainly visible in sources as late as 946, and a locally managed provincial government department (*kebii-dokoro*) administering kebiishi activities can be seen by 1106. The period between is

---

*Definitions of the term *zaichō kanjin* vary widely. In this study, I use the phrase to refer to local men who served as regular or surrogate regular officials in the on-site offices of the provincial government, and who legally (local political and social realities notwithstanding) held their positions at the sufferance of the provincial governor, rather than the central court.

murky. The term kebii-dokoro appears in the historical record as early as 965, but it is questionable whether this refers to a true zaichō kanjin–staffed department, since the officer mentioned was clearly appointed by the Council of State. This example probably represents an intermediary stage in the metamorphosis of the provincial kebiishi post. It does, in any case, show that by 965 the agency through which the kebiishi operated was already being called the kebii-dokoro in some instances. What appears to have occurred was a gradual transformation of the provincial kebiishi from a centrally to a locally controlled post, which raises the question of why such a change should have taken place.[31]

Provincial kebiishi were first unveiled in 855, when a court history reported the appointment of one Ise Morotsugu in Yamato. The entry is short and somewhat cryptic, but its language indicates that it was probably not the first appointment of this sort. If that is so, the provincial kebiishi post would have appeared at about the same time as the kebiishi-chō appeared in the capital. This fact has led Ōae Akira to posit a connection between them. The kebiishi in the capital, he argues, were charged with keeping the peace in the city but were not allowed to venture outside its gates without special permission. But since felons often fled or assembled just outside these jurisdictional limits, peacekeeping inside of Heian-kyō mandated some form of police officer operating in the rest of the capital region as well. Provincial kebiishi were thus conceived of as an expansion of the central office; they were created in order to reinforce the activities of the capital forces.[32]

While this argument is attractive, it must stand or fall mainly on its own internal logic. There are no sources that attest to, or even hint at, such a beginning for the provincial kebiishi post. There is, moreover, no evidence to indicate the sort of chain-of-command relationship between the central and provincial kebiishi one would expect if the two were connected. Provincial kebiishi appear to have operated as independent entities within their own jurisdiction. Further, as we have already observed, the central kebiishi-chō's response to the problem of criminals fleeing the capital was to seek permission for its officers to venture outside the city; there should have been no need for that request had agents—the provincial kebiishi—been operating in the provinces.

In any event, provincial kebiishi appointments do not appear to have been made in accord with an integrated, *a priori* plan. Rather, new posts were created in sporadic, piecemeal fashion in various provinces between the 850's (or earlier) and the late 870's. The number of officers posted was not always the same. Although in most known cases a single kebiishi was designated, Kazusa was assigned two and Musashi one per *gun*. Apparently, kebiishi were appointed by the Council of State on an as-needed basis, in response to requests by provincial governors.[33]

The usual reason cited in these requests was the rise of banditry within the province. As indicated in the preceding chapter, the depredations of bandit bands in the east and of pirates in the west, often led by members of the provincial elite, became a major problem in the early ninth century and had become virtually endemic by the time it closed. Dealing with these outlaws, it would seem, was of sufficient difficulty to prompt provincial governors to apply for special officers to assist in their control. The court answered by appointing kebiishi "to investigate evil doings within the province and eliminate bandits among the people: in short to be the teeth and claws of the governor and the controlling agent of the people."[34]

Initially, the men appointed as provincial kebiishi were of

low or low-middle court rank. The late ninth and early tenth centuries, however, witnessed a devaluation of the office. In 894, the court found it necessary to order an end to the appointment of men without court rank and the dismissal of those already appointed.[35] By 914, the situation had become worse, prompting one critic to lament that the occupants of these posts were "all peasants of the province in which they hold office":

> They simply buy their posts. They waste public salaries and cannot carry out their duties; they are only empty holders of the title. . . . Like pictures of rice cake that cannot be eaten, they are officials made of wood, who cannot speak.[36]

Within two decades of this complaint, the office was already being referred to as a department of the provincial government; at some unknown stage thereafter, the central government divested itself entirely of responsibility for the position.

To understand these events, we must take a Darwinian view of the problem. During the ninth and tenth centuries, the court was fashioning, largely by trial and error, a new provincial military and police system to replace the one it had created at the beginning of the eighth century. Two major principles guided these efforts. The first was to ensure that the new military institution maintained a close symmetry to conditions in rural society. The ritsuryō military system had been created by fiat, but in forging a new one, great pains were taken to accommodate it to the current state of affairs in the countryside. The second principle was that the authority and formal (if not actual) control over the key officers of the new system were to remain in the hands of the central government. Thus when, during the middle decades of the ninth century, the court was beset with pleas from provincial officials for help in coping with bandits and pirates, it responded with the creation of the provincial kebiishi post. The new officers were assigned only to those provinces where they were specifically needed, and their appointments were directly controlled by the Council of State. The name for the new post was presumably modeled on the central kebiishi title, also recently created.

During this same period, the court was also experimenting with another title, that of ōryōshi. Although ōryōshi originated in a primarily military context, and the kebiishi post appears to have been more of a police position, it is clear that the troops led by both officers must have been drawn from essentially the same source and probably by much the same method. By the close of the ninth century, the ōryōshi title had shown itself to be the more effective and viable of the two, primarily, it would appear, because it proved to be more attractive to the warrior leaders of provincial society.

In the absence of conclusive evidence, one can only speculate why this should have been the case. As we shall see, the ōryōshi title originated as a commission for officers who led special military units from eastern provinces to other provinces where they were needed as reinforcements, and was often held by men who also held appointments as provincial officials. The kebiishi, by contrast, were from the start simply provincial versions of a police officer in the capital. Perhaps, in the eyes of provincial warrior leaders, these differences made the ōryō-shi title more prestigious and consequently more desirable.

In any case, it appears that by the 890's the senior members of rural society had lost interest in being kebiishi. As this occurred, the court too lost interest in the kebiishi title and began to focus its attention on the ōryōshi post. Provincial kebiishi were never abolished; they were simply allowed to become the property of the provincial government.

EARLY ŌRYŌSHI

If the provincial kebiishi were an experiment that failed, the court found far greater success with the post that rendered them obsolete—that of ōryōshi. The title, which first appeared in the late eighth century, was used sporadically until the early 900's, when after undergoing a fundamental redefinition, it became a cornerstone of the Heian period military and police system.

Though there are fewer than a dozen extant references to ōryōshi during the eighth and ninth centuries, a close examination of them permits a number of conclusions on the origins of the office.[37] It is evident, first of all, that the post was a military office from its inception. In every case in which it appears, "ōryōshi" designated an officer who led troops in some capacity. And in nearly every instance, court orders for the appointment of ōryōshi emphasized the martial qualities of those to be appointed. Provincial governors were instructed to select "men of valor" to lead men of "spirit and courage" and men "skilled with bow and horse."[38]

A typical example of an early ōryōshi appointment occurred in 783, when a Council of State edict complained that matters had once again gotten out of hand on the northern frontier, and that the provincial regiments of Dewa and Mutsu were not up to handling the job. Each of the provinces of the bandō, depending on its size, was ordered to recruit from 500 to 1,000 men of fighting quality from among the sons of district officials and other provincial elites. These were to be equipped and trained in the skills of war. One "particularly able" official from each province was to be selected and trained to manage the entire operation. He was to rush to the front with his troops, and then report back. Only one officer was deputized in each province. The duration of these appointments is difficult to judge, but the conditions under which the early ōryōshi were designated suggest that the commission was originally temporary. Nearly all those appointed as ōryōshi were middle-level provincial officials—secretaries (jō) or clerks (sakan).[39]

Some authors have argued that ōryōshi were established only to handle the job of moving troops from their home provinces to other regions where they might be required as reinforcements—that they were transport rather than true military officers.[40] But this does not seem to be a problem of sufficient magnitude to warrant the creation of a new office.

Yumino Masatake notes that the Yōrō Codes used the verb buryō to indicate the transport of soldiers, corpses, prisoners, and so forth from province to province, from province to capital, and from capital to province. The title buryōshi (also read "kotori no tsukai") appears in some sources for the officer who discharged this function. There is no logical reason why the movement of columns of reinforcements between provinces should not also have been managed by officers designated as buryōshi. Why, then, was the new title created? Yumino concludes that ōryōshi emerged as a specialized kind of buryōshi. That is, ōryōshi dealt with transportation only in a military context.[41]

Although a division of functions along these lines is certainly likely, that still does not explain why the new title was created. Besides, "ōryōshi" did not completely replace "buryōshi" in even military contexts; examples of its use in this context can be found as late as 1058.[42] The strong implication is that ōryōshi were created for a purpose other than simply to move troops from province to province. Ōryōshi appear to have been involved in the recruitment and training of troops as well, and may in fact have served as the primary officers for the companies under them. Inoue Mitsuo is emphatic that the first ōryōshi did not participate on the battlefield. With one exception, he argues, these early ōryōshi are never portrayed as leading troops in combat. The exception is the 894 case of an ōryōshi on the southwestern island of Tsushima, who led an attack on marauders from Silla, the dominant power on the Korean peninsula at the time. In this instance, says Inoue, the man was acting in his capacity as a district official, not as an ōryōshi.[43]

This last point is difficult to accept. The source cited by Inoue states that the district official and a ranking priest of a temple on the island "were designated as *ōryōshi*. They assembled a hundred troops into twenty units and cut off the movement of the pirates into strategic areas."[44] If the district official here was leading troops by virtue of his civil post, rather than his ōryōshi title, it would follow that the priest's exercise of military authority stemmed from his clerical position, which seems unlikely. Moreover, it does not follow that because the sources do not record any battlefield exploits of eighth- and ninth-century ōryōshi, these officers did not participate in combat. There are simply too many gaps in the battle accounts to allow such a conclusion. The emphasis on the need for martial skills in many of these passages makes it more logical to assume that ōryōshi were active as leaders of troops on, as well as off, the battlefield.[45]

On the basis of the foregoing, then, it appears that the ōryōshi post was designed to exploit the military talents of rural elites. The companies that followed ōryōshi during the ninth century were composed of expert fighting men drawn from the ranks of the provincial gentry. At least one source indicates that ōryōshi were called on to lead a similar sort of force even before the provincial regiments were abolished.[46] This strongly suggests a connection between the office and the type of soldier it was intended to manage. By the late eighth century, the court had come to recognize the inherent weakness of its current army and had begun to seek means of first supplementing and later replacing most of the provincial regiments with a more elite force. Focusing its attention on the martially skilled provincial aristocracy, the court instructed governors to mobilize these armed gentry for temporary duty when they were needed. In situations where only limited numbers of men were called up, this would not have posed special difficulties. But when units of 500 men or more, drawn from all over the province, were needed as wartime reinforcements, some type of supervisory post was called for. To ensure that such captains would be of higher position and status than the men they commanded, provincial government officials were selected for the job. The court created the title of ōryōshi to license such civil officials to act in a military capacity.

ŌRYŌSHI IN THE MID-TENTH CENTURY

In the twelfth month of 939, an ascendant and somewhat quixotic warrior of Shimōsa province named Taira Masakado began to style himself the New Emperor, and set about building a new capital near his home and appointing officials to staff his new court. Masakado's declaration, the most direct challenge to the sovereignty of the imperial throne in two centuries, was the climax to a decade or more of conflicts with kinsmen and local rivals, but until 939 he had managed to keep his quarrels within the boundaries of imperial law. In that year, his career took a radical turn when he entered the province of Hitachi at the head of 1,000 men, ostensibly to plead the case of one of his followers, Fujiwara Haruaki, with Acting Assistant Governor Fujiwara Korechika.

Whatever Masakado's initial intentions were in leading armed troops into Hitachi, he ended by attacking and occupying the provincial government headquarters. With this action, he had crossed the proverbial line: no longer could the court view him as simply a powerful provincial warrior at odds with local rivals; his capture of a provincial government headquarters had put him in rebellion against the state. Having left himself no avenue of retreat, Masakado elected to surge forward, seizing, in rapid succession, the provincial governments of Shimotsuke, Kōzuke, Musashi, Kazusa, Awa, Sagami, Izu, and Shimōsa.

For all this, the reign of the New Emperor was not very long. Within a month of his assumption of the title, the court in Heian-kyō had issued an edict calling for his destruction, a mandate that was enthusiastically taken up by an old enemy, his cousin Taira Sadamori—and by several other warriors specifically commissioned for the purpose. On the fourteenth day of the second month of 940, "the punishment of Heaven descended upon Masakado."[47] As he squared off against government forces in northwestern Shimōsa, "his horse forgot how to gallop as the wind in flight; the man lost his [martial] skills. Struck by an arrow from the gods, in the end the New Emperor perished alone, like Ch'ih Yu battling on the plain of Cho-lu."*

The campaign against Masakado involved a completely different form of military organization from that used in north-

* *Shōmonki*, p. 129. Ch'ih Yu was a rebel from Chinese mythology who met his end in a battle with the illustrious Yellow Emperor near Cho-lu, a plain in Hopei province.

ern Japan only a half century earlier. Conscripted provincial armies no longer played a major role; they were replaced by forces knit together from privately organized bands of fighting men. Rural society had changed; the embryonic warrior order of the eighth and ninth centuries was rapidly evolving into the samurai caste of the medieval age. Keeping pace with this change, the ōryōshi post too had evolved.

Various sources identify at least five men as ōryōshi in connection with the Masakado episode, but tell us very little about most of them.[48] Only one of them, in any event, seems to have played a major role: the much-mentioned Fujiwara Hidesato, the "ōryōshi of Shimotsuke," who made his first appearance in the conflict during the second month of 940, when he joined with Taira Sadamori to lead a force of some 4,000 men in an attack against Masakado. From this point forward, Hidesato became the most important figure in the campaign. He is the only one of the principals arrayed against Masakado who held the ōryōshi title—Sadamori's involvement in the affair seems to have been essentially private, stemming from a desire to avenge the death of his father in 935 at the hands of Masakado.[49]

Hidesato, long considered the archetypical warrior of his age, had already assembled a substantial network of private fighting men by the time Masakado's revolt began. A scion of a branch of the Fujiwara that had long maintained a base in Shimotsuke, he appears to have gotten himself into trouble early in his career, prompting the governor of Shimotsuke to request his banishment in 916. Some time between this date and 940, he must have managed to redeem himself enough to secure appointment as an ōryōshi.[50]

The relationship between Hidesato's background and his role in the conflict has been suggested by Inoue Mitsuo. If the court was to control a threat such as Masakado's, he contends, it needed to draw the support of others like him, that is, the leaders of large private warrior networks in the provinces. This support, in turn, was dependent on the central government's being able to convince such men that it was in their own interest to support the state, rather than join forces with the would-be Masakados. This could be accomplished only by giving the warriors a stake in the survival of the polity, by making them a part of it and thus linking their personal success to its success.[51]

The ōryōshi title appears to have been one of the prime devices the court used to this end. To this were added rewards in the form of rank, office, and land granted for the meritorious performance of assigned tasks. It was necessary to reward a man like Hidesato with juicier plums than needed to be offered to someone like Sadamori, whose interest in fighting Masakado was already inseparably bound up with the court's. Consequently, Hidesato was raised to Junior Fourth Rank, Lower Grade, and given lucrative governorships in Shimotsuke and Musashi, while Sadamori was awarded only Junior Fifth Rank, Lower Grade, and the much less profitable assistant directorship of the Right Imperial Stables (*uma no suke*).[52]

In this connection, remarks Inoue, it is interesting to contrast Hidesato with Masakado. Although both men came from similar backgrounds and had similar goals, that is, the expansion of their personal power and wealth, they sought to realize these goals by different means. Hidesato carved himself a niche within the system, a new role in an old system; Masakado attempted to establish another version of the system with himself at its head, an old role in a new system. Thus while Hidesato was capable of being coopted by the court, Masakado was not, and needed to be destroyed.[53]

The ōryōshi of the first half of the tenth century, then, were elite provincial warriors, the leaders of private military organizations, coopted by the court to fight on its behalf.[54] Although many of these figures also held positions within the provincial government, an additional title was needed for them to function for the court in a military capacity. The decision to bestow the ōryōshi title on them may have stemmed in part from the fact that such men were not qualified, by reason of rank and pedigree, for other military titles of sufficient prestige.[55]

It is clear that the ōryōshi of the 930's and 940's were substantially different from those of the eighth and ninth centuries. This raises the question of what relationship, if any, existed between the earlier and later forms of the office.[56] In my own view, the post as it now existed ought to be considered a natural outgrowth of the earlier one. As we have seen, the title was designed from its inception to take advantage of the martial talents of the provincial elite. Originally, this involved using these proto-warriors within armies that were raised through mainly public means. By the early tenth century, however, the private warrior organizations of the provincial aristocracy had become the most important military power in the countryside. The ōryōshi title, therefore, while continuing to be given to members of essentially the same class, now served a different purpose: to legitimize the use of the private martial resources of the provincial warrior order in the name of the state.

EARLY TSUIBUSHI

Masakado was not the only major military problem the court had to cope with in the late 930's. Throughout this decade, southwestern Japan was plagued by the raids of a sizable confederation of pirate bands led by a onetime provincial official named Fujiwara Sumitomo. Pirate activities in and around the Inland Sea had been a steadily growing nuisance since the middle of the ninth century. By the second quarter of the tenth, they had become a problem of serious proportions. Sumitomo seems to have exploited a combination of local connections and illustrious pedigree to make an already difficult situation far worse. Born into an elite family of Iyo province, on the southwestern coast of Shikoku, he was adopted by Fujiwara Yoshinori, the scion of a court lineage of high-intermediate rank. After a brief stint as a provincial secretary in Iyo, Sumitomo elected to abandon his government career and concentrate his energies on organizing the pirates of his home region into a coalition under his leadership. Making his base on Hiburi Island off Iyo, he assembled more than a thousand boats and crews, which he directed in raids on government shipments and private treasures up and down the coast. At his peak, he virtually controlled the entire Inland Sea.

Government efforts to control Sumitomo met with mixed success at best until the summer of 941, when forces under Ono Yoshifuru and Okura Harusane caught the pirate leader and most of his fleet in Hakata Bay, on the northwest coast of Kyushu, fresh from an unusually destructive raid on the dazaifu. In the ensuing battle, several hundred pirates were killed, and over 800 of their boats captured. Sumitomo himself was able to escape, only to be apprehended in his native Iyo by Tachibana Tōyasu. Sources disagree on whether he was killed during this capture or died later in prison.[57]

The 930's and 940's were also witness to the proliferation of another important extra-codal military title—*tsuibushi*. The earliest unambiguous reference to the title is a record of the appointment of a *tsuibu kaizoku shi* ("Envoy for the Pursuit and

Capture of Pirates") in 932.[58] This suggests that the tsuibushi post might have been created in the 930's to deal with Fujiwara Sumitomo and other of the pirates active along the Inland Sea.[59] But a plausible case can be made for an earlier date. For one thing, widespread pirate activity was not a new phenomenon in the 930's, although Sumitomo's leadership appears to have brought about a qualitative change in the nature of the problem. For another, the term tsuibu appears often in early Heian historical sources and can be traced back to the early eighth century. A particularly intriguing use is in a court history's entry for 862, where the pirates in the west were said to be boldly seizing both public and private property, attacking tax boats, and murdering local residents. It goes on to state that orders had been sent to twelve provinces along the Inland Sea calling for the "pursuit and apprehension" (tsuibu) of these villains. Still, although circumstances described in this passage are consistent in many respects with those attending later appearances of tsuibushi, it cannot be concluded with certainty that this is an early reference to the office. "Tsuibu" was a general term meaning "to pursue and apprehend" and is also found in what are plainly ōryōshi appointments.[60]

All of the men appointed as tsuibushi before 956 were central nobles who held titles within imperial guard units, either the kon'efu or the emonfu. Officers of these units had, on occasion, been sent into the kinai region on military/police errands since the early ninth century. The tsuibushi post was probably originally conceived as an extension of this practice.[61]

Unlike ōryōshi, who were appointed to individual provinces, the first tsuibushi had jurisdiction over the old imperial circuits (dō).[62] A source dated 941 raises some interesting questions about the terms of early tsuibushi appointments. It records a debate by the Council of State over the appropriate way

to handle the arrival of Ono Yoshifuru, tsuibushi of the Nankai and San'yō circuits. When Seitōshi Taishōgun ("Field Marshal and Envoy for the Pacification of the East") Fujiwara Tadabumi had returned to the capital in the previous year, it was
recalled, an official of the Department of Shrines (*jingikan*)
was sent out to meet him and cancel his commission. Perhaps,
then, this procedure should be followed for Yoshifuru? But,
came the objection, an examination of the precedents concerning returning "*tsuibushi* of the various circuits" showed that
while taishōgun posts had often been canceled in this manner,
there were no examples of cancelations of tsuibushi commissions. At this, the Right Major Controller (*udaiben*), Fujiwara
Arihira, suggested that the post need not be canceled.[63] The fact
that Yoshifuru was returning to the capital, and that the Council discussed canceling his title after the fashion of the taishōgun, indicates that tsuibushi was a temporary commission,
given with a specific purpose in mind, rather than a standing
office. The implications of the decision that the title need not
be canceled are less self-evident. Perhaps it was felt that the
commission expired automatically on completion of the mission, and hence did not require formal cancelation.

These first tsuibushi, in any event, differed from the ōryōshi
of the same period in social background, area of jurisdiction,
length of service, and mission. Ōryōshi were provincial warriors, appointed on a standing basis to individual provinces;
tsuibushi were central court figures, appointed over circuits
and charged with a specific task. At least one author believes
that in some circumstances ōryōshi served under tsuibushi.[64]
What is not so clear is why the government should feel the need
to put still another kind of officer in the field. The answer appears to lie in a combination of factors involving matters of
precedent and practical military necessity.

Masakado in the east represented a completely different military problem from that posed by the pirates in the west, for he was a landholder with a firm, identifiable base and deep roots in the provincial economy and society. It was from this position that he drew his military strength. To fight him, the court needed to coopt the private military resources of other provincial warrior leaders, such as Hidesato. Pirates like Sumitomo, on the other hand, were a fluid threat. Widespread and operating in complete disregard for provincial borders, they "drifted north and south like floating grasses, committed only to profit and yearning naught for their homes. Like birds, they scattered when pursued and regathered when given respite."[65] Suppressing them called for a coordinated effort over a multiprovince area. This need was best met by posting officers over large jurisdictions, such as the circuits. Commissions of this level could not be handed to provincial warriors for reasons of status and precedent. Protocol demanded that the new officers be central nobles.

This ruled out the ōryōshi title, which had already been assigned a different sort of function, was associated with men of insufficient pedigree, and, in any case, conveyed only provincewide authority. Other existing titles, such as taishōgun (field marshal), which would have carried the necessary prestige and geographical scope, were unsuitable owing to the nature of the pirate threat. One source, in summarizing the Masakado and Sumitomo affairs, remarks that "in the east a taishōgun was dispatched; in the west tsuibushi were dispatched."[66] Inoue has pointed out the significance of this juxtaposition of tsuibushi as the counterpart of the taishōgun in the east, even though there was, in fact, an officer called the *seisai taishōgun* ("Field Marshal for the Pacification of the West"). The title taishōgun, he observes, had always been reserved as a commission to defend the empire as the proxy of the emperor. A taishōgun was therefore an appropriate sort of officer to send against someone like Masakado, who was seeking to overthrow the state. Sumitomo and the other pirates, however, were no threat to the state polity; they were not rebels at all, merely criminals. A taishōgun commission was thus not warranted in their case. In short, faced with a situation that called for a type of officer for which no suitable title existed, the court simply created a new one—tsuibushi.[67]

ŌRYŌSHI AND TSUIBUSHI IN THE ELEVENTH AND
TWELFTH CENTURIES

In the first two decades following its inception, the office of tsuibushi underwent a rapid and thoroughgoing evolution. By the second half of the tenth century, the distinction between tsuibushi and ōryōshi had virtually disappeared. A document dated 956 appointing a tsuibushi in Ōmi, for instance, is practically identical in form and content to one of 952 appointing an ōryōshi in Izumo. Similarly, in a petition of 952, the governor of Echizen speaks without distinction of the activities of the tsuibushi and ōryōshi in his province. From the 950's onward, both tsuibushi and ōryōshi were appointed on a standing basis, had jurisdiction over a single province, and held similar law enforcement responsibilities. Although tsuibushi had previously been chosen from among the central nobility, the title, like that of ōryōshi, was now assigned to provincial warriors.[68]

In the wake of the Masakado and Sumitomo disturbances, the tsuibushi and ōryōshi emerged as the government's principal law enforcement tools in the countryside. Documents requesting ōryōshi or tsuibushi appointments dwell at length on the helplessness of the province in the face of bandits and pirates without such officers, attesting to the importance of the two posts. The tsuibushi and ōryōshi appear to have been involved in all aspects of provincial peacekeeping, from investigation to apprehension and even punishment. An early-eleventh-century tsuibushi in Yamashiro, for instance, was instructed to investigate an alleged attack on some provincial residents, and to apprehend and forward the guilty parties for judgment. Another tsuibushi, in 1126, took it on himself to cut the grain and burn down several houses belonging to a man accused of being delinquent with his taxes.[69]

Although the ōryōshi and tsuibushi were usually local figures serving in their home provinces, they were appointed by the central, not the provincial, government. The normal procedure called for the provincial governor (or his representative) to select a suitable candidate and then petition the Council of State on his behalf. The Council would then consider the request and issue an edict ordering the appointment. The process was hardly expeditious—it commonly took eight to ten months from start to finish, and occasionally as much as three years—but it allowed the court to maintain a voice in military and police affairs in the provinces. Appointments continued to be made by the Council of State well into the thirteenth century.[70]

On occasion, provincial governors or assistant governors requested the ōryōshi title for themselves. Instances of this sort were not confined to a particular era, but occurred across the whole period from the mid-tenth to the mid-thirteenth century. In some cases, the governor asked to be made the ōryōshi of a neighboring province, as well as his own; applications of this sort were always refused.[71]

Fukuda Toyohiko believes that the governors who sought these offices had limited private warrior followings of their own and saw this as a way to gain the muscle they needed to reinforce their rule. The fact that many of these petitions also requested the assignment of twenty to thirty military retainers (*zuihyō*) tends to support that theory. But the motive might have simply been to forestall real or potential military rivals in or near one's bailiwick. A document of 1005 quotes the complaint of an assistant governor of Kōzuke that officials of neighboring provinces had been crossing into his jurisdiction at the head of private troops and causing serious destruction of property. The document goes on to note that the assistant governor had asked to be named ōryōshi of Shimotsuke, Musashi, Kazusa, and Hitachi.[72]

I have not found any instance of a governor asking to be named tsuibushi. It is not clear why this should be the case. Perhaps it was simply a matter of tradition. Since the first ōryōshi commissions were given as joint appointments to provincial officials, the court may have felt bound by the precedents it had set; no such precedents existed for the tsuibushi post. Thus provincial officials who desired military titles would have been constrained to apply for ōryōshi rather than tsuibushi posts.[73]

All those appointments, then, and the majority of ōryōshi appointments as well, were given to provincial warrior leaders. Nearly all the petitions for these posts heavily emphasize the character and especially the martial abilities of the candidate. A document of 956 appointing one Kōga Koreshige as tsuibushi in Ōmi, for example, remarked that when Kanehira, the previous officer, had died earlier in the year, the first man selected to replace him was not acceptable because he was old and "not of warrior status." Koreshige, by contrast, was loyal, honest, unswerving, and "adept with both brush and sword."[74]

Provincial warriors were, of course, precisely the same group whose members were in the greatest need of being controlled. Having no other military resources of its own, the court continued, as it had since the middle of the eighth century, to depend on the very class that was most active in outlawry to preserve the peace. As one might predict in these circumstances, not every last ōryōshi or tsuibushi was entirely conscientious in his peacekeeping duty. A petition of 952 from the governor of Echizen, for instance, complained that the ōryōshi and tsuibushi in his province had been "borrowing the prestige of their offices," running rampant in the province, and even attacking innocent people. Thus the countryside was not at peace but was the site of "grief and lamentation." The governor therefore asked the court to cancel the appointments of these officers. Should future conditions warrant it, he said, petitions for new appointments could be made. Or again, an appeal of 998 from Shikida Estate in Bizen accused a local ōryōshi of plotting with a malevolent boathand to murder the captain and steal the cargo of a boat carrying tax goods to the capital, after the vessel had been caught in a storm off Settsu.[75]

Clearly, the integrity of the average tsuibushi or ōryōshi was no higher (although presumably no lower) than that of the average American frontier sheriff. The provincial elite, as has often been observed, were engaged in the business of self-aggrandizement. Those who were designated as peace officers were often not above trading on the prestige and authority of their office to intimidate provincial residents for their own gain. A few were even amenable to engaging in out-and-out criminal activity themselves.

The similarity of the later ōryōshi and tsuibushi, in terms of jurisdiction, duties, and background of appointees, leads us to wonder why both titles were retained. What differences, if any, can be discerned between the two offices? The best-known theory is the one advanced by Shimomukai Tatsu-hiko—that ōryōshi and tsuibushi differed in their regions of appointment. Tsuibushi, he argues, were found mostly in the kinai, in southwestern Honshu, and in Shikoku, and ōryōshi mostly in other regions.[76] But this does not seem to have been the case. Although the extreme northeast was the exclusive preserve of the ōryōshi, and tsuibushi dominated in the kinai, it is difficult to distinguish any other strong regional pattern to the two offices. Tsui-bushi and ōryōshi were often found in provinces that bordered one another, and both types of officer can be identified in at least two provinces.[77] (The distribution of these officials from about 944 to 1180 is shown in Figure 7.)[78] Nevertheless, the two posts were not identical. Ōryōshi titles could be held as joint appointments by governors or assistant governors; there is no evidence of these officials ever becoming tsuibushi. And ōr-yōshi were responsible only to the governor of their province and to the Council of State; tsuibushi were also answerable to the kebiishi-chō on certain occasions.

There is a clear continuity of development between the office of ōryōshi as it existed in the early tenth century and its eleventh- to twelfth-century counterpart. The tsuibushi post, however, evolved into a radically different post after it first appeared in the 930's and 940's. As originally conceived, the tsuibushi title was a temporary commission, a device by which the court dispatched special officers from the capital to handle pirate activity in the countryside. By the second half of the tenth century, the office had become a near clone of the ōryōshi office.

Inoue has suggested that this change reflected a loss of interest by the court in provincial affairs following the Masakado-Sumitomo upheavals. In the aftermath of these

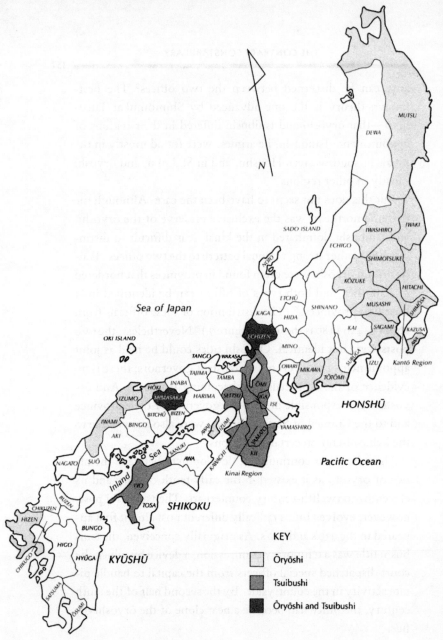

FIGURE 7. Provinces of known *ōryōshi* and *tsuibushi* postings, ca. 944–1180.

events, he says, the nobility in the capital did not really care what took place in the countryside so long as the tax revenues continued to flow in.[79] Given the extreme rapidity of the change, however—it occurred in less than a decade—this is not entirely convincing. Moreover, as we will see in the next section, the court continued to send out officers armed with special commissions to deal with rebels and lawbreakers throughout the Heian period.

TSUITŌSHI

Tsuitōshi ("Envoy to Pursue and Strike Down"), the fourth major title in the late Heian military/police system, was used for the first time in 941 and on many occasions thereafter.[80] A typical example of a tsuitōshi in action is the case of Taira Masamori, commissioned by the court in 1108 to "pursue and strike down" Minamoto Yoshichika. Yoshichika, a son of "Hachiman Tarō" Yoshiie, had been appointed governor of Tsushima several years earlier. He proved to be a thoroughly corrupt official and was exiled to Oki for stealing government property and murdering local residents. He fled to Izumo, where he killed the governor's deputy (*mokudai*) and again engaged in the theft of government property. The court responded by naming Masamori, the governor of Inaba, tsuitōshi, with orders to go after the miscreant. Assembling men from various bordering provinces, Masamori attacked Yoshichika and took his head. As a reward for his efforts, he was made governor of Tajima.*

---

*Chūyūki, 1108/1/19, 1/29. This incident did much to raise Taira prestige at the expense of the Seiwa Genji in the eyes of the court. An interesting postscript to this story took place nine years later. In 1117, the court began to hear rumors of an indigent priest who was wandering about northeastern Japan claiming to be Yoshichika. After repeated efforts to track him down, the man

Here, and in similar cases, the man who served as tsuitōshi was a member of one of the major central warrior (*miyako no musha*) houses. He was, in most instances, the governor of the province in which the disturbance took place, or of a nearby province, and was appointed for a specific mission, for which he was usually rewarded later with other provincial governorships.[81]

The tsuitōshi title bears a strong resemblance to the tsuibushi title as it was originally conceived. Like tsuibushi, tsuitōshi was a temporary commission used for officers dispatched by the court on specific missions. The major difference between the two, in fact, was that the circuit (*dō*) was no longer designated as the formal area of authority. Apparently, the title tsuitōshi was adopted to fill the gap left by the inflation of the tsuibushi office during the second half of the tenth century. Once the government began to assign tsuibushi to individual provinces, the title was no longer available to serve as the sort of emergency commission it had been designated to be. Thus, thereafter, when the court needed to grant special police powers to specific warrior leaders for specific missions, it simply called them "tsuitōshi," a title that was similar in meaning to, but had been hitherto less often used than, tsuibushi.

THE PROVINCIAL MILITARY/POLICE SYSTEM

The cardinal feature of the late Heian military and police system was that final authority and formal control rested with the imperial court. All major officers continued to be appointed by the court; all but the most minor criminal problems were first

---

was finally captured in Shimōsa the following spring. He did not of course prove to be the real Yoshichika (*Chōya gunsai*, pp. 286–87, 1117/5/5 Kebiishi-chō kudashibumi; *Denryaku*, 1117/8/1; *Chūyūki*, 1118/2/5).

reported upward, and the appropriate action was decided on and ordered by the Council of State. Despite considerable institutional changes, the underlying principles and the basic framework of the system remained much the same as they had been in the early eighth century.

Under the ritsuryō system, any violations of the law outside the capital were first to be reported to the local district government office. District officials were empowered to dispose of most misdemeanors (that is, crimes punishable by light or heavy beating) themselves. More serious crimes were reported to the provincial governor, who was authorized to handle minor felonies (crimes punishable by a period of labor service). For major felonies—armed robbery, murder, and rebellion— governors were required to advise the Council of State of the situation and await its instructions. Only the central government could authorize the mobilization of troops to apprehend the felon or pass judgment on him following his capture.[82]

A murder incident that took place in Yamato in 999 shows that this same procedure was still employed. The crime was first reported to the local district official, who notified the governor, who in turn informed the Council of State. The Council of State then authorized the use of troops to inquire into the matter and apprehend those responsible. Upon investigation, a number of suspects were rounded up and forwarded, along with the evidence against them, to the Council of State for judgment.[83]

Court orders to capture criminals or suppress rebellions were issued by the Council of State in the form of *tsuibu kanpu*, or "Warrants of Pursuit and Capture."[84] These warrants carried with them six basic powers:

1. Authorized the mobilizing of troops

2. Gave the commander full authority over his troops, including the right to punish those who violated orders or failed to report for duty

3. Authorized the commander to take whatever action he deemed necessary to accomplish his mission, including the use of deadly force

4. Canceled any immunity from arrest or prosecution enjoyed by monks, high-ranking courtiers, and other people of privileged position

5. Authorized the government forces to commandeer food and supplies as needed

6. Authorized rewards for warriors who fought on behalf of the government.[85]

Any form of military activity undertaken without a tsuibu kanpu was considered private warfare and subject to strict punishment. "To muster more than twenty warriors without a special order has been forbidden by law again and again," noted one source, while a petition to the Council of State reminded that body that "the mustering of private warriors has been repeatedly forbidden by the nobility."[86] People violated this rule at their peril, as Minamoto Yorichika, governor of Yamato, and Minamoto Yorifusa, former governor of Kaga, learned when their private skirmish in 1049 resulted in their exile to Tosa and Oki, respectively.[87]

It was the provincial government that held the primary responsibility for carrying out the pursue-and-capture orders of the Council of State. In virtually all cases, even those in which tsuitōshi were designated, tsuibu kanpu were issued first to the province(s) where the disturbance took place.[88] The ever-increasing complexity of political, economic, and social conditions in the hinterlands, however, rapidly brought about a much more intricate military chain-of-command network. By the late eleventh century, Council of State instructions could result in the mobilization of provincial warriors through any of at least three channels.

The most intriguing complication to the system was caused by the development of the tsuitōshi office. As explained above, those appointed tsuitōshi were *miyako no musha*, leaders of the principal warrior houses who maintained extensive ties to both rural and capital society, and who spent most of their careers serving as provincial officials. Such men commanded sizable private warrior followings, which were often scattered through several provinces. When called to government military service, they brought their own forces with them, mobilizing provincial bushi directly, through their personal connections. Tsuitōshi commissions were never issued in isolation, however. Orders to aid and cooperate in the operation were always simultaneously sent to the provinces involved. Designation as a tsuitōshi, which put a warrior in charge of the entire campaign, thus put him at the head of two overlapping chains of command: those warriors who followed him directly and those who were called up by the provincial governments under him.[89]

Military and police procedures were further complicated by the development of immunity privileges by various estates, or shōen. Once government agents came to be denied access to such lands, the court found it necessary to petition the shōen owner for the extradition of criminals hiding within estate borders.[90] There is a considerable body of evidence suggesting that this problem may have led to the creation of private estate versions of the ōryōshi and tsuibushi posts.[91]

The three channels through which the court might mobilize provincial warriors are shown in Figure 8. A fourth channel sometimes came into play. Occasionally, complaints about

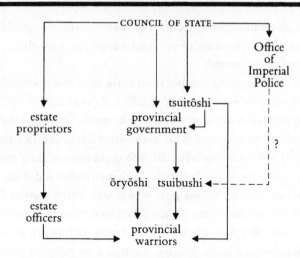

FIGURE 8. Chains of command in the provincial military and police system of the 11th and 12th centuries.

troubles in the kinai or nearby provinces were handled by the Office of Imperial Police. In such instances, the kebiishi-chō might issue instructions to provincial tsuibushi to investigate the case and arrest any suspects.[92] This does not necessarily indicate a special relationship between the Office of Imperial Police and the tsuibushi. For though there is no evidence of kebiishi-chō orders addressed to ōryōshi, neither is there any of such orders being addressed to tsuibushi outside the capital region, and no ōryōshi is known to have been appointed in the kinai. It is likely, in other words, that these orders came about only because the problem fell within the geographical scope of the Imperial Police's authority.

The preceding discussion has been lengthy and, at times, a bit technical. The fundamental conclusions toward which I have tried to argue, however, can be readily summarized in a few paragraphs.

At the turn of the ninth century, the central government took a major step toward dismantling the military institutions it had created at the beginning of the imperial era. But it was only the mechanisms of the old system that were cast off at this time. The central nobility did not simply throw up its collective hands and abandon the provinces to fend for themselves in military and police matters. Fully cognizant of the importance of control over this function of government to the survival of the state polity, the court unceasingly strove to keep its fighting men in tight rein. Many of the basic principles and procedures of the imperial military and police system were retained into the early medieval era.

Nevertheless, during the early ninth century, the state found itself faced with an institutional vacuum in this domain. The armed forces had been scuttled to improve the efficiency of the whole system. But though the government knew in principle what it wanted—to replace unreliable peasant soldiers with a martially skilled elite drawn from the upper tier of rural society and the lower tier of the court nobility—it had done away with the old provincial regiments without working out how best to tap into the new proto-warrior group. The Heian military system was built piece by piece during a century and a half or more of trial-and-error experimentation. Various officerships and mobilization methods were modified or abandoned until a workable mechanism was finally achieved. The cornerstones of the new system—the posts of ōryōshi, tsuibushi, and tsui-tōshi—were in place by the mid-tenth century, but the system continued to evolve and adapt to an ever-changing provincial reality until the imperial court lost the last of its governing power, some time during the fifteenth century.

The evolution of supernumerary military posts during the Heian period reflects the growth of the warrior order. The relationship between these two processes was, in fact, reciprocal:

commissioning provincial leaders with titles of this sort inevitably had a catalytic effect on the development of private martial organizations under these leaders, which in turn led to the introduction of new assignments and the modification of existing ones. It would be a mistake, however, to view this correlative evolution as a situation in which the central nobility, in a scramble to stay one step ahead of a warrior class that was steadily encroaching on court authority, attempted to buy off bushi leaders with ad hoc military commissions. These offices were not devised to keep a rising military order at bay (although they proved efficacious in this regard). Rather, they were established in an effort to upgrade the provincial military and police system. (At least two of these titles were in use long before the emergence, or resurgence, of local power could possibly have been construed as a threat to central authority.) Subsequent changes to these posts were made with the same goal in mind. The growth of private warrior networks may have resulted in new law enforcement problems in the countryside, but to the extent to which these same networks could be coopted by the central government, it also contributed to the increased efficiency of the court's answer to these problems.

CONCLUSION:

REASSESSING

THE HEIAN WARRIOR

But above all, it is most conducive to the greatness of empire for a nation to profess the skill of arms as its principal glory and most honorable employ.

FRANCIS BACON

He shall turn soldier, and rather depend on the outside of his head than on the lining.

WILLIAM CONGREVE, *LOVE FOR LOVE*

Few themes in Japanese history are as fundamental or as compelling as the transition from the classical age to the medieval age. Classical Japan—the Heian and Nara periods—was politically ruled, economically controlled, and socially dominated by civil authority, the court nobility; medieval Japan was politically, economically, and socially the age of the samurai. Over the course of the past two and a half decades, historians have radically and dramatically revised their thinking on how it was, and when it was, that the one epoch gave way to the other.

Up to a generation ago, scholars viewed the events of the Gempei War and the founding of the Kamakura shogunate as signaling both the demise of the classical age and the onset of the medieval era, equating the establishment of a warrior government with the presence of a feudal state ruled by warriors. So profound and thoroughgoing a transformation could not, of course, have occurred at a stroke; and so these historians looked backward, to the Heian period, for the changes and developments that made possible the rapid inauguration of a warrior regime.

Thus until fairly recently, Western scholarship on Heian Japan portrayed a polity and a society that were, for the most part, synonymous with the world depicted in Murasaki Shikibu's tenth-century classic, *The Tale of Genji*.[1] The Heian period was viewed as a time of tremendous cultural flowering side by side with horrendous institutional breakdown, a time when the legal framework of the imperial state was abandoned bit by bit. The capital became increasingly a universe unto itself as the court nobility, a class of "pampered minions and bepowdered poetasters, . . . an ever-pullulating brood of greedy, needy, frivolous dilettanti—as often as not foully licentious, utterly effeminate, incapable of any worthy achievement, but withal the polished exponents of high breeding and correct 'form,'" divorced itself ever further from political affairs and concerns of governance outside the confines of Heian-kyō.[2]

This characterization, which continues to dominate many survey histories and introductory courses, contrasted the effete, idyllic central aristocracy with the stalwart, practical warrior class that was developing in the provinces: the court had lost control over the political and economic life of the country;

while courtiers occupied themselves "going through the forms
and ceremonies of little more than a sham government and de-
voting their energies more to the arts of poetry-writing and
lovemaking than to governing," a hardier military aristocracy
was taking over in the countryside.[3]

By mid-Heian times (to continue this scenario), the imperial
state had ceased to exist other than in name. All that was
needed to bring even this to an end was a catalyst, something
to awaken provincial warriors to the fact that not only the emperor but his entire court had no clothes, and that it was they,
not the courtiers in the capital, who had become the real figures
of power in Japan. The long-delayed stimulus finally came in
the events of the Hōgen and Heiji incidents of the late 1150's.
The result was the supplanting of the court by the warrior class
and the onset of the medieval (feudal) age.

But despite the curious pertinacity of this view in Western
textbooks and introductory histories, the trend of the last
quarter century among specialists in the period has been toward a radically different portrait of the Heian state and a substantially revised chronology for the onset of warrior rule.
Historians have now come to view the Kamakura period—the
late twelfth, thirteenth, and early fourteenth centuries—as a
time of transition between the classical and medieval ages. The
creation of the Kamakura shogunate is now seen as marking
not the end of the ascendancy of the civil court nobility, but
merely the beginning of the end.

The reappraisal of developments during the Heian period
began in earnest with the appearance of John W. Hall's *Government and Local Power* in 1966. Hall, the first Western historian since Asakawa Kan'ichi in the opening decades of the
twentieth century to make serious use of documents, diaries
by leading court figures, and other nonliterary sources, re-

jected the notion of a court composed of lackadaisical fops interested only in poetry, sexual adventurism, and matters of fashion. He pointed instead to the vigorous political and economic activity of both the imperial government and the great aristocratic houses and religious institutions of which it was constituted. Hall stressed that what occurred during the Heian period was not the decay or atrophy of central government institutions, but their evolution and modification.

Scholars have subsequently built extensively on Hall's discoveries, stressing the adaptability and resiliency of the imperial court as a ruling body and as the seat of governing authority. Court dominion has been shown to have been far from the verge of collapse in the 1180's. Virtually unchallenged before Minamoto Yoritomo issued his call to arms during that decade, the nobility's supremacy was only gradually whittled away over the course of the next several generations. Courtiers remained able to compete for power and influence with warriors until at least the early fourteenth century.[4]

The revamped scholarship on the Heian and Kamakura periods, then, indicates that the early development of Japan's warrior class was signally different from what it was formerly supposed to have been. The notion that the bushi had achieved virtually independent control of the countryside by late Heian times has been set aside. It has been shown instead that the civil nobility was able to maintain tight constraints on the autonomy of Heian warriors in matters of governance and landholding, and that warriors were only beginning to break out of these constraints during the early Kamakura period. The revised view, in other words, makes the rise of the warrior class as a political and economic power a tale of the thirteenth through sixteenth centuries, not of the eleventh and twelfth.

Yet in spite of this fundamental reassessment of the political and economic strength of the warrior order that appeared during the Heian period, Western historians' perceptions of the origins of that order and of the military affairs of the Heian state have not altered appreciably since the 1950's.* The notion that the bushi arose when imperial court incompetence and lack of interest in maintaining a workable military and police system in the countryside forced provincial residents to take up arms for themselves has remained a part of the received wisdom.

But does it not seem odd that a ruling body that proved so adept at preserving its preeminence in political and economic affairs could have chosen to ignore so fundamental a sphere of government activity as military and police matters? And odder still that, if the court truly had lost control of coercive military force during the early Heian period, the warriors to whom this control had passed could have taken so long and found it so difficult to assert themselves?

The material I have presented in this volume, I believe, adds a long-needed third leg to the easel supporting the new portrait of early warrior development in Japan. While previous authors have described the mechanisms by which Heian warriors and other provincial powers-that-be were kept politically and economically bound to the court nobility, I have attempted to show that the state no more abandoned interest in or control of military and police matters than it did of any other fundamental aspects of governance. Rather, law enforcement and defense, like most operations of government during the Heian era, simply became privatized, contracted out to professionals. I have argued that the evolution of military institutions in Japan between the seventh and twelfth centuries followed a con-

*Let me stress the word Western. Scholars in Japan have been reconsidering this matter for several decades.

sistent and relatively steady pattern, a pattern characterized by ever-increasing reliance on the privately fostered martial skills and resources of provincial elites and of the lower tiers of the central aristocracy. I have further argued that this trend is visible from the inception of the imperial state military system, and that throughout the Heian period the central government jealously—and successfully—reserved for itself the exclusive right to sanction the use of armed force.

Around the turn of the eighth century, the imperial house and its supporters created an elaborate battery of military institutions modeled in large measure on those of T'ang China. These institutions were not simply adopted wholesale; they were carefully adapted to meet Japanese needs. Unfortunately, the various goals and requirements of the state were often in conflict with each other. As a result, the imperial state military system incorporated a number of rather unhappy compromises. The needs and priorities of the Japanese state in the 690's were, moreover, not the same as those of the mid-700's and later; problems inherent in the system at its inception were thus exacerbated by changing conditions.

The most important shortcoming of the imperial military was that it was predominantly an infantry force in a day when the premier military technology was mounted archery. This infantry-heavy balance was partly a matter of design and partly a matter of necessity. The imperial armies had been contrived to meet two major threats—invasion from the continent and regional challenges to the prerogatives of the imperial house or central court—and the court's solution to meeting those threats, the large-scale, direct mobilization of the peasantry, dictated that the bulk of the state's forces would be infantry. The state did try to maintain as large a cavalry component as possible, but the effort ran afoul of major logistical difficulties, in particular the formidable time and expense required to train recruits in the extremely complex skill of operating a bow and arrow from horseback. It was simply not practical to attempt to develop large numbers of cavalrymen out of short-term, peasant conscripts. The court addressed these problems by drawing cavalry troops only from among those who already possessed the necessary skills, and by making care of the state's war-horses the responsibility of private parties. This, in turn, ensured that the paramount units of the armed forces would be composed almost exclusively of provincial elites and central aristocrats.

By the mid-eighth century, both the threat of a Chinese invasion and the threat of challenges to the central polity had dwindled sufficiently to allow the court to reevaluate its martial needs and to begin to restructure its armed forces. First, the provincial regiments were supplemented with new types of cavalry forces drawn predominantly from among provincial elites. Then, in 792, the regiments were eliminated in most of the country; henceforth the state's military and police apparatus came more and more to be centered on the privately cultivated martial skills of an order of professional mercenaries. For the next century and a half, the court tinkered and experimented with the mechanisms through which it used and directed its new soldiery until a workable system was achieved during the middle of the tenth century. Adjustments to the system continued until the very end of the classical era, as the court moved to keep pace with the evolution of the new warrior order.

The incentive for provincial elites and lower-tier central nobles to develop private skills-at-arms came from two main sources: state military policy, and the growing private competition for wealth and influence among various parties and factions in both the capital and the provinces. Both served to create continually expanding opportunities for advancement for those with martial talent. The two sources of incentive tended to reinforce one another; similarly, the court's efforts to keep abreast of warrior development by adjusting the mechanisms through which it coopted and supervised private warrior resources provided a stimulus to their further development and improvement.

The descendants—both genealogical and institutional—of the professional warriors of Heian times were to become the masters of Japan's medieval and early modern epochs. And yet until the very end of the twelfth century, these fighting men were the servants, not the adversaries, of the court and the state. This situation, which appears so enigmatic in hindsight, seems much less so when considered in the context of the times. For as the foregoing chapters illustrate, the nascent warrior order of the Heian age was constrained from without by the same public (state) and private (court noble) policies that encouraged its development, and from within by the inability of its members to forge secure and enduring bonds between them.

The complex and even cumbersome procedures through which police and military affairs were handled in early Japan were designed with an important purpose in mind, that is, to ensure that control of this vital aspect of governance remained as firmly as possible in the hands of the central government. During the late seventh century, when these procedures were first laid down, the imperial court was still struggling to assert its preeminence over the regional nobility. While the initial threat to central authority posed by this group had subsided by the mid-700's, it reappeared a century and a half later in a different guise. By the end of the ninth century, most of the state's military dirty work was being done by private forces directed by private warriors operating in the name of the government. This raised the real possibility of the court falling under the domination of its own military servants, in the manner of Victor Frankenstein and his famous brainchild. The central nobility was well aware of this danger, and the state's military policies throughout the Heian period were carefully designed to minimize it. Like the landholding system of the same era, the Heian military and police system readily responded and adapted to changing circumstances in the provinces, while the court jealously guarded its exclusive right to oversee and direct it.

Most Western authors, in their efforts to portray the emergence of the bushi during late Heian, and the founding of the Kamakura shogunate as precisely the sort of Frankenstein-and-monster scenario described above, have completely missed this point. Stephen Turnbull, for example, argues that the government set a "very dangerous precedent" when it refused to reward Minamoto Yoshiie for his services in the Latter Three Years' War of 1083–87 on the grounds that he had never been ordered to undertake the campaign in the first place:

> If Yoshiie was to be regarded as a suppressor of rebels, then it was essential that he should be seen to be acting on the government's behalf. If the Latter Three Years' War was to be regarded as a private war between the Minamoto and the Kiyowara, then the government were in fact sanctioning a *droit de guerre*, as no steps were taken to punish them. In such ways the government revealed their utter lack of understanding of the changed conditions of life in Japan.[5]

In fact, precisely the opposite is true. Although the results of Yoshiie's expedition were essentially in the state's best interests, he had chosen to fight Kiyowara Iehira entirely on his own initiative, after the court had turned down his petition for a warrant sanctioning the action. To have rewarded him for this would have been to recognize a fait accompli that would have established exactly the sort of right of velitation to which Turnbull refers. Yoshiie violated prescribed procedures and thus no reward could be forthcoming. Perhaps, however, because his campaign was helpful to the state, or perhaps because of his tremendous personal popularity in both the provinces and at court, he was able to avoid punishment. In like manner, a governor of Kii was reprimanded for conducting a manhunt in 849 without first seeking authorization from the court.[6]

Turnbull, and other scholars who have expressed similar views of Heian warrior development, have of course a tremendous advantage over the court nobility of the time: they know the medieval outcome of the story. A hindsight analysis of the court's handling of Yoshiie as indicative of courtier naïveté in provincial affairs is deceptively attractive. It does not accord very well, however, with the evidence I have presented on military and police policy and procedures during Heian.

As a group, Heian warriors viewed the central government as a ferocious pet dog views its owner. For if the beast was potentially dangerous, it was also thoroughly domesticated. The idea that they somehow might survive without a master seldom occurred to them. There is no evidence that warriors were becoming more and more independent of the court as the Heian period rolled on. There was no discernible increase in either the frequency or the severity of bandit activity; and if private wars between bushi were beginning to threaten central authority, the sources do not reflect it. Until Minamoto Yoritomo's epoch-making usurpation of power in the 1180's, the civil nobility was able to keep warriors at heel by setting them against themselves. Bushi were made to compete with each other for the titles that permitted them to exercise armed force and for the rewards that accompanied military service to the court. Wherever powerful warriors, such as Taira Masakado or Taira Tadatsune, dared to rise and challenge the central government's authority, there were always peers and rivals, a Taira Sadamori, a Fujiwara Hidesato, a Taira Naokata, or a Minamoto Yorinobu, who were readily persuaded that cooperation with the state was a surer path to success. The specter of the warrior-dominated polity that characterized the later medieval era was not apparent even as late as the 1170's.

REFERENCE MATERIAL

NOTES

For complete authors' names, titles, and publication data on works cited in short form in these Notes, see the Bibliography, pp. 227–55.

INTRODUCTION

1. Jien, quoted in Brown and Ishida, p. 144.

2. Strictly speaking, "bushi" is a historiographical, not a historical, term when applied to the warriors of the Heian period. The contemporary pronunciation of the two Chinese characters we now read as bushi was "*mononofu*." Heian warriors were also referred to as *musha, tsuwamono,* and a handful of other names.

3. These events have been the subject of a tremendous volume of scholarship in both Japan and the West. In English, see Asakawa, "Founding of the Shogunate"; Cholley, "Rise and Fall of a Great Military Clan"; Mass, *Warrior Government,* pp. 15–93; E. Reischauer, "Heiji Monogatari"; Shinoda, *Founding of the Kamakura Shogunate,* pp. 35–147; Wilson, *Hōgen Monogatari*; and McCullough, *Tale of the Heike.*

4. For Asakawa's views on this question, see "Founding" (1933) and "The Origin of Feudal Land Tenure in Japan" (1914). Sansom's treatment can be found in *A History of Japan to 1334* (1958), pp. 99–263.

5. Sansom, p. 104.

6. Hall, *Government and Local Power*, pp. 130–54. The idea that the arming of the rural elite was in fact a return to an old pattern was not completely original to Hall. It was first proposed by Ōmori Kingorō in his *Buke jidai no kenkyū* (1924).

7. See especially Kiley, "Estate and Property"; Mass, *Warrior Government*; Hurst, *Insei*; and Arnesen, "Struggle for Lordship."

CHAPTER ONE

1. Shinoda, *Founding*, pp. 27–28.

2. Hall, *Japan*, p. 54.

3. Varley, *Japanese Culture*, title of chap. 3.

4. The manner in which Chinese government institutions were modified to meet Japanese needs has become an important topic of discussion among scholars in recent years. Various facets of this process are described in Borgen; D. Morris; Piggott; and Batten, "State." On the differences between the T'ang and Japanese military systems, see Noda, *Ritsuryō kokka*; Crump, " 'Borrowed' T'ang Titles"; and Crump, "T'ang Penal Law."

5. For details on the political structure and events of this period, see Kiley, "State."

6. For an overview of the Japanese literature on *kuni no miyatsuko*, see Niino. For descriptions in English, see Batten, "State," pp. 53–64; and Vargo.

7. Batten, "State," pp. 10–14.

8. *Nihon shoki*, 591/11/4, 602/2/1.

9. For details on the *kuni no miyatsuko* military system and its evolution into the ritsuryō army, see Naoki, *Nihon kodai heiseishi*, pp. 172–92; Sasayama, *Kodai kokka*, pp. 12–74; and Yamanouchi, "Ritsuryōsei gundan no seiritsu."

10. For an overview of Japanese scholarship on the Jinshin War, see Hoshino Ryōsaku. On the background and conduct of the war, see Mizuno, "Jinshin no ran"; Naoki, *Jinshin no ran*; and Hurst, "Emperor."

11. *Nihon shoki*, 684/intercalary 4/5; translation by Aston, part 2, p. 363.

12. *Nihon shoki*, 685/11/4; Yamanouchi, "Ritsuryōsei gundan no seiritsu," pp. 26–34. The quoted passage is from *Nihon shoki*, 689/intercalary 8/10.

13. *Ryō no gige*, pp. 186, 194–95; *Ryō no shūge*, 1: 98–104, 164–65.

14. According to Mutō (pp. 108–10), in the population registers from the early 700's he analyzed, the average age of those listed as heishi was around 30.

15. *Ryō no gige*, pp. 183, 186. The names on the roster were classified into three groups according to wealth (the purpose for this division is unknown), and special note was made of men with criminal records, men serving on foreign campaigns, and men serving in frontier garrisons.

16. Ibid., p. 122.

17. Quoted in *Shoku nihongi*, 704/6/3.

18. That is, assuming the first watch of the first year of our accounting began on the first day of the first month, the thirty-sixth change of watch would have taken place either five or six days before the end of the year. The first change of watch of the subsequent year would then have occurred on either the fourth or the fifth day of the first month. This would have been followed by 34 additional changes of watch, which would have

ended on the final day of the twelfth month, after which a new two-year cycle would have begun.

19. *Ryō no gige*, pp. 183–84.

20. Ibid., p. 186.

21. The Yōrō Codes classify three sizes of gundan: 1,000 men, 600–1,000 men, and regiments of 500 men or fewer (ibid., p. 183). The codes do not actually specify either the total number of regiments countrywide or a limit of one regiment per province. Predictably, therefore, this point has been questioned by some Japanese historians. But the consensus favors the one-per-province norm. For an overview of the debate, see Yamanouchi, "Ritsuryō gundan ni kansuru," pp. 34–36.

22. *Ryō no gige*, pp. 183–84, 190–91.

23. Ibid., pp. 60–61, 183, 185.

24. Ibid., pp. 183, 185; *Ruijū sandaikyaku*, 2: 549 (733/11/14 choku, quoted in 810/5/11 daijōkanpu).

25. Hashimoto, *Ritsuryō gundansei no kenkyū*, pp. 9–27. For an example of a gunki serving outside his home province, see *Shoku nihongi*, 716/5/14.

26. Noda, "Nihon ritsuryō gunsei," pp. 33–38; Hashimoto, *Ritsuryō gundansei no kenkyū*, p. 22.

27. *Ryō no gige*, pp. 63, 185, 189.

28. *Nihon shoki*, 646/1/1, 664/12/12. For a discussion of the unreliability of the *Nihon shoki* for the events surrounding the Taika coup, see Hara. Further information on sakimori can be found in Ikemori, "Shokoku sakimori"; Shioda; and Tanaka. Chinpei are described in Takahashi Takashi, "Mutsu-Dewa"; Sasaki; and Takahashi Tomio, "Tōhoku kodai shijō."

29. *Shoku nihongi*, 737/4/14; Takahashi Takashi, "Mutsu-Dewa," pp. 23–24.

30. *Shoku nihongi*, 730/9/28; *Ryō no gige*, p. 60. The thesis that sakimori were limited to Kyushu, Iki, and Tsushima is argued by Ikemori, "Shokoku sakimori"; and Tanaka. The case

for the second thesis is made in Naoki, "Tōgoku no seijiteki chii"; and Yamanouchi, "Sakimori."

31. *Ryō no gige*, p. 185; *Shoku nihongi*, 757/8/27. The latter source informs us that hitherto, "for sakimori, heishi of the bandō provinces had been designated and sent" to the frontier. This point is discussed further in Ikemori, "Shokoku sakimori." The theory that the pre-Taika Yamato royal house used the bandō as its primary military base is detailed in Naoki, *Nihon kodai heiseishi*, pp. 128–31.

32. *Ryō no gige*, pp. 185–86, 198.

33. Ibid., pp. 199–200.

34. Ibid., pp. 198, 200; Kudō, "Tōhoku kodaishi"; Takahashi Tomio, "Tōhoku kodai shijō." The first appearances of stockades in the sources are *Nihon shoki*, 647/12/30 and 648/4/1, reporting the establishment of outposts in Echigo.

35. *Shoku nihongi*, 724/2/25, 759/9/26, 768/9/22, 769/1/30, 775/10/13. The term chinjō appears for the first time in *Shoku nihongi*, 722/intercalary 4/25. The theory that chinpei were recruited mainly from the bandō is discussed in Sasaki Tsunebito, p. 1.

36. *Shoku nihongi*, 766/4/7, 768/9/22, 769/1/30; Takahashi Takashi, "Mutsu-Dewa," p. 28; *Ruijū sandaikyaku*, 2: 548–49 (795/11/22 daijōkan sō). This development is described in detail in Batten, "State," pp. 185–96 (sakimori); and Sasaki Tsunebito, pp. 12–14 (chinpei).

37. *Ryō no shūge*, 1: 99; Batten, "State," pp. 27–28; Shimomukai, "Nihon ritsuryō gunsei," pp. 30–31.

38. *Ryō no gige*, pp. 187–89; Shimomukai, "Nihon ritsuryō gunsei," p. 35. The *Ryō no gige* (p. 185) informs us that settō originally came into use as substitutes for scepters given to imperial emissaries in earlier times. The scepters, it relates, were made from the tails of oxen.

39. *Ryō no gige*, pp. 187, 190 (Gunbōryō, Kokushi buryō eji

sakimori no jō, Shin kunfu no jō). The possibility that each battalion contained several regiments is discussed in Shimo-mukai, "Nihon ritsuryō gunsei," p. 36.

40. Sasayama, *Kodai kokka*, pp. 67–70.

41. Ibid., p. 56; *Ryō no shūge*, p. 673. More on kadobe and mononobe can be found in Sasayama, *Nihon kodai efu*, pp. 27–31; and Miller, "Study."

42. *Ryō no gige*, pp. 185–86; *Shoku nihongi*, 722/2/23, 757/4/4, 766/2/27; *Ruijū sandaikyaku*, 2: 557 (722/2/23 choku); Hashimoto, *Ritsuryō gundansei no kenkyū*, pp. 45–47.

43. *Ryō no gige*, pp. 185, 187, 188.

44. Ibid., pp. 157, 192–93, 195–96.

45. Sasayama, *Nihon kodai efu*, pp. 41–42.

46. Sasayama, *Kodai kokka*, pp. 67–70.

CHAPTER TWO

1. See, for example, Shinoda, *Founding*, pp. 27–29.

2. For explanations of the ritsuryō tax system, see D. Morris; and Batten, "State."

3. *Shoku nihongi*, 709/10/14, 711/9/2, 722/2/23, 780/3/16. On absconding and other tax-resistance devices during the 8th century, see Farris, *Population*, pp. 118–31; Nishiyama; Kado-waki; and Yoshie. Dana Robert Morris offers an insightful treatment of the evolution of the tax system in "Peasant Economy."

4. English-language summaries of the controversy surrounding the so-called Horserider Thesis can be found in Kiley, "State"; Ledyard; Edwards; Egami, "Formation"; and Mizuno, "Origin." Egami and Mizuno argue for an invasion in the 3d century, Kiley and Ledyard for one in the 4th or 5th. Edwards; Kobayashi Yukio; Sonoda; and Naoki, *Nihon kodai heiseishi*, pp. 192–208, all contend that the art of horsemanship reached Japan without a continental invasion.

5. Sasama, pp. 2–12. Curiously, cavalry does not appear to have been prominent in the Japanese armies sent to Korea during the 5th century. A relief force sent to aid Paekche against Koryŏ in 554, for example, consisted of 1,000 troops, 100 horses, and 40 ships (*Nihon shoki*, 554/1/7). But as Sonoda, pp. 6–8, suggests, this may owe more to the difficulties of transporting horses to Korea and back than to a preferred style of warfare.

6. It was mainly cavalry that carried the day for Tenmu and his supporters, even though foot soldiers accounted for the majority of the troops on both sides (*Nihon shoki*, 672/6/24, 6/29, 7/2, 7/9, 7/23).

7. Nakamura, pp. 221–22; Sonoda, pp. 6–8. Hirotsugu's rebellion receives extensive treatment in Batten, "State," pp. 172–79. Nakamaro's is discussed at length by Piggott, pp. 61–72.

8. *Ryō no gige*, pp. 185, 193, 195–96; *Shoku nihongi*, 709/10/26, 714/11/11.

9. A lively discussion of Japanese scholarship on the conscription formula appears in Yamanouchi, "Ritsuryō gundan ni kansuru." For the debate on Ishio's thesis, see Yoneda, "Taihō ryō zengo"; Yamanouchi, "Ritsuryōsei gundan heishi"; and Naoki, "Ikko, ichi heishi."

10. *Ryō no gige*, p. 183.

11. Ibid., pp. 183–84, 274. For a detailed examination of the state-operated system of pastures, see Nishioka, "Bushi kaikyū."

12. Suzuki Takeo.

13. *Shoku nihongi*, 704/6/3; *Ryō no gige*, pp. 63, 184–85, 190–91; *Ruijū sandaikyaku*, 2: 553 (753/10/21 daijōkanpu). While the Yōrō Codes mandated that each heishi provide his own weapons and equipment, the state probably ended up providing most of the goods (see Sasayama, *Kodai kokka*, p.

65). Studies of the training of ritsuryō soldiers include Hashimoto, *Ritsuryō gundansei no kenkyū*, pp. 119–34; Koguchi, "Ritsuryō gundansei"; Koguchi, "Sekichō"; and Kita, "Gundanshi." For information on the weapons and tactics of the ritsuryō military, see Ueda; Sasayama, "Bunken"; Mizuno Yū, "Jinshin no ran"; Nakamura; Inoue Mitsuo, *Heian jidai no gunji seido*, pp. 73–103; Morita, "Kodai sentō"; and Toda, "Kokuga gunsei."

14. Sasama, pp. 425–26; Morita, "Kodai sentō," pp. 177–79.

15. *Honchō monzui*, pp. 51–52 (914/4/28 Miyoshi Kiyotsura iken fuji).

16. *Nihon shoki*, 672/7/22; *Ruijū sandaikyaku*, 1: 216–17 (901/4/5 daijōkanpu); *Ryō no gige*, p. 185.

17. *Honchō monzui*, p. 51 (914/4/28 Miyoshi Kiyotsura iken fuji).

18. *Nihon shoki*, 672/7/22.

19. *Ruijū sandaikyaku*, 1: 209–10 (837/2/8 Mutsu no kuni ge).

20. Ibid., pp. 209–17, 219–20 (daijōkanpu dated 814/5/21, 837/2/8, 838/7/25, 869/3/7, 11/29, 870/5/19, 871/8/16, 875/1/13, 879/2/5, 880/8/7, 8/12, 894/8/21, 9/13, 895/7/20, 11/2, 12/9, 901/4/5).

21. *Honchō monzui*, pp. 51–52 (914/4/28 Miyoshi Kiyotsura iken fuji).

22. On the An Lu-shan rebellion, see Pulleyblank.

23. *Shoku nihongi*, 704/6/3; *Ruijū sandaikyaku*, 2: 553 (753/10/21 daijōkanpu).

24. *Shoku nihongi*, 719/10/14; Yamanouchi, "Ritsuryō gundansei no suii," pp. 13–15; Nakata, pp. 36–38; *Dainihon komonjo*, 1: 385 (729 Shima no kuni yuyōchō).

25. *Ruijū sandaikyaku*, 2: 548–49 (739/5/25 hyōbushōfu, quoted in 802/12 daijōkanpu); *Shoku nihongi*, 746/12/10;

Noda, "Ritsuryō kokka"; Shinoda, *Founding*, p. 28; Farris, *Population*, pp. 65–66; Yamanouchi, "Ritsuryō gundansei no suii," pp. 15–16.

26. *Shoku nihongi*, 780/3/16, 783/6/6, 788/3/3.

27. *Ruijū sandaikyaku*, 2: 547–48 (792/6/7 daijōkanpu).

28. Ibid., pp. 548–49 (802/12 daijōkanpu); Nagato had been included in the list of places where gundan were retained in 739.

29. *Ryō no gige*, pp. 197–98, 200; *Shoku nihongi*, 737/4/14; Hayashi Rokurō, *Kodai makki*, pp. 44–55. The changes in court policy toward the inhabitants of the northeastern frontier are discussed at length in Takahashi Tomio, "Kodai kokka."

30. *Shoku nihongi*, 774/7/23, 7/25, 775/10/13, 778/6/25, 780/2/2, 2/11; Muraoka, "8 seikimatsu 'seii'"; Hayashi Rokurō, *Kodai makki*, pp. 44–61; Oyama, "Kodai makki," pp. 249–50.

31. Similar conclusions are reached by Muraoka, "Enryaku 11 nen."

32. *Shoku nihon kōki*, 837/2/8.

33. Ibid. The uses, strengths, and weaknesses of cavalry and infantry are discussed at length in Jones, pp. 39–85; Jomini, pp. 277–327; and Altham, vol. 1. See also Halleck, pp. 256–75.

34. *Shoku nihongi*, 737/4/14, 740/10/23; *Ruijū sandaikyaku*, 2: 547 (780/7/26).

35. *Ruijū sandaikyaku*, 2: 558–59 (792/6/14 daijōkanpu).

36. Nishioka, "Bushi kaikyū." See also Hall, *Government and Local Power*, pp. 132–33. The influence of Nishioka's thesis on later scholarship is discussed in Seki, 1: 170–72.

37. For example, *Sandai jitsuroku*, 878/4/28.

38. *Ruijū sandaikyaku*, 2: 518 (797/8/16 daijōkanpu); *Nihon Montoku tennō jitsuroku*, 857/4/23.

39. See, for example, Yamanouchi, "Kondeisei o meguru

shomondai"; Hirano Tomohiko, "Kondeisei seiritsu"; Inoue Mitsuo, *Heian jidai no gunji seido*, pp. 29–54; and Nagai, "Kondeisei ni tsuite."

40. *Ruijū sandaikyaku*, 2: 559 (797/11/29 daijōkanpu); *Nihon kiryaku*, 804/9/22, 810/9/7.

41. *Nihon shoki*, 642/7/9, 663/6, 663/8/13; at the time the word "kondei" was read as *chikara no hito*, which could also be written with a number of other character combinations. Aston translates it as "stout fellows" (part 2, pp. 174, 279).

42. *Ruijū sandaikyaku*, 2: 560 (733/11/14 daijōkanpu, quoted in 810/5/11 daijōkanpu); *Dainihon komonjo*, 1: 331–32, 387–89, 391–93, 440–41, 450, 504–5, 621–22 (725, 729–34 Ōmi no kuni shinan gun keichō); *Shoku nihongi*, 734/4/23, 738/5/3. See also Inoue Mitsuo, *Heian jidai no gunji seido*, p. 35.

43. *Shoku nihongi*, 762/2/12.

44. *Ruijū sandaikyaku*, 2: 560 (866/11/17 daijōkanpu).

45. *Heian ibun*, doc. 4178.

46. Batten, "State," pp. 18–30.

47. Morita, "Heian zenki o chūshin"; Sasayama, *Nihon kodai efu*, pp. 96–97. For an example of an amnesty edict, see *Shoku nihongi*, 707/7/17 or 717/11/17. Details on the political machinations of the period are given in Hurst, *Insei*, pp. 36–101; and Piggott, pp. 22–90.

48. Quoted in *Shoku nihongi*, 728/4/25.

49. My treatment of the process of central military evolution in the 8th century owes much to the studies of Naoki ("Kodai tennō") and Sasayama (*Kodai kokka* and *Nihon kodai efu*).

50. *Shoku nihongi*, 707/7/21.

51. Hurst, *Insei*, pp. 40–43.

52. *Shoku nihongi*, 722/intercalary 4/25; Sasayama, *Nihon kodai efu*, pp. 83–84, 96–97; Sasayama, *Kodai kokka*, p. 103;

Piggott, p. 47. On the background and early rise of the Fuji-wara, see Piggott, pp. 17–82.

53. *Ruijū sandaikyaku*, 1: 156 (728/7/21); *Shoku nihongi*, 728/8/1, 8/30; *Ryō no gige*, pp. 8–15. Some scholars have questioned the relationship between the jutō toneri ryō and the chūefu, but I find little room for doubt. The term jutō toneri ryō disappears abruptly from the sources around 727, and "chūefu" appears the following year. Troops for both units are referred to in various sources by the nickname *azuma toneri*. Moreover, the first commander of the chūefu, Fujiwara Fusa-saki, had been serving as the head of the jutō toneri ryō since 722. It seems clear, then, that the jutō toneri ryō was either absorbed by or converted into the chūefu (cf. Sasayama, *Nihon kodai efu*, pp. 92–94).

54. According to the *Ryō no shūge*, 3: 694, by 738 night-patrol duty, originally performed by the hyōefu and the ejifu, was being shared by the left and right hyōefu and the chūefu. Sasayama believes the hyōefu had been moved into the gap created by deserting eji, leaving the chūefu, which was essentially similar to the hyōefu in terms of personnel, to take up the slack for those units (*Nihon kodai efu*, pp. 84–85).

55. See Farris, *Population*, pp. 50–73.

56. See Hurst, *Insei*, pp. 36–101. Hurst's thesis is that the women who ascended the imperial throne did so only as care-takers, to preserve the succession for sons or grandsons. This view has met with some challenge in recent years (see, for example, Tsurumi), but this does not alter the basic point that the selection of Abe represented the first time in Japanese history that a daughter had been named as heir in preference to a son.

57. *Shoku nihongi*, 744/intercalary 1/11, 745/9/17, 746/2/7.

58. Recorded in ibid., 769/10/1. Sasayama and Naoki both believe that the "men from the east" referred to must have been

the jutō toneri (Naoki, "Kodai tennō," pp. 25–26; Sasayama, *Nihon kodai efu*, pp. 155–65).

59. *Shoku nihongi*, 756/7/27.

60. Hurst, *Insei*, p. 45.

61. *Shoku nihongi*, 764/9/18.

62. Ibid., 759/12/2; Hurst, *Insei*, p. 45; Sasayama, *Kodai kokka*, pp. 123–25.

63. *Ruijū sandaikyaku*, 1: 156 (765/2/3); *Shoku nihongi*, 765/2/3.

64. *Shoku nihongi*, 770/6/10, 772/2/16, 805/12/7; *Ruijū sandaikyaku*, 1: 184–85 (808/7/20 daijōkan chō). In point of fact, the chūefu no longer existed under that name, having been renamed the right kon'efu the previous year.

65. *Ruijū sandaikyaku*, 1: 156, 184–85 (807/4/22 choku, 808/7/20 daijōkan chō); *Nihon kōki*, 808/7/22; *Nihon kiryaku*, 811/11/28.

66. *Ryō no gige*, pp. 6–23.

67. Ibid., pp. 190–91.

68. The *Ryō no gige* (p. 191) states: "For those without previous *kun'i*, one point shall raise their rank to twelfth *tō*. For those of sixth *tō* [equivalent to junior fifth rank] or above, a promotion of one *tō* shall be given for every two points earned. For those already holding second *tō* or higher, three points shall qualify for promotion of one *tō*."

69. *Ryō no gige*, pp. 75–76, 196–97. The chōnai/shijin system is discussed in detail by Hurst, *Insei*, pp. 19–35.

70. Sasayama, *Kodai kokka*, pp. 129–30. For a discussion of Dōkyō and his career, see Bender.

CHAPTER THREE

1. Hall, *Government and Local Power*, pp. 116–28.

2. In kasagake, mounted competitors shot at targets made

of leather. In yabusame (which is still practiced at Shintō shrines all over Japan), archers gallop on horseback down a path about 300–400 meters long, shooting at a series of three square wooden targets mounted on poles about a meter high. In yatsumato, mounted archers shot at a series of eight targets scattered about the shooting grounds. And in sanzaku, archers shot at targets placed on posts about one meter (three *shaku*) high. The nature of tahasami is unclear, but the characters used to write the word indicate that it may have involved shooting at handheld targets.

3. *Shin sarugakki*, p. 138.

4. Japanese historians refer to the differences between the Heian and Nara polities as a transformation from the *ritsuryō kokka* to the *ōchō kokka*. Morita, *Ōchō seiji*, gives an excellent overview of this transformation. For a survey of Japanese historiography on the topic, see Morita, *Kenkyūshi ōchō kokka*. Extensive treatment of the changing relationship between center and provinces is also provided by D. R. Morris; and Batten, "State."

5. This account of the changes in the Japanese tax system draws heavily on D. Morris, pp. 163–205.

6. Yoneda, *Kodai kokka*, pp. 145–46; D. R. Morris, pp. 189–204.

7. *Ruijū sandaikyaku*, 2: 623–64 (835/10/18 daijōkanpu, quoted in 867/11/20 daijōkanpu).

8. Ibid., pp. 606, 617–18 (896/4/2 daijōkanpu, 905/8/25 daijōkanpu).

9. Morita, *Zuryō*, pp. 136–38.

10. *Ruijū sandaikyaku*, 2: 598 (863/3/15 daijōkanpu); Morita, *Zuryō*, pp. 50–52, 107–17. Morita lists 20 petitions calling for the dismissal of governors between 974 and 1052.

11. *Heian ibun*, doc. 339.

12. Kiley, "Estate and Property," pp. 110–11.

13. Hurst, "Structure," pp. 47–59.

14. *Ruijū sandaikyaku*, 2: 638 (Settsu no kuni ge, quoted in 860/9/20 daijōkanpu).

15. Ibid., p. 617 (894/11/30 daijōkanpu).

16. The single best explanation of the commendation process—and of the shōen phenomenon in general—remains Nagahara's *Shōen*. In English, see Nagahara, "Land Ownership"; Arnesen, "Struggle for Lordship"; Kiley, "Property and Political Authority"; and E. Sato, "Early Development."

17. *Ruijū sandaikyaku*, 2: 619–21 (797/4/29 daijōkanpu, quoted in 891/9/11 daijōkanpu; 842/8/15 daijōkanpu, quoted in 895/11/7 daijōkanpu; 891/9/11 daijōkanpu; 895/11/7 daijōkanpu); *Sandai jitsuroku*, 884/8/4.

18. Morita, *Zuryō*, pp. 139–43; Takahashi Masaaki, *Kiyomori izen*, p. 14.

19. *Shoku nihongi*, 777/1/25; *Chōya gunsai*, p. 430 (890/8/5 chinyū chō); *Sonpi bunmyaku*, 2: 419; *Sandai jitsuroku*, 877/3/10. This example is used by Hodate ("Kodai makki," pp. 7–12), who in turn drew it from Toda, "Kyū seki tōgoku shōen to sono kōtsu keitai," *Seiji keizai shigaku*, 110 (1975).

20. *Ruijū kokushi*, 798/2/1; *Shoku nihon kōki*, 838/2/9, 2/10, 2/12, 839/4/2; *Ruijū sandaikyaku*, 2: 614, 640–41 (840/2/25 daijōkanpu, 867/3/24 daijōkanpu); *Shoku nihon kōki*, 850/2/3, 857/3/18; *Nihon Montoku tennō jitsuroku*, 857/3/16, 858/2/22; *Sandai jitsuroku*, 861/11/6, 862/5/20, 866/4/11, 870/12/2; etc. Bandits were active nationwide; pirates along the inland sea; see Okuno, "Heian jidai," pp. 14–15.

21. *Sandai jitsuroku*, 870/12/2; *Ruijū sandaikyaku*, 2: 565 (Kōzuke no kuni ge, quoted in 899/9/19 daijōkanpu), 2: 620–21 (891/9/11 daijōkanpu), 2: 623–24 (867/12/20 daijōkanpu).

22. *Ruijū sandaikyaku*, 2: 614 (867/3/24 daijōkanpu).

23. Ibid., pp. 623–24 (835/10/18 daijōkanpu, quoted in 867/ 12/20 daijōkanpu, 894/7/16 daijōkanpu).

24. *Chōya gunsai*, p. 525; *Heian ibun*, doc. 339; *Konjaku monogatari shū*, 19.4, 28.2.

25. *Hokuzanshō*, ura monjo 996/11/25; *Shin sarugakki*, p. 148; *Chōya gunsai*, pp. 523–24; *Konjaku monogatari shū*, 19.4.

26. *Chōya gunsai*, pp. 518–24.

27. *Heian ibun*, doc. 339.

28. *Chōya gunsai*, p. 510 (956/6/21 Suruga kokushi ge); *Sandai jitsuroku*, 877/3/10, 8/7; *Nihon kiryaku*, 811/7/8; *Nihon kōki*, 811/7/8.

29. See, for example, *Nihon kiryaku*, 810/9/11, 811/6/3; *Shoku nihon kōki*, 843/1/5; and *Nihon Montoku tennō jitsuroku*, 850/11/6, 852/2/27.

30. *Sandai jitsuroku*, 877/3/10.

31. *Sandai jitsuroku*, 887/8/7; *Nihon kōki*, 811/7/8.

32. *Konjaku monogatari shū*, 19.4.

33. On the trend toward hereditary positions, see Satō Shin'ichi, pp. 41–62.

34. *Konjaku monogatari shū*, 19.7; similar statements can be found in *Konjaku monogatari shū*, 23.15, 25.7.

35. Mass, "Kamakura Bakufu," p. 49; Yasuda, *Bushi sekai*, p. 6.

36. *Sonpi bunmyaku*, 3: 57–62. The Seiwa Genji have been the subject of numerous studies by Japanese historians. Two works I found particularly helpful are Oboroya, *Seiwa genji*; and Yasuda, *Bushi sekai*. Of special interest is Oboroya's discussion of the imperial family's habit of disposing of extraneous relatives by granting them surnames (such as Taira or Minamoto) and demoting them from princely to commoner status (pp. 21–27). Intriguingly, the ancestry of this lineage has been disputed by some historians, who suggest that Tsune-

moto was in fact descended from Emperor Yōzei (r. 877–84), not Seiwa. See Takeuchi, *Bushi no tōjō*, pp. 40–43. For a short summary of the controversy, see Hurst, "Structure," p. 50n.

37. *Sonpi bunmyaku*, 2: 267–68, 385–86; Noguchi, *Bandō bushidan*, pp. 16–17. Noguchi cites *Azuma kagami*, 1209/12/15. Further information on the bandō Fujiwara can be found in Noguchi, pp. 16–46; and Takahashi Tomio, *Hiraizumi*.

38. *Sonpi bunmyaku*, 4: 1–4, 11–38; Takahashi Masaaki, "Masakado," p. 26; Morita, *Zuryō*, pp. 139–40. Some scholars have questioned whether the warrior Taira are truly an off-shoot of the Kammu Heishi. The Heishi genealogies in the *Sonpi bunmyaku* are considered the least reliable section of the work and contain numerous errors. But as Yasuda, *Bushi sekai*, pp. 68–69, observes, failing any way to correct most of these errors, we have little choice but to accept the general outline of the genealogy.

39. *Sonpi bunmyaku*, 2: 268, 386–411.

40. *Honchō seiki*, 995/3/6 (the other warrior was a Taira, Koremasa's son Koretoki); *Chūyūki*, 1095/10/23, 1104/10/30; *Denryaku*, 1107/10/6; Yasuda, *Bushi sekai*, pp. 11–12.

41. *Mutsuwaki*, p. 23.

42. Ibid., p. 25. The *Mutsuwaki* gives Yoshiie's battlefield skill and courage as the source of his nickname. But many modern scholars disagree, arguing instead that the "Hachiman" refers to the Hachiman Shrine in Iwashimizu, where his coming of age ceremony was performed, and the "Tarō" to his status as Yoriyoshi's eldest son. See H. McCullough, "Tale of Mutsu," p. 207, n. 32.

43. *Hyakurenshō*, 1091/6/12, 1092/5/12. For some details on this incident, see Mass, *Warrior Government*, p. 37.

44. *Chūyūki*, 1108/1/29.

45. Takahashi Masaaki, *Kiyomori izen*, p. 94; Takahashi cites

Chūyūki, 1108/4/1, as an illustration of the parity between the Taira and the Minamoto. Another case in point is related in *Chūyūki*, 1113/4/30, where Taira Masamori is said to have been placed in charge of "Taira and Minamoto warriors of world renown." Ironically, Taira fortunes owed much to Minamoto misfortunes: Masamori's reputation began with his successful campaign against Minamoto Yoshiie's son Yoshichika in 1108.

46. The history of the term bushidan is discussed in Seki, 1: 144. Wilson's translation of "ikusa" appears in "Way of the Bow and Arrow." A few of the most common terms for warrior followers besides rōtō, rōjū, and jūsha are *banrui, jūrui, kenin, zuishin*, and *jūhei*. Little or no consistency of usage can be discerned in Heian documents in most cases. Some sources do distinguish banrui from jūrui (*Shōmonki*, for example), but provide too little information to piece out the distinction between them. Nevertheless, Japanese scholars have directed considerable energy toward uncovering the specific meanings of banrui, jūrui, et al., although to date little consensus has emerged. See Fukuda, "Ōchō gunji kikō," pp. 85–95; Yoshida, "Heian chūki," pp. 2–12; and Haruda.

47. Yasuda, *Bushidan*, p. 17.

48. Ibid., pp. 21–36, 52–58. In this context, Yasuda contrasts the martial following of Taira Masakado with that of his kinsman and opponent Taira Sadamori. Sadamori, he maintains, was the leader of a true bushidan; Masakado was not.

49. Yasuda's views on bushidan and their position in the historiography of bushidan are discussed in Seki, 2: 11–83. Ishii Susumu expresses an opinion similar to mine in *Chūsei bushidan*, pp. 114–15.

50. *Ruijū sandaikyaku*, 2: 547 (780/7/26 choku).

51. The earliest reference I have discovered is *Nihon shoki*, 642/1/15.

52. Okuno, "Heian jidai," p. 7. The first appearance of "guntō" is *Ruijū kokushi*, 798/2/1. The term tōzoku continued to appear sporadically after this date; see, for example, *Shoku nihon kōki*, 840/2/23, 850/1/26.

53. *Sandai jitsuroku*, 870/12/2, 878/6/7; *Ruijū sandaikyaku*, 2: 565 (Kōzuke no kuni ge, quoted in 899/9/19 daijōkanpu).

54. *Sandai jitsuroku*, 884/8/4.

55. Complaints about the phenomenon of the armed forces of elites did not disappear completely, however. See, for example, *Heian ibun*, doc. 682, a daijōkanpu dated 1050/7/22.

56. *Shōmonki*, pp. 125–27; *Konjaku monogatari shū*, 23.14, 25.3, 25.5; Yasuda, *Bushidan*, pp. 20–90, 119–44; Haruda; Yoshida, "Heian chūki"; Fukuda, "Ōchō," pp. 85–88, 99–110; Nagahara, *Nihon hōken shakai ron*, pp. 78–93; Ishimoda, *Kodai makki*, pp. 40–55; Matsumoto Shinpachirō, pp. 10–14. The quotation is from *Shōmonki*, p. 101, describing the entourage of Taira Masakado; the numbers reported are no doubt grossly exaggerated, but even so the ratio of direct to rear vassals is noteworthy.

57. The instability of horizontal alliances in Japan is discussed in other contexts in Endō, pp. 13–15; and Miyagawa and Kiley.

58. The so-called "seven leagues of Musashi" are discussed in detail in Yasuda, *Bushi sekai*, pp. 28–38; and Ishii Susumu, *Kamakura bushi*, pp. 91–94.

59. Ishii Susumu, *Kamakura bushi*, p. 64; Yasuda, *Bushi sekai*, p. 34.

60. A case in point is Taira Masakado; see *Shōmonki*, pp. 101, 117–19.

61. On the warrior leaders' dependence on their court connections, see Mass, *Warrior Government*, pp. 33–35, 45–54.

62. *Shōmonki*, pp. 105–7.

63. On the warrior ethic of Heian times, see Friday, "Mononofu"; Wilson, "Way of the Bow and Arrow"; and Kobayashi Hiroko, pp. 88–170.

64. *Konjaku monogatari shū,* 19.4, 25.6, 25.9, 25.10, 28.2; *Nihon kiryaku,* 989/11/23; *Hokuzanshō,* ura monjo 996/11/25; *Midō kampakki,* 1017/3/11; *Sakeiki,* 1021/6/3.

65. *Konjaku monogatari shū,* 25.9; *Nihon kiryaku,* 1029/2/8, 1030/9/2, 1031/4/28; *Sakeiki,* 1028/6/21, 8/5, 8/16, 1030/6/23.

66. Japanese scholars have used this technique to reconstruct the late-12th-century warbands of several eastern warrior houses, including those of the Oyama, Ōta, Saeki, Chiba, Nakamura, Kamakura, Hatano, Yamanouchi, and Namitano. For recent work in this area, see Noguchi, pp. 82–173; Ishii Susumu, *Kamakura bushi,* pp. 58–157; and Yasuda, *Bushi sekai,* pp. 1–41.

67. Toshitsuna is thought to have been descended from Hidesato's fifth son, Chitsune, through his son Fumihisa and grandson Kanemitsu (although, according to the *Sonpi bunmyaku,* some old texts identify Kanemitsu as Fumihisa's younger brother, rather than his son). Nariyuki was Kanemitsu's great-grandson, and Toshitsuna was legally Nariyuki's grandson, albeit biologically his great-grandson, since Nariyuki adopted his grandson (by his son Naritsuna) Ietsuna. The timing of the arrival of Toshitsuna's forebears in Ashikaga District and of their adoption of the Ashikaga surname is only an estimate. Nariyuki's grandfather Yoriyuki was active around the turn of the 11th century; Nariyuki's eldest son, Naritsuna, and grandson Ietsuna are known to have competed in sumo tournaments in 1111 and 1158, respectively; allowing 15 to 30 years between generations, Nariyuki was probably born between the 1030's and 1060's. Nariyuki's father, Kaneyuki, carried the surname of Fuchina, from an area in south-

eastern Kōzuke. The name was passed down to him from his uncle Kanesuke, a onetime assistant governor of Kōzuke (the *Sonpi bunmyaku* notes that Kanesuke may have been Kaneyuki's elder brother, not his uncle). Kaneyuki's family appears to have left the Fuchina area during his or the succeeding generation. His son Kanenari was known as Azuma *no kami*, suggesting that he resided in the Azuma District of northwestern Kōzuke; none of Kaneyuki's progeny continued the Fuchina surname. (*Sonpi bunmyaku*, 2: 386–88, 399, 404–7; *Shōyūki*, 996/5/2; *Chōshūki*, 1111/8/21; *Heihanki*, 1158/6/27; Noguchi, pp. 38–41, 82, 102–3.)

68. *Azuma kagami*, 1181/9/7; Noguchi, pp. 105–7. The *Gempei seisuiki* (quoted in Noguchi, p. 105) lists among this force the collateral houses of Onoji and Heyako of Shimotsuke and the Saki and Naname of Kōzuke, along with eight rōtō: Kaneko Bonjirō, Ōka Angorō, Tone Shirō, Tanaka Tōda, Obuzuma Jirō, Chinzei Hachi, Kiryū Rokurō, and Ubagoya Jirō. Various versions of the *Heike monogatari* (quoted in Noguchi, p. 107) add to the list of collaterals the Ōko, Ōya, Fukamatsu, and Yamanoue of Kōzuke and the Yoshimizu of Shimotsuke.

69. *Sonpi bunmyaku*, 2: 399–401, 3: 236. Yoshikuni established a *betsugyō* or *betsumyō* in Ashikaga. For information on this form of landholding, see Arnesen, "Struggle for Lordship." Tomomasa was descended from Masamitsu, the grandson of Kaneyuki's younger brother, Yukitaka.

70. The 1142 date for the founding of the estate comes from a document believed to have been written during the early Kamakura period (reproduced in the *Kindai Ashikaga-shi shi*, 1: 136). The *Tochigi-kenshi* (*tsūshihen*, 3: 17) argues that the estate was created by the Minamoto-line Ashikaga, but if the document quoted in the *Kindai Ashikaga-shi shi* is to be believed, the

first scion of the Genshō Ashikaga who can be identified with Ashikaga Estate is Yoshikuni's grandson Yoshikane (1147–96). Noguchi (p. 102) believes the manor was founded by Nariyuki, of the Fujiwara line, but this would place the founding of the estate nearly 100 years earlier than the date specified in the document cited above. Unfortunately, Noguchi does not address this point.

71. *Azuma kagami*, 1181/9/7.

72. Ibid., intercalary 2/23.

73. This passage, from the Enkyōbon version of the *Heike monogatari*, is reproduced in Noguchi, p. 109.

74. Ibid., pp. 108–10.

75. *Azuma kagami*, 1181/9/18.

76. *Sonpi bunmyaku*, 4: 11–12; *Heian ibun*, doc. 2586; *Sakeiki*, 1028/8/1, 8/4; *Shōyūki*, 1028/8/1, 8/2, 8/4, 8/8; *Nihon kiryaku*, 1029/6/13.

77. *Sakeiki*, 1031/6/27; Noguchi, p. 116. For details on Tadatsune's rebellion, see Noguchi, pp. 47–72; and Ishimoda, "Taira Tadatsune."

78. *Heian ibun*, doc. 640.

79. *Azuma kagami*, 1180/8/24, 9/19, 1184/1/17; Noguchi, pp. 124–30.

80. Noguchi, p. 124. *Sonpi bunmyaku* (4: 13) lists Tsuneharu (called Tsunetoki in the genealogy) and his heirs as "assistant governors" (*suke*), rather than "acting assistant governors" (*gon no suke*) but this is probably an error, since that would have effectively made them governors (the governorship of Kazusa being a customary sinecure of an imperial prince). It is highly unlikely that provincial figures like Tsuneharu and his progeny would have been appointed to a post of such high prestige. On this point, see Noguchi, p. 116.

81. *Heian ibun*, doc. 2586. The estate had originally been be-

queathed to Tsunezumi's cousin and adopted brother Tsune-shige by his (Tsunezumi's) father, Tsuneharu. Thus Tsunezumi felt the estate to be rightfully his. His efforts to seize it from Tsunetane failed, however, although he must have managed to retain some residual rights over the land, since *Azuma kagami*, 1184/1/17, identifies one "Sōma Kyūrō Tsunekiyo" as a younger brother of Hirotsune. This case is discussed in detail in Noguchi, pp. 117–18; and Mass, *Warrior Government*, pp. 48–52.

82. *Azuma kagami*, 1184/1/1, 1/17, 3/13.

83. Ishii Susumu, *Kamakura bushi*, pp. 71–72. As noted, descendants of the old regional nobility are believed to have often adopted the surnames of powerful court families. The Kikuchi of Kyushu, who claimed descent from Dazaifu Acting Governor-General Fujiwara Takaie, and the Hatano of Sagami, ostensibly progeny of Fujiwara Hidesato, are two examples for which this can be conclusively demonstrated to have occurred.

84. The incident is recounted in the *Ōshū gosannenki*, paraphrased by Ishii Susumu, *Kamakura bushi*, pp. 69–70.

85. *Heian ibun*, doc. 2548.

86. *Azuma kagami*, 1180/8/24, 8/26. Yoshizumi served as shugo of Sagami from 1194 to 1200. The post of shugo is discussed at length in Mass, *Warrior Government*, pp. 93–102, 203–29.

87. *Azuma kagami*, 1209/12/15. In 1209, Yoshiaki's grandson Yoshimura stated that his family had hereditarily performed "miscellaneous services" (*zōji*) in the Sagami provincial office since the Tenji era (1124–26), a claim that was duly recognized by the shogunate. This service was the reason for Yoshiaki's nickname, Miura no Suke, which appears in the *Sonpi bunmyaku* (4: 14) and other sources. The appellation does

not refer to the formal post of assistant governor of Sagami; see Noguchi, p. 149; and Ishii Susumu, *Kamakura bushi*, pp. 73–75.

88. *Heian ibun*, doc. 2548; Noguchi, p. 149; Ishii Susumu, *Kamakura bushi*, p. 77.

89. Noguchi, pp. 152–53.

90. See, for example, Yasuda, "Bushidan no keisei," pp. 127–28.

91. As in the case of patron-client relationships between court nobles, a warrior entering the service of another presented his new master with his name placard (*myōbu*; see *Heian ibun*, doc. 2467; and *Konjaku monogatari shū*, 25.9). But there is no evidence that he ever received any written confirmation in exchange. On the vassalage system created by Yoritomo and his successors, see Mass, "Kamakura Bakufu."

92. See Mass, *Warrior Government*, pp. 36–54, for a discussion of the difficulties the Minamoto ran into in their efforts to create major networks.

93. See, for instance, Hall, *Government and Local Power*, pp. 134–38; and Shinoda, *Founding*, p. 34.

94. The relationship between Ashikaga Toshitsuna and Oyama Tomomasa is a case in point. Others are the Taira Masakado Rebellion of the mid-10th century, the Taira Tadatsune Insurrection of the mid-11th century, and the Hōgen Incident and the Gempei War of the late 12th century. See also *Denryaku*, 1101/7/3; *Hyakurenshō*, 1091/6/12; and *Shōyūki*, 1005/8/5.

95. Mass, *Lordship*, p. 26.

96. *Konjaku monogatari shū*, 25.6.

97. *Mutsuwaki*, p. 23.

98. *Konjaku monogatari shū*, 25.5.

99. Mass, *Lordship*, pp. 9–37.

100. Noguchi, pp. 86–101.

101. Mass, *Warrior Government*, pp. 59–123, details a number of cases in which related houses fought on opposite sides during the Gempei War.

102. *Heian ibun*, docs. 1663, 1681, 4652; *Denryaku*, 1113/3/13; *Chūyūki*, 1114/1/17, 5/16, 6/8, 6/30, 7/18, 7/22, 8/13, 8/16, 8/21, 9/3, 9/4. I am indebted to Cornelius J. Kiley for calling the Kunifusa-Yukinaka case to my attention.

103. See, for example, *Shōmonki*, pp. 79, 125–29; *Konjaku monogatari shū*, 25.9; *Mutsuwaki*, pp. 23–24, 26, 28; *Chōya gunsai*, p. 284 (1058/3/29 daijōkanpu); and *Chūyūki*, 1114/5/6.

104. *Mutsuwaki*, pp. 25–26.

105. See Takahashi Masaaki, "Bushi no hassei to sono seikaku."

CHAPTER FOUR

1. Much of the following chapter is based on Friday, "Teeth and Claws."

2. See, for example, Hall, *Government and Local Power*, pp. 131–34; and Shinoda, *Founding*, pp. 33–34.

3. See Mass, *Warrior Government*, and Kiley, "Estate and Property," on the relationship between the imperial court and the rights of provincial warriors over land.

4. See, for example, *Sandai jitsuroku*, 879/6/26; *Ruijū sandaikyaku*, 2: 566–67 (894/8/9 daijōkanpu); and *Nihon kiryaku*, 947/2/14.

5. Many scholars have identified the kondei as the new, more select military that was intended to replace the gundan. But for the reasons discussed in Chap. 2, this hypothesis must be rejected.

6. For elaborations of this theory, see Morita, "Heian zenki

o chūshin"; Muraoka, "Enryaku 11"; Hashimoto, "Ritsuryō gundansei to kihei"; and Matsumoto Masaharu, "Gunji."

7. *Ryō no gige*, pp. 303–4. Hirano Tomohiko, one of the earliest and staunchest exponents of the jinpei hypothesis (see "Kondeisei seiritsu"), has since recanted. (In an earlier treatment of this issue, I erroneously cited Hirano as an advocate of the theory; the volume in which he published his new position in fact appeared a few months before my own article went to press. See Friday, "Teeth and Claws," pp. 158–59.) He now rejects both the idea that the ritsuryō system provided for separate institutions to cope with domestic and foreign threats to the peace and the notion that district officials played a regular role in the imperial military apparatus. See his paper "Ritsuryō chihō gunsei."

8. See *Sandai jitsuroku*, 862/5/20, for example.

9. *Ryō no gige*, p. 304; Shimomukai, "Ōchō kokka gunsei kenkyū," pp. 309–10. In his recent apostasy, Hirano also acknowledges this last point (see "Ritsuryō chihō gunsei," p. 200).

10. *Sandai jitsuroku*, 883/2/9.

11. *Honchō seiki*, 941/9/19; *Nihon kiryaku*, 947/2/14. On 10th-century warrior organization, see Takahashi Masaaki, "Masakado"; Yoshida, "Masakado"; Haruda; and Fukuda, "Ōchō gunji kikō."

12. The earliest use of the term kebiishi-chō I know of is in an 895/12/22 daijōkanpu, quoted in *Seiji yōryaku*, pp. 688–91. It is clear, however, that the office was in place long before this. The close ties between the emonfu and the kebiishi-chō are discussed in Satō Shin'ichi, pp. 18–19. The kebiishi-chō has been well studied. A few of the works I have found particularly useful are Uwayokote, "Heian chūki"; Inoue Mitsuo, *Heian jidai*

no gunji seido, pp. 104–31; Watanabe, "Kebiishi no kenkyū"; Ōae, *Ritsuryō seika*; and Morita, "Kebiishi no kenkyū." The only detailed Western-language treatment of kebiishi to date is Hérail, *Fonctions et fonctionnaires*, pp. 480–97.

13. *Seiji yōryaku*, pp. 517–18; *Heian ibun*, doc. 520.

14. Quoted in *Seiji yōryaku*, p. 517.

15. *Nihon Montoku tennō jitsuroku*, 850/11/5. This is the earliest instance in which the term kebiishi is used specifically; it may not, however, have been the first kebiishi appointment. *Nihon kōki*, 805/11/7, refers to one Ki Hamakimi, a Junior Clerk (*shōsakan*) of the left hyōefu, as a "*shi*" assigned to investigate an alleged incident of murder by poisoning. Though the chronicle does not explicitly identify Hamakimi as such, a popular index to the *Nihon kōki* cites this entry as a reference to kebiishi (*Rikkokushi sakuin*, 3: 157). If Hamakimi was a kebiishi, the Office of Imperial Police could not have been wholly a subunit of the emonfu, since he was a member of the hyōefu.

16. *Kugyō bunin*, 1: 103; *Shoku nihon kōki*, 837/10/1; *Seiji yōryaku*, p. 517. Inoue Mitsuo and Satō Shin'ichi have both suggested that the first kebiishi suke was appointed in 824, ten years before the appointment of the first bettō (Inoue Mitsuo, *Heian jidai no gunji seido*, p. 106; Satō Shin'ichi, p. 18). But neither reveals his source for this information, and I have been unable to discover a reference to the post earlier than the 837 cited in *Shoku Nihon kōki*.

17. *Kugyō bunin*, 1: 103–509; *Seiji yōryaku*, pp. 529–30. Of a total of 82 bettō appointments made between 834 and 1184, 48 held concurrent posts as *emonfu no kami*, 32 as *hyōefu no kami*, and two as *kon'efu no chūjō*. Two were of the second court rank, 17 of the fourth rank, and the rest of the third rank. Thirty-eight were sangi, 34 were *gon no chūnagon*, and 10 were chūnagon. Fifty-seven of the appointees were Fujiwara, 16 Mina-

moto, and 5 Taira; the other 4 were a Fumiya, Tomo, Sahara, and Ōe. Inoue, *Heian jidai no gunji seido*, pp. 116–17, provides a chronological list of kebiishi bettō, with their years of appointment, concurrent appointments, and court ranks.

18. *Chōya gunsai*, pp. 240–41 (1089/1/23 Kazusa Yoshisada kebiishi mōshibumi); *Shōyūki*, 1021/8/24, 1024/3/11; *Denryaku*, 1113/3/13; *Chūyūki*, 1095/10/23, 1104/10/30; *Dainihonshi*, 16: 43–132; Uwayokote, "Heian chūki," pp. 526–27; Morita, "Kebiishi," pp. 15–17; Morita, "Heian chūki," p. 55. Some of the best information on kebiishi jō and sakan can be found in the series of appointment documents and petitions for appointment reproduced in *Chōya gunsai*, pp. 240–42, 257–58.

19. *Seiji yōryaku*, pp. 517–18; *Engi shiki*, pp. 963–64; 1003/11/28 kebiishi bettō sen, quoted in *Seiji yōryaku*, pp. 530–31; Horiuchi, pp. 346–50. Of the 18 group chiefs listed in the *Engi shiki* (p. 963), four (two left and two right) were designated as overseers and two (one left and one right) as superintendents of records; four were assigned as attendants to the assistant director, four as attendants to the secretaries, two as attendants to the clerks, and two as attendants to the sergeants.

20. *Ryō no gige*, pp. 55–59, 311. The law enforcement activities of the danjōdai and the kyōshiki are discussed in Ōae, pp. 14–15.

21. Inoue Mitsuo, *Heian jidai no gunji seido*, pp. 107–11; Ōae, pp. 14–23; Morita, "Kebiishi seiritsu"; Satō Shin'ichi, pp. 19–23.

22. *Ryō no gige*, p. 55.

23. *Ruijū sandaikyaku*, 2: 645 (820/12/11 senji, quoted in 832/7/9 daijōkanpu).

24. Ibid. (820/11[?]/25 kebiishi ge, quoted in 832/7/9 daijōkanpu).

25. Quoted in *Shoku Nihon kōki*, 839/6/6.

26. *Seiji yōryaku*, p. 689 (kebiishi bettō ge, quoted in 895/12/22 daijōkanpu).

27. Ibid., p. 517; *Nihon Montoku tennō jitsuroku*, 857/3/16; *Sandai jitsuroku*, 874/12/26.

28. *Heian ibun*, docs. 372, 374, ho 7, 682; *Chōya gunsai*, pp. 262–63 (1025 Ubenkan kudashibumi, and 1025 Sabenkan kudashibumi). The actual investigation of incidents occurring outside the capital was usually handled by provincial *tsuibushi* rather than the kebiishi themselves.

29. *Heian ibun*, doc. 520.

30. A number of sources support both points; see, for example, *Sankeiki*, 1021/5/11; and *Shōyūki*, 1028/7/19.

31. *Besshū fusenshō*, pp. 23–24 (946/3/13 daijōkanpu); *Heian ibun*, doc. 1999; *Saigūki*, 2: 240 (965/?/13); Watanabe, p. 344; Ōae, pp. 276–77. On the relationship between the *zaichō kanjin* and the provincial government, see Morita, *Zuryō*, pp. 193–207. On the relationship between those two bodies and the provincial kebiishi, see Watanabe, pp. 343–57; and Ōae, pp. 275–77.

32. *Nihon Montoku tennō jitsuroku*, 855/3/26; Ōae, pp. 270–71.

33. *Sandai jitsuroku*, 861/11/16, 867/12/4, 876/7/8, 877/12/21, 878/2/13; *Nihon Montoku tennō jitsuroku*, 855/3/26; *Besshū fusenshō*, pp. 22–23 (949/1/21 Ōmi kokushi ge). Several authorities have reached conclusions similar to mine, including Watanabe, p. 340; Ōae, pp. 271–73; Kuroda, p. 6.

34. *Honchō monzui*, pp. 51–52 (914/4/28 Miyoshi Kiyotsura iken fuji).

35. *Nihon Montoku tennō jitsuroku*, 855/3/26, 857/8/7; *Sandai jitsuroku*, 879/10/22; *Ruijū sandaikyaku*, 1: 234–35 (894/9/18 daijōkanpu).

36. *Honchō monzui*, pp. 51–52 (914/4/28 Miyoshi Kiyotsura iken fuji).

37. Detailed discussions of these early sources can be found in Friday, "Teeth and Claws," pp. 163–67; and Friday, "Hired Swords," pp. 229–36.

38. *Shoku nihongi*, 759/11/9.

39. Ibid., 783/6/6; *Sandai jitsuroku*, 876/4/4, 4/28, 6/7, 7/10, 878/4/4, 4/28, 6/7, 7/10, 879/6/26; *Ruijū sandaikyaku*, 2: 548 (795/11/22 daijōkanpu); *Fusō ryakki*, 894/9/5. Jō and sakan were the third- and fourth-ranking posts in the provincial government hierarchy, after governor (kami) and assistant governor (suke). In large provinces, the posts were often divided into senior (*dai*) and junior (*shō*) offices. The convention of choosing provincial officials as ōryōshi was not absolute; in at least one case, a district officer was so designated (*Fusō ryakki*, 894/9/5). It is not clear how long ōryōshi remained a temporary appointment. Takeuchi Rizō ("Zaichō kanjin," pp. 27–28) believes ōryōshi had become a permanent office by at least the third quarter of the 9th century; Fukuda Toyohiko ("Ōchō gunji kikō," p. 107) thinks it was temporary until the mid-940's.

40. Inoue Mitsuo, *Heian jidai no gunji seido*, pp. 136–38; Shimomukai, "Ōryōshi," pp. 19–22.

41. Yumino. For examples of buryō in the ritsuryō codes, see *Ryō no gige*, pp. 186–87.

42. *Chōya gunsai*, p. 28 (1058/3/29 daijōkanpu).

43. Inoue Mitsuo, *Heian jidai no gunji seido*, pp. 138–41.

44. *Fusō ryakki*, 894/9/5.

45. Yumino (pp. 228–29) reaches a similar conclusion, arguing that a field command had always been an essential part of the ōryōshi office.

46. *Shoku nihongi*, 783/6/6.

47. *Konjaku monogatari shū*, 25.1. For an overview of the historical literature on Masakado, see Saeki et al. For English-language accounts, see Stramigioli; and Rabinovitch.

48. The sources and the information they give about the ō-ryōshi active in 939–40 are detailed in Friday, "Teeth and Claws," pp. 167–68.

49. *Shōmonki*, p. 121; Inoue Mitsuo, *Heian jidai no gunji seido*, p. 149.

50. *Nihon kiryaku*, 916/8/12. Hidesato was also the subject of an investigation in Shimotsuke in 929 (*Fusō ryakki*, 929/5/ 20, as quoted in *Dainihon shiryō*). *Azuma kagami*, 1209/12/15, claims that Hidesato's father and grandfather had also held the ōryōshi title. On Hidesato and his warrior organization, see Noguchi, pp. 16–46.

51. Inoue Mitsuo, *Heian jidai no gunji seido*, pp. 149–50.

52. *Nihon kiryaku*, 940/3/9; *Fusō ryakki*, 940/3/9.

53. Inoue Mitsuo, *Heian jidai no gunji seido*, pp. 150–51.

54. Fujiwara Tadanobu, who is identified as an ōryōshi by the *Shōmonki* (p. 133), is an exception here, and seems to have been an exception to most of the generalizations that can be made about the ōryōshi of the period. But since this is the only source that calls him an ōryōshi, the possibility that the compilers mislabeled him cannot be ignored.

55. Hidesato was later appointed *chinjufu* shōgun, but this occurred after his promotion to the fourth rank. The provincial kebiishi post would not have been of high enough status by this time for what were essentially the colonels and brigadiers of the government's army.

56. Inoue Mitsuo (*Heian jidai no gunji seido*, pp. 146–47) sees the later form as a reinvention: though the essence of the office had been completely redefined, the Masakado-era ōryōshi developed out of the earlier billet. But Shimomukai ("Ōryōshi,"

pp. 24–26) contends that Hidesato and the others represent the birth of a completely different type of ōryōshi, one that bore no relationship to the earlier type beyond its name.

57. For details on Sumitomo and his career, see Hayashi Rokurō, *Kodai makki*; and Minamoto.

58. *Teishin kōki*, 932/4/28. Tsuibushi subsequently appear in a number of sources for 940–41. The title was subject to considerable variation in these early years, appearing in several other guises: *tsuibu kaizoku shi, tsuibu kyōzoku shi*, and *tsuibu nankai kyōzoku shi*, among others. As Inoue Mitsuo (*Heian jidai no gunji seido*, pp. 185–86) has observed, however, there are really only two patterns: "*X* tsuibushi," where the variable is the region of the appointment, and "tsuibu *X* shi," where the variable is the object of pursuit. There is no evidence to suggest a difference of function between the title-holders.

59. This is the conclusion reached by Inoue Mitsuo, *Heian jidai no gunji seido*, pp. 13–14.

60. *Ryō no gige*, pp. 303–4; *Shoku nihongi*, 766 addendum; *Sandai jitsuroku*, 862/5/28; *Honchō seiki*, 939/6/21; *Chōya gunsai*, p. 511 (950/2/20 Shimōsa kokushi ge).

61. *Shoku nihongi*, 838/2/10; *Sandai jitsuroku*, 881/5/13. The backgrounds of those appointed as tsuibushi have also been noted by Shimomukai, "Ōryōshi," p. 29; and Inoue Mitsuo, *Heian jidai no gunji seido*, pp. 13–14.

62. *Nihon kiryaku*, 940/1/1; *Honchō seiki*, 941/8/7. *Nihon kiryaku*, 940/10/22, also mentions a "dazaifu tsuibushi"; Inoue Mitsuo (*Heian jidai no gunji seido*, pp. 185–86) believes the jurisdiction of this officer included the whole of the Saikaidō, that is, Kyushu and the islands of Iki and Tsushima. Shimomukai ("Ōryōshi," p. 30) identifies nine tsuibushi appointments made between 932 and 941, eight of which had jurisdiction over one or more circuits. The remaining appointment

was that of a "*suimon tsuibushi*," appointed to Musashi in 939 (*Honchō seiki*, 939/6/7).

63. *Honchō seiki*, 941/8/7.

64. Shimomukai, "Ōryōshi," pp. 22, 31. Though this point deserves careful consideration, it is based on the linking of two passages, *Teishin kōki*, 940/1/13, and *Nihon kiryaku*, 940/1/1, both of which are ambiguous and not all that obviously connected.

65. *Sandai jitsuroku*, 867/11/10. The quoted passage does not of course refer specifically to Sumitomo and his gang but concerns the pirates of several decades earlier; nevertheless, the military problem posed by the pirates was essentially the same.

66. *Honchō seiki*, 941/11/5.

67. Inoue Mitsuo, *Heian jidai no gunji seido*, pp. 187–89. On the *seisai taishōgun*, see *Nihon kiryaku*, 941/5/19. On the title taishōgun, see Noda, *Ritsuryō kokka no gunjisei*, pp. 106–7. In addition to tsuibushi, a number of similar titles appear in the sources around the time of Sumitomo's troublemaking. *Fusō ryakki*, 933/12/17; *Nihon kiryaku*, 940/8/27; *Honchō seiki*, 941/11/5; and *Fusō ryakki*, 940/12/26, mention the appointment of several "*keikoshi*" in response to pirate activity. In *Honchō seiki*, 941/11/29, Minamoto Tsunemoto is identified by this title, as well as by "*tsuitō kyōzoku shi*," while *Fusō ryakki*, 940/12/26, calls him a tsuibushi. *Nihon kiryaku*, 941/8/7, speaks of Ono Yoshifuru as a "*seitōshi*," but earlier passages call him "*sei nankai zokushi*" (941/5/19) and mention his appointment as San'yōdō tsuibushi (940/1/1). *Honchō seiki*, 941/10/23, observes the posting of keikoshi, ōryōshi, and *gekishushi* to the various provinces of the San'yōdō and Nankaidō. While little can be said about any of these titles, it is clear that the court was still experimenting with the mechanics of its new military/police system.

68. *Chōya gunsai*, pp. 512–14 (952/3/2 Echizen kokushi ge, 952/11/9 daijōkanpu, 956/6/13 daijōkanpu).

69. *Chōya gunsai*, p. 511 (1006/4/11 Awaji kokushi ge); *Ruijū fusenshō*, p. 175 (992/10/18 daijōkanpu). *Heian ibun*, docs. *ho* 7, 2090. An appointment document usually quoted at length from the document requesting the appointment.

70. For examples of appointment documents, see *Chōya gunsai*, pp. 512–13 (952/11/9 daijōkanpu, 956/6/13 daijōkanpu); and *Ruijū fusenshō*, pp. 175–76 (1006/3/9 daijōkanpu). For documents requesting appointments, see *Chōya gunsai*, p. 511 (950/2/20 Shimōsa no kami Fujiwara Ariyuki mōshibumi, 1006/4/11 Awaji kokushi ge). The appointment process is outlined in *Saigūki*, pp. 244, 282; and *Hokuzanshō*, p. 451. *Kamakura ibun*, doc. 3827, records the Council of State's appointment of an ōryōshi in Dewa in 1229. An interesting sidebar is the 1184 appointment of Fujiwara (Masuda) Kanetaka as ōryōshi of Iwami by Kajiwara Kagetoki, acting in the name of the future shōgun Minamoto Yoritomo (*Heian ibun*, doc. 4175). While not made by the daijōkan, the appointment was still central in origin.

71. *Chōya gunsai*, p. 511 (950/2/20 Shimōsa no kami Fujiwara Ariyuki mōshibumi); *Chōshūki*, 1130/9/4; *Kamakura ibun*, doc. 3827; *Hokuzanshō*, p. 588; *Heian ibun*, doc. 439.

72. Fukuda, "Ōchō gunji kikō," pp. 107–9; *Chōya gunsai*, p. 511 (950/2/20 Shimōsa no kami Fujiwara Ariyuki mōshibumi); *Heian ibun*, doc. 439; *Chūyūki*, 1133/2/28.

73. There is one instance of someone being designated *tsuibu nakaidō shi* and simultaneously made governor of Iyo (936/5/26; *Gunshō ruiju, wakabu* doc. 285 [*Kokin wakashū mokuroku*]). But the sequence here was the opposite of that for the early ōryōshi appointments. The appointee, Ki no Yoshihito, was not a provincial official granted an extra title, but was

given the governorship of Iyo for precisely the same purpose as the tsuibushi title: to suppress pirate activity in and around the province.

74. *Chōya gunsai*, p. 512 (956/6/13 daijōkanpu).

75. Ibid., pp. 513–14 (952/3/2 Echizen kokushi ge); *Heian ibun*, doc. 374. There is some doubt whether the ōryōshi in the Shikida Estate case really held the office; the appellation may have simply been a nickname. A similar case is documented in *Shōyūki*, 1028/7/19, 7/20, 7/22, 8/11, 8/15, 8/17.

76. Shimomukai, "Ōryōshi," p. 31.

77. One example is the 952 case just cited, in which the governor of Echizen asked the court to cancel the ōryōshi and tsuibushi commissions in his province. His use of the two titles is borne out by an authoritative genealogy (*Sonpi bunmyaku*, 2: 315), which describes one Fujiwara Koresuke as "the ōryōshi of Echizen" and his nephew Kuniaki as "Echizen *no kuni no tsuibushi*." The other province that seems to have had both is Mimasaka. See the reference to a tsuibushi in *Chōya gunsai*, pp. 512–13 (952/11/9 daijōkanpu); and the reference to an ōryōshi in "Jihanki," 1099/3/28.

78. In constructing the Fig. 7 map, I limited the provinces to those in which ōryōshi or tsuibushi can be identified from contemporary (pre-Kamakura) sources. The *Azuma kagami* and some genealogies from the Kamakura, Muromachi, and *sengoku* eras suggest that both offices were more widespread.

79. Inoue Mitsuo, *Heian jidai no gunji seido*, pp. 105–7.

80. *Honchō seiki*, 941/11/29.

81. There were exceptions, as in the case of commissions given to Taira Naokata and Nakahara Narimichi to capture Taira Tadatsune (*Sankaiki*, 1028/6/21).

82. *Ryō no gige*, pp. 186, 311–12.

83. *Heian ibun*, doc. 385.

84. Such warrants were alternatively called *tsuibu senji, tsuitō kanpu*, or *tsuitō senji*. For an example, see *Heian ibun*, doc. 4573.

85. *Heian ibun*, docs. 385, 520, 795, 797; *Chōshūki*, 1094/3/8, 1113/9/30, 1135/4/8; *Mutsuwaki*, pp. 23–24; *Chūyūki*, 1095/10/23, 1108/1/19; *Fusō ryakki*, 1057/8/10; *Sankaiki*, 1031/6/7. The powers granted by tsuibu kanpu are discussed in detail by Shimomukai, "Ōchō kokka gunsei kenkyū," pp. 308–19.

86. *Chūyūki*, 1104/6/24; *Heian ibun*, doc. 1627. As we saw in Chap. 2, the injunction against raising more than 20 troops without a court order dates back to the ritsuryō codes.

87. *Fusō ryakki*, 1049/12/28.

88. See, for example, *Shoku Nihon kōki*, 838/2/9, 2/10, 848/2/10; *Sandai jitsuroku*, 866/4/11, 883/2/9; *Teishin kōki*, 938/5/23; *Nihon kiryaku*, 969/4/3; *Shōyūki*, 1027/2/10; and *Chōshūki*, 1113/3/4, 1135 4/8. The normal procedure apparently called for tsuibu kanpu to be given to the governors of the provinces in question; there is no evidence that the Council of State ever issued military instructions directly to ōryōshi or tsuibushi.

89. *Shōyūki*, 1030/9/6; *Chūyūki*, 1108/1/29, 1135/4/8; *Chōshūki*, 1135/4/8. See Toda, "Kokuga gunsei," pp. 26–27.

90. *Heian ibun*, doc. 385; *Chōshūki*, 1113/9/30.

91. The signatures of men who identify themselves as ōryōshi or tsuibushi are found on documents relating to intraestate affairs. Often these are mixed in among the signatures of men who are clearly shōen officers (see *Heian ibun*, docs. 1103, 1923, 2754, and 3492). Evidence of this sort dates the first shōen tsuibushi or ōryōshi back to the 1070's. See Shimomukai, "Ōryōshi," pp. 26–27; and Inoue Mitsuo, *Heian jidai no gunji seido*, pp. 167–68.

92. *Heian ibun*, docs. 384, ho 7.

CONCLUSION

1. One of the works that most directly equates Genji's court with the reality of the Heian central government is Ivan Morris's *The World of the Shining Prince*. In spite of several flaws, the work remains fascinating reading and a source of much useful information on Heian court society.

2. Murdoch, *History of Japan*, 1: 230. Some may think it unkind of me to cite Murdoch in this context—after all, it should hardly be surprising that the interpretations of a work published 80 years ago would be out of date. But I quote Murdoch here out of affection, for his is simply an unusually colorful exposition of a view that continues to appear in survey and introductory histories today. Compare, for example, this passage from a recent work: "At the end of the twelfth century, Japan was swept violently out of the age of aristocratic, courtly government and into the age of feudal, military rule. The process of change had been gradual; the violent upheaval was merely the final stage, the final struggle for supremacy between two rival military families that had already established their power. . . . The hallmark of Heian culture was a pacific, aristocratic aestheticism, courtly almost beyond belief, in which . . . success, both in society and in one's career, depended on the ability to dress well, comport oneself correctly, compose poetry, write in a good hand, perform music, and display sensitivity to the beauty and sadness of nature in its changing seasons and to the feelings of one's fellow aristocrats. Wit, decorum, good taste, and gentleness were valued. Rude violence was abhorred. Officers of the guards coveted the high social standing that went with their military titles, but they would have been shocked at the idea of having to fight." (Phillip T. Harries, *The Poetic Memoirs*

of Lady Daibu [Stanford, Calif.: Stanford University Press, 1980], p. 5.)

3. E. Reischauer, *Japan*, p. 41.

4. Among the more important studies developing this theme are Hurst, *Insei*, and "Kōbu Polity"; Kiley, "Estate and Property," and "Imperial Court"; Mass, *Warrior Government*, *Development of Kamakura Rule*, and *Lordship*; Gay, "Muromachi Rule"; and Goble, "Go-Daigo."

5. Turnbull, *Samurai*, pp. 24–25.

6. *Shoku Nihon kōki*, 849/intercalary 12/21.

GLOSSARY

Bandō 坂東. Literally, "East of the Barrier"; eastern Japan, the provinces of Sagami, Musashi, Kazusa, Shimōsa, Hitachi, Kōzuke, Shimotsuke, and Mutsu; Awa and Dewa are also sometimes included in this list.

Bettō 別当. The director or chief administrator of any of several extra-code central government offices, the chancellory (*mandokoro*) of a high-ranking noble house, a religious institution, or an estate (*shōen*) headquarters.

Bushi 武士. A generic term for Japanese warriors.

Bushidan 武士団. A historiographical term for the private military organizations of warriors of the Heian and Kamakura periods.

Chakushi 嫡子. Designated principal heir; *chakushi* succeeded their fathers as heads of their families and inherited the most important hereditary rights and properties; they were usually, but not necessarily, the eldest sons.

Chinjufu 鎮守府. The Pacification Headquarters established in Dewa during the early 8th century as part of the government's efforts to subdue the *emishi* (q.v.); originally called the Chinjō.

Chinpei 鎮兵. "Pacification Soldiers"; special garrison troops drawn from the provincial regiments and stationed in the northeastern frontier region.

Chūefu 中衛府. One of the Six Guard units that made up the central military institutions of the Heian period; established in 707 as the *jutō toneri ryō* (q.v.) and renamed the *chūefu* in 728; in 807 it was again renamed, this time becoming the right *kon'efu* (q.v.).

Chūjō 中将. Middle General; the number two post in the left and right *kon'efu* (q.v.), the *chūefu* (q.v.), and the *gaiefu* (q.v.).

Circuits, see *dō*.

Daijōkan 太政官. Council of State; the supreme legislative and policy-making body under the *ritsuryō* (q.v.) codes; responsible for debating issues, recommending courses of action to the emperor, and issuing edicts in the name of the emperor.

Daiki 大毅. Colonel; the designation for the officer in charge of large *ritsuryō* provincial regiments (of more than one *gunki*, q.v.).

Dazaifu 大宰府. A supraprovincial government office with jurisdiction over Kyushu, Iki, and Tsushima.

Dō 道. Also called *michi*; an administrative grouping of provinces under the *ritsuryō* system (q.v.); there were seven *dō* (called circuits in the text), each named for a major travel route originating in the capital and passing through each of the provinces in the circuit: the Tōkaidō, Tōsandō, Hokurikudō, San'indō, San'yōdō, Nankaidō, and Saikaidō (q.v. all), plus the capital region (*kinai*, q.v.).

Eji 衛士. Troops serving guard duty in the capital in the left or right *ejifu* (q.v.) or the *emonfu* (q.v.); *eji* were drawn from among the conscripts on the provincial regimental rosters.

Ejifu 衛士府. Two of the original Five Guards (*goefu*; q.v.) units that made up the *ritsuryō* central military; the right and left *ejifu* were combined with the *emonfu* (q.v.) in 808 and then renamed the right and left *emonfu* in 811.

Emishi 蝦夷. Also called the *ezo* or the *ebisu*; a tribal people who once inhabited much of eastern Japan; although of similar racial stock to the Yamato Japanese, they differed in language and custom, and fiercely resisted the court's efforts to extend its authority into their homeland.

Emonfu 衛門府. One of the original Five Guards (*goefu*; q.v.) units that made up the *ritsuryō* central military; the *emonfu* was combined with the left and right *ejifu* (q.v.) in 808; in 811 the two *ejifu* were renamed the left and right *emonfu*.

Fukushōgun 副将軍. Lieutenant General; the number two post (above *gunken* and below *shōgun*; q.v.) in the command staff of the *ritsuryō* expeditionary armies.

Gaiefu 外衛府. An imperial guard unit established by Empress Kōken/Shōtoku in 765; it was abolished in 772.

Go 伍. A squad; a five-man unit within the *ritsuryō* provincial regiments.

Goefu 五衛府. The Five Guards; the military units established under the *ritsuryō* codes (q.v.) for the defense of the imperial palace and the capital.

Gun 軍. An army within an expeditionary force; under the *ritsuryō* system, an expeditionary force would be composed of from one to three *gun*, each numbering between 3,000 and 12,000 men.

Gun 郡. District; an administrative subdivision of a province; provinces included at least two and as many as 20 *gun*; an average province contained around 10.

Gundan 軍団. The provincial regiments established under the *ritsuryō* system; *gundan* were administrative organizations, not standing garrisons or tactical units.

Gunji 郡司. District Official; the officers in charge of a *gun* (q.v. district).

Gunken 軍監. Major General; the number three post (above *gunsō* and below *fukushōgun*; q.v.) in a *ritsuryō* expeditionary army.

Gunki 軍毅. Colonel (also called *ki*); the officer in charge of the *ritsuryō* provincial regiments; in large regiments *gunki* were divided into *daiki* and *shōki* (q.v.).

Gunsō 軍曹. Brigadier General; the number four post (above *rokuji* and below *gunken*; q.v.) in the *ritsuryō* expeditionary armies.

Haniwa 埴輪. A collective term for the clay figurines found in the great tombs (*kofun*) of the 3d and 4th centuries.

Heian-kyō 平安京. The imperial capital from 794 to 1868; present-day Kyoto.

Heijō 平城. The imperial capital from 710 to 794; near present-day Nara.

Heishi 兵士. A conscript soldier enrolled in one of the provincial regiments under the *ritsuryō* codes (q.v.).

Hokurikudō 北陸道. One of the seven circuits (*dō*) under the *ritsuryō* system (q.v.); the provinces of Wakasa, Echizen, Etchū, Echigo, Kaga, Noto, and Sado.

Hyōe 兵衛. The troopers who manned the left and right *hyōefu* (q.v.); *hyōe* were drawn from the provincial and lower central nobility.

Hyōefu 兵衛府. Two of the original Five Guards (*goefu*; q.v.) units that made up the *ritsuryō* central military; the left and right *hyōefu* survived the transformation of the *ritsuryō* central military to the Six Guards (*rokuefu*; q.v.) of Heian and later times.

In 院. The retired or abdicated emperor.

Jin 陣. Battalion; the largest subdivisions of the *ritsuryō* expeditionary armies; battalions were the tactical equivalents of the regiments, which were administrative units.

Jutōe 授刀衛. An imperial guard unit reconstituted by Empress Kōken/Shōtoku in 759. See also *kon'efu*.

Jutō toneri 授刀舎人. The name applies to the troops who manned the *jutōe* and the *jutō toneri ryō* (q.v.). Also, the name of an imperial guard unit established in 746 by Emperor Shōmu and renamed the *jutōe* (q.v.).

Jutō toneri ryō 授刀舎人寮. An imperial guard unit established by Empress Genmei in 707; in 728, it was renamed the *chūefu* (q.v.).

Ka 火. Campfire; a ten-man unit within the *ritsuryō* provincial regiments.

Kantō 関東. The great plain of eastern Japan centered on the modern cities of Tokyo and Yokohama; the provinces of Hitachi, Shimotsuke, Kōzuke, Musashi, Sagami, Shimōsa, Kazusa, and Awa.

Kebii-dokoro 検非違所. A department in the provincial government office (*zaichō*) during the late Heian period.

Kebiishi 検非違使. "Envoy to Investigate Oddities"; members of the Imperial Police in the capital; also, a provincial military/police post established in the mid-9th century.

Kebiishi-chō 検非違使庁. The Office of Imperial Police; the primary policing agency for the capital; established around 820 as a special unit within the left and right *emonfu* (q.v.), and given its own independent administrative apparatus by the 930's.

Kinai 畿内. The capital region around Heijō (q.v.) and Heian-kyō (q.v.); the provinces of Yamato, Yamashiro, Kawachi, Settsu, and Izumi; this region had a special legal status in many areas of governance.

Kondei 健児. Literally, "stalwart youth"; any of several incarnations of units established at various times during the 8th century to augment the imperial court's military and police system in the countryside.

Kon'efu 近衛府. One of the Six Guards (*rokuefu*; q.v.) units that made up the central military institutions of the Heian period; established in 746 by Emperor Shōmu as the *jutō toneri* (q.v.) and renamed the *jutōe* (q.v.) by Empress Kōken/Shōtoku in 759; in 765, it was reconstituted as the *kon'efu*; in 807, it was again renamed, this time becoming the left *kon'efu*.

Kugyō 公卿. The highest ranking members of the central nobility.

Kuni no miyatsuko 国造. Provincial Patriarchs; posts awarded on a permanent and hereditary basis by the Yamato court to prominent regional chieftains who acknowledged the authority of the court during the pre-*ritsuryō* (q.v.) period; although nominally officials of the Yamato sovereign, in practice they were largely beyond the court's authority.

Kun'i 勲位. Merit rank or military merit rank; under the *ritsuryō* codes (q.v.), a system of ranks that paralleled the normal court ranks but in which promotions were based on meritorious performance in military campaigns.

Kyōi 校尉. Warrant Officer First Class; the number three post (above *rosochi* and below *taishō*; q.v.) in the *ritsuryō* provincial regiments.

Miyako no musha 都の武者. Warriors of the capital; central nobles of the provincial governor class (men of the fourth or fifth court rank) who used the profession of arms as a vehicle for more general career advancement; sometimes called the samurai in English-language sources.

Mokudai 目代. The personal deputy of an absentee provincial

governor; often the main link between central authority and the provincial government.

Nankaidō 南海道. One of the seven circuits (*dō*) under the *ritsuryō* system (q.v.); the provinces of Kii, Awaji, Awa, Sanuki, Iyo, and Tosa.

Ōryōshi 押領使. "Envoy to Subdue the Territory"; one of the two main titles granted warriors under the Heian period provincial military and police system.

Ōyumi 弩. The "artillery" piece of the *ritsuryō* military; no clear descriptions or drawings survive, but it appears to have been a kind of large, multiple-arrow-launching crossbow.

Ritsuryō 律令. The legal codes that defined the structure and operation of the imperial state. There were four such codes: the Ōmi Codes of 668, the Kiyomihara Codes of 689, the Taihō Codes of 702, and the Yōrō Codes of 718. Only the Yōrō Codes remain extant.

Rokuefu 六衛府. The Six Guards; the central military and guard units of the Heian and later periods.

Rokuji 録事. Major; the lowest post (below *gunsō*; q.v.) in the *ritsuryō* expeditionary armies.

Rosochi 旅師. Warrant Officer Second Class; the number four post (above *taishō* and below *kyōi*; q.v.) in the *ritsuryō* provincial regiments.

Rōtō 郎党. One of the higher-ranking retainers in the entourage of a career provincial governor; performed as general functionaries in the provincial government. Also, the warrior followers of provincial governors, high-ranking courtiers, or renowned warriors.

Rusudokoro 留守所. Absentee Office; the agency within a provincial government headquarters that received the orders and communiques of governors who remained in the capital.

Saikaidō 西海道. One of the seven circuits (*dō*) under the *ritsuryō* system (q.v.); the provinces of Chikuzen, Chikugo, Buzen, Bungo, Hizen, Higo, Hyūgo, Satsuma, and Ōsumi on the island of Kyushu, plus the island provinces of Tsushima and Iki.

Sakimori 防人. "Defenders of the Edge"; under the *ritsuryō* codes (q.v.), special garrison troops drawn from the provincial regiments and stationed in the southwestern frontier region.

San'indō 山陰道. One of the seven circuits (*dō*) under the *ritsuryō* system (q.v.); the provinces of Tango, Tanba, Tajima, Inaba, Hōki, Izumo, Iwami, and Oki.

San'yōdō 山陽道. One of the seven circuits (*dō*) under the *ritsuryō* system (q.v.); the provinces of Harima, Mimasaka, Bizen, Bitchū, Bingo, Aki, Suō, and Nagato.

Sekkanke 摂関家. Regent's House; the sublineage of the northern branch of the Fujiwara house that came to hold in heredity the posts of *sesshō* (a regent for an emperor still in his/her minority) and *kampaku* (a "regent" for an adult emperor).

Shōen 荘園. A landed estate, normally held in proprietorship by a high-ranking member of the central nobility or by one of the great religious institutions; the dominant form of landholding and land administration from the 11th through the 14th century, its full history runs from the 8th through the 16th.

Shōgun 将軍. General; the top post in the *ritsuryō* expeditionary armies. In very large expeditionary forces composed of two or more armies (*gun*; q.v.), *shōgun* were under the command of *taishōgun* (q.v.).

Shōken 将監. Captain; the number four post (above *shōshō* and below *shōsō*; q.v.) in the left and right *kon'efu*, the *chūefu*, and the *gaiefu* (q.v. all 3); sometimes translated as Lieutenant.

Shōki 小毅. Lieutenant Colonel; the number two post (above *kyōi* and below *daiki*; q.v.) in *ritsuryō* provincial regiments of 600 men or more.

Shōshō 少将. Lesser General; the number three post (above *shōken* and below *chūjō*; q.v.) in the left and right *kon'efu*, the *chūefu*, and the *gaiefu* (q.v. all 3); sometimes translated as Lesser Captain.

Shōsō 将曹. Lieutenant; the number five post (below *shōken*; q.v.) in the left and right *kon'efu*, the *chūefu*, and the *gaiefu* (q.v. all 3).

Shuchō 主帳. Clerk; a post within the *ritsuryō* provincial regiments.

Tai 隊. Company; a 50-man unit with the *ritsuryō* provincial regiments; the fundamental tactical units of the *ritsuryō* provincial military, *tai* were either infantry (*hotai*) or cavalry (*kitai*) companies.

Taihō Codes 大宝. The *ritsuryō* codes (q.v.) promulgated in 702; no longer extant.

Taishō 隊正. Warrant Officer Third Class; the lowest post (below *rosochi*; q.v.) in the administrative/command structure of the *ritsuryō* provincial regiments.

Taishō 大将. Grand General; the top post (above *chūjō*; q.v.) in the left and right *kon'efu*, the *chūefu*, and the *gaiefu* (q.v. all 3); sometimes translated as Major Captain.

Taishōgun 大将軍. Field Marshal; the top post in a *ritsuryō* expeditionary force; *taishōgun* were appointed to command the entire expeditionary force when it consisted of three armies (*gun*; q.v.).

Tōkaidō 東海道. One of the seven circuits (*dō*) under the *ritsuryō* system (q.v.); the provinces of Ise, Iga, Shima, Owari, Mikawa, Tōtōmi, Suruga, Kai, Izu, Sagami, Awa, Kazusa, Shimōsa, Hitachi, and Musashi.

Tōsandō 東山道. One of the seven circuits (*dō*) under the *ritsuryō* system (q.v.); the provinces of Ōmi, Mino, Hida, Kōzuke, Shimotsuke, Mutsu, and Dewa.

Tsuibushi 追捕使. "Envoy to Pursue and Capture"; one of the three main titles granted warriors under the Heian period provincial military and police system.

Tsuitōshi 追討使. "Envoy to Pursue and Strike Down"; a temporary deputation used by the court from the mid–Heian period to grant special military or police powers to warrior leaders for specific missions.

Yōrō Codes 養老. The only extant set of *ritsuryō* (q.v.) codes; created in 718.

Zaichō kanjin 在庁官人. On-site provincial official; the local men who served as regular or surrogate regular officials in the on-site offices (*zaichō* or *rusudokoro*, q.v.) of the provincial government, and who legally (local political and social realities notwithstanding) held their positions at the sufferance of the provincial governor, rather than the central government.

BIBLIOGRAPHY

PRIMARY SOURCES

Azuma kagami. 4 vols. In *Shintei zōho kokushi taikei.* Tokyo: Yoshikawa kōbunkan, 1968.

Besshū fusenshō. In *Kokushi taikei.* Tokyo: Yoshikawa kōbunkan, 1964.

Chōshūki. 2 vols. In *Zōho shiryō taisei.* Kyoto: Rinsen shoten, 1965.

Chōya gunsai. In *Kokushi taikei.* Tokyo: Yoshikawa kōbunkan, 1964.

Chūyūki. 7 vols. In *Zōho shiryō taisei.* Kyoto: Rinsen shoten, 1965.

Dainihon komonjo. Vol. 1. Ed. Tōkyō daigaku shiryō hensanjo. Tokyo: Tōkyō daigaku shuppan kai, 1901–

Dainihon shiryō. Series 1–3. Tokyo: Tōkyō daigaku shuppan kai, 1901– .

Denryaku. 5 vols. In *Dainihon kokiroku.* Tokyo: Iwanami shoten, 1960–70.

Engi shiki. In *Shintei zōhō kokushi taikei.* Tokyo: Yoshikawa kōbunkan, 1937.

Fusō ryakki. In *Kokushi taikei.* Tokyo: Yoshikawa kōbunkan, 1965.

Gonki. 2 vols. In *Zōho shiryō taisei.* Kyoto: Rinsen shoten, 1965.

Heian ibun. Ed. Takeuchi Rizō. 15 vols. Tokyo: Tōkyōdō, 1965– .

Heihanki. In *Zōho shiryō taisei.* Kyoto: Rinsen shoten, 1965.

Hokuzanshō. In *Kojitsu sōsho.* Tokyo: Yoshikawa kōbunkan, 1954.

Honchō monzui. In *Kokushi taikei.* Tokyo: Yoshikawa kōbunkan, 1964.

Honchō seiki. In *Kokushi taikei.* Tokyo: Yoshikawa kōbunkan, 1964.

Hyakurenshō. In *Kokushi taikei.* Tokyo: Yoshikawa kōbunkan, 1965.

"Jihanki." 32 vols. In "Kunaichō shoryōbu kiyō." In the collection of the Tōkyō daigaku shiryō hensanjo. Unpublished.

Kamakura ibun. Ed. Takeuchi Rizō. 54 vols. Tokyo: Tōkyōdō, 1971– .

Kokin wakashū mokuroku. In *Shinkō gunsho ruiji.* Tokyo: Shoku gunshoruijū kanseikai, 1941.

Konjaku monogatari shū. 5 vols. In *Nihon koten bungaku zenshū.* Tokyo: Shōgakkan, 1971.

Kugyō bunin. 5 vols. In *Shintei zōhō kokushi taikei.* Tokyo: Yoshikawa kōbunkan, 1928.

Midō kampakki. 3 vols. In *Dainihon kokiroku.* Tokyo: Iwanami shoten, 1952.

Mutsuwaki. In *Gunsho ruijū.* Tokyo: Shoku gunshoruijū kanseikai, 1941.

Nihon kiryaku. 3 vols. In *Shintei zōho kokushi taikei.* Tokyo: Yoshikawa kōbunkan, 1985.

Nihon kōki. In *Shintei zōho kokushi taikei.* Tokyo: Yoshikawa kōbunkan, 1984.

Nihon Montoku tennō jitsuroku. In *Shintei zōho kokushi taikei.* Tokyo: Yoshikawa kōbunkan, 1984.

Nihon shoki. 2 vols. In *Shintei zōho kokushi taikei.* Tokyo: Yoshikawa kōbunkan, 1985.

Ritsu. In *Shintei zōho kokushi taikei.* Tokyo: Yoshikawa kōbunkan, 1982.

Ruijū fusenshō. In *Kokushi taikei.* Tokyo: Yoshikawa kōbunkan, 1964.

Ruijū kokushi. 5 vols. In *Shintei zōho kokushi taikei.* Tokyo: Yoshikawa kōbunkan, 1986.

Ruijū sandaikyaku. 2 vols. In *Shintei zōho kokushi taikei.* Tokyo: Yoshikawa kōbunkan, 1983.

Ryō no gige. In *Shintei zōho kokushi taikei.* Tokyo: Yoshikawa kōbunkan, 1985.

Ryō no shūge. 4 vols. In *Shintei zōho kokushi taikei.* Tokyo: Yoshikawa kōbunkan, 1985.

Saigūki. In *Shiseki shūran.* Tokyo: Kondō kappansho, 1902.

Sakeiki. In *Zōho shiryō taisei.* Kyoto: Rinsen shoten, 1965.

Sandai jitsuroku. 2 vols. In *Shintei zōho kokushi taikei.* Tokyo: Yoshikawa kōbunkan, 1986.

Sankaiki. 3 vols. In *Zōho shiryō taisei.* Kyoto: Rinsen shoten, 1965.

Seiji yōryaku. In *Shintei zōho kokushi taikei.* Tokyo: Yoshikawa kōbunkan, 1984.

Shin sarugakki. In *Nihon shisō taikei 8, kodai seiji shakai shisō.* Tokyo: Iwanami shoten, 1986.

Shoku nihongi. 2 vols. In *Shintei zōho kokushi taikei.* Tokyo: Yoshikawa kōbunkan, 1986.

Shoku nihon kōki. In *Shintei zōho kokushi taikei.* Tokyo: Yoshikawa kōbunkan, 1987.

Shōmonki. In *Shinsen Nihon koten bunko.* Tokyo: Gendai shi-chōsha, 1975.

Shōyūki. 7 vols. In *Dainihon kokiroku.* Tokyo: Iwanami shoten, 1959.

Sonpi bunmyaku. 5 vols. In *Shintei zōho kokushi taikei.* Tokyo: Yoshikawa kōbunkan, 1983.

Teishin kōki. In *Dainihon kokiroku.* Tokyo: Iwanami shoten, 1956.

SECONDARY SOURCES

Altham, E. A. *The Principles of War.* Vol. 1. London: Macmillan, 1914.

Arnesen, Peter J. "The Struggle for Lordship in Late Heian Japan: The Case of Aki," *Journal of Japanese Studies,* 10, no. 1 (1984): 101–41.

Arnn, Barbara L. "Local Legends of the Gempei War: Reflections of Medieval Japanese History," *Asian Folk Studies,* 38, no. 2 (1979): 1–10.

Asakawa Kan'ichi. "The Founding of the Shogunate by Minamoto No Yoritomo" (1933). In *Land and Society in Medieval Japan,* ed. Committee for the Publication of Dr. K. Asakawa's Works, pp. 269–89. Tokyo: Japan Society for the Promotion of Science, 1965.

———. *Land and Society in Medieval Japan,* ed. Committee for the Publication of Dr. K. Asakawa's Works. Tokyo: Japan Society for the Promotion of Science, 1965.

———. "The Origin of Feudal Land Tenure in Japan" (1914). In *Land and Society in Medieval Japan,* ed. Committee for the Publication of Dr. K. Asakawa's Works, pp. 139–62. Tokyo: Japan Society for the Promotion of Science, 1965.

Aston, W. G. *Nihongi: Chronicles of Japan from the Earliest Times to 697 AD*. 2 vols. in one. Rutland, Vt.: Tuttle, 1972. Originally published in 1896.

Batten, Bruce L. "Foreign Threat and Domestic Reform: The Emergence of the Ritsuryō State," *Monumenta Nipponica*, 41, no. 2 (1986): 199–219.

————. "State and Frontier in Early Japan, 645–1185: The Case of Kyushu." Ph.D. dissertation, Stanford University, 1989.

Bender, Ross. "The Hachiman Cult and the Dōkyō Incident," *Monumenta Nipponica*, 34, no. 2 (1979): 125–53.

Bock, Felicia, tr. *Engi-shiki: Procedures of the Engi Era Books I–IV*. Tokyo: Monumenta Nipponica Monograph, 1970.

Borgen, Robert. *Sugawara No Michizane and the Early Heian Court*. Cambridge, Mass.: Harvard University Press, 1985.

Brown, Delmer, and Ishida Ichirō, trs. and eds. *The Future and the Past: A Translation and Study of the Gukansho, an Interpretive History of Japan Written in 1219*. Berkeley: University of California Press, 1979.

Butler, Kenneth. "The Heike Monogatari and the Japanese Warrior Ethic," *Harvard Journal of Asian Studies*, no. 29 (1969): 93–108.

Cholley, Jene-Rene. "The Rise and Fall of a Great Military Clan: Taira No Kiyomori." In Murakami Hyoe and Thomas J. Harper, eds., *Great Historical Figures of Japan*, pp. 72–78. Tokyo: Japan Culture Institute, 1978.

Crump, James I., Jr. "'Borrowed' T'ang Titles and Offices in the Yōrō Codes," *Occasional Papers*, University of Michigan Center for Japanese Studies, 1952.

————. "T'ang Penal Law in Early Japan," *Occasional Papers*, University of Michigan Center for Japanese Studies, 1953.

Dainihonshi. Vol. 16. Tokyo: Tokugawa-ke zōpan, 1928.

Davis, David L. "The Evolution of *Bushidō* to the Year 1500," *Journal of the Oriental Society of Australia*, no. 13 (1978): 38–56.

Edwards, Walter. "Event and Process in the Founding of Japan," *Journal of Japanese Studies*, 9, no. 2 (1983): 265–95.

Egami Namio. "The Formation of the People and the Origin of the State in Japan," *Memoirs of the Tōyō Bunkō*, no. 23 (1964): 35–70.

———. *Kiba minzoku kokka: Nihon kodaishi e no apurochi*. Tokyo: Chūō kōronsha, 1967.

Egami Namio, Wajima Seiichi, Mikami Hideo, and Nagatani Bugenjin. "Nihon kodai kokka no keisei," *Tōyō bunka*, no. 6 (1951).

Endō Yukio. "Shuba no tō no kōdō to seikaku." In *Nihon kodai shi ron'en*, ed. Endō Yukio sensei shōju kinen kai, pp. 3–17. Tokyo: Kokusho kangyōkai, 1983.

Farris, William Wayne. "From Soldier to Samurai," *Transactions of the International Conference of Orientalists in Japan*, 28, no. 9 (1984): 34–39.

———. *Population, Disease, and Land in Early Japan, 645–900*. Cambridge, Mass.: Harvard University Press, 1985.

Friday, Karl. "Hired Swords: The Rise of Private Warrior Power in Early Japan." Ph.D. dissertation, Stanford University, 1989.

———. "Mononofu: The Warrior of Heian Japan." M.A. thesis, University of Kansas, 1983.

———. "Teeth and Claws: Provincial Warriors and the Heian Court," *Monumenta Nipponica*, 43, no. 2 (1988): 153–85.

Fukuda Toyohiko. "Ōchō gunji kikō to nairan." In *Iwanami kōza Nihon rekishi 4 (kodai)*, pp. 81–120. Tokyo: Iwanami shoten, 1976.

―――. "Tetsu to uma to Taira Masakado," *Gekkan hyakka*, no. 196 (1974): 6–11.

Gay, Suzanne. "Muromachi Rule in Kyoto: Administrative and Judicial Aspects." In Jeffrey P. Mass and William Hauser, eds., *The Bakufu in Japanese History*, pp. 49–66. Stanford, Calif.: Stanford University Press, 1985.

Goble, Andrew E. "Go-Daigo and the Kemmu Restoration." Ph.D. dissertation, Stanford University, 1987.

Haga Noboru. "Emishi to henkyō," *Hikaku bunka*, no. 2 (1986): 1–38.

Hall, John W. *Government and Local Power in Japan, 500–1700: A Study Based on Bizen Province*. Princeton, N.J.: Princeton University Press, 1966.

―――. *Japan: From Prehistory to Modern Times*. Tokyo: Tuttle, 1971.

―――. "Kyoto as Historical Background." In John W. Hall and Jeffrey P. Mass, eds., *Medieval Japan: Essays in Institutional History*, pp. 3–38. New Haven, Conn.: Yale University Press, 1974.

―――. "Reflections on Murakami Yasusuke's 'Ie Society as a Pattern,'" *Journal of Japanese Studies*, 11, no. 1 (1985): 47–65.

―――. "Terms and Concepts in Japanese Medieval History: An Inquiry Into the Problems of Translation," *Journal of Japanese Studies*, 9, no. 1 (1983): 1–32.

Hall, John W., and Jeffrey P. Mass, eds. *Medieval Japan: Essays in Institutional History*. New Haven, Conn.: Yale University Press, 1974.

Halleck, H. W. *Elements of Military Science*. Westport, Conn.: Greenwood Press, 1971. Originally published in 1846.

Hara Hidesaburō. "Taika ishin ron hihan josetsu (ge)–ritsuryōseiteki jinmin shihai no seiritsu katei o ronjite iwayuru 'taika ishin' no sonzai o utagau—," *Nihonshi kenkyū,* no. 88 (1967): 23–48.

Haruda Takayoshi. "Masakado no ran ni okeru buryoku soshiki: toku ni banrui ni," *Shigen,* 2, no. 3 (1967): 44–51.

Hashimoto Yū. "Kodai heisei to gunji kunren: Koguchi Yasuo-shi no ron ni sesshite," *Shokunihongi kenkyū,* no. 213 (1981): 1–11.

———. *Ritsuryō gundansei no kenkyū.* Osaka: Hashimoto shi ikōshū kangyōkai, 1982.

———. "Ritsuryō gundansei to kihei," *Shokunihongi kenkyū,* no. 217 (1981): 29–38.

Hattō Sanae. "Kodai ni okeru kazoku to kyōdōtai," *Rekishi hyōron,* no. 424 (1985): 14–23.

Hayashi Rokurō. *Kodai makki no hanran.* Tokyo: Kyōiku sha, 1977.

———. *Shōmonki.* Tokyo: Imaizumi seibunsha, 1975.

Hayashi Tatsusaburō. *Hōken shakai seiritsushi.* Tokyo: Chikuma shobō, 1987.

Hérail, Francine. *Fonctions et fonctionnaires: Japonais au début du XIe siècle.* Paris: Bibliothèque Japonaise, 1971.

———. *Yodo No Tsukai: Ou le système des quatre envoyés.* Paris: Presses Universitaires de France, 1966.

Hirakawa Minami. "Fushū to ezō." In *Nihon kodai no seiji to bunka,* ed. Aoki Kazuo sensei kanreki kinen kai, pp. 265–318. Tokyo: Yoshikawa kōbunkan, 1987.

———. "Tōhoku daisensō jidai." In Takahashi Takashi, ed., *Kodai no chihōshi,* vol. 6, pp. 156–92. Tokyo: Asakura shoten, 1978.

Hirano Kunio. "The Yamato State and Korea in the Fourth and Fifth Centuries," *Acta Asiatica,* no. 31 (1977): 51–82.

Hirano Tomohiko. "Kondeisei seiritsu no haikei to sono yakuwari." In Saeki Arikiyo, ed., *Nihon kodaishi ronkō*, pp. 271–316. Tokyo: Yoshikawa kōbunkan, 1980.

———. "Ritsuryō chihō gunsei kenkyū no ichi shiten: gunji no buryoku hatsudō o megutte." In Saeki Arikiyo, ed., *Nihon kodai chūseishi ronkō*, pp. 193–224. Tokyo: Yoshikawa kōbunkan, 1987.

Hodate Michihisa. "Kodai makki no tōgoku to ryūjū kizoku." In *Chūsei tōgokushi no kenkyū*, ed. Chūsei tōgokushi kenkyūkai, pp. 3–22. Tokyo: Tōkyō daigaku shuppankai, 1988.

Horiuchi Kazuaki. "Heian chūki no kebiishi no buryoku ni tsuite." In Yamaō Yukihisa, ed., *Ronkyū Nihon kodai shi*, pp. 341–62. Tokyo: Gakuseisha, 1979.

Hoshino Hitoshi. "Shugo, jitō kō," *Shigaku zasshi*, 25, no. 29 (1918).

Hoshino Ryōsaku. *Kenkyūshi jinshin no ran*. Tokyo: Yoshikawa kōbunkan, 1973.

Hurst, G. Cameron, III. "The Development of Insei: A Problem in Japanese History and Historiography." In John W. Hall and Jeffrey P. Mass, eds., *Medieval Japan: Essays in Institutional History*, pp. 60–90. New Haven, Conn.: Yale University Press, 1974.

———. "An Emperor Who Reigned as Well as Ruled: Temmu Tennō." In Murakami Hyoe and Thomas J. Harper, eds., *Great Historical Figures of Japan*, pp. 16–27. Tokyo: Japan Culture Institute, 1978.

———. *Insei: Abdicated Sovereigns in the Politics of Late Heian Japan, 1086–1185*. New York: Columbia University Press, 1976.

———. "The Kōbu Polity: Court-Bakufu Relations in Kamakura Japan." In Jeffrey P. Mass, ed., *Court and Bakufu in Japan*, pp. 3–28. New Haven, Conn.: Yale University Press, 1982.

――――. "The Structure of the Heian Court: Some Thoughts on 'Familial Authority' in Medieval Japan." In John W. Hall and Jeffrey P. Mass, eds., *Medieval Japan: Essays in Institutional History*, pp. 39–59. New Haven, Conn.: Yale University Press, 1974.

Iida Takesato. *Nihon shoki tsūyaku.* Tokyo: Naigai shokō, 1930.

Iida Yukiko. *Hōgen, heiji no ran.* Tokyo: Kyōikusha, 1979.

Ijima Shigeru. *Nihon senheishi.* Tokyo: Kaihatsusha, 1943.

Ikemori Seikichi. "Shokoku sakimori to Tsukushi sakimori," *Nihon rekishi*, no. 253 (1969): 13–21.

Inoue Mitsuo. *Heian jidai no gunji seido no kenkyū.* Tokyo: Yoshikawa kōbunkan, 1980.

――――. "Heian jidai no tsuibushi," *Komonjo kenkyū*, no. 2 (1969): 38–59.

――――. "Kebiishi no seiritsu to sekkan seiji," *Nihonshi kenkyū*, no. 93 (1967): 31–49.

――――. "Masakado no ran to chūō kizoku," *Shirin*, 50, no. 6 (1967): 1–26.

――――. "Nara jidai no kondei," *Nihon rekishi*, no. 276 (1971): 28–41.

――――. "Ōryōshi no kenkyū," *Nihonshi kenkyū*, no. 101 (1968).

Inoue Mitsusada. "Kōgo nenseki to taishizoku saku." In Inoue, *Nihon kodaishi no shomondai*, pp. 259–320. Tokyo: Shisōsha, 1949.

――――. "Ritsuryō System in Early Japan," *Acta Asiatica*, no. 31 (1977): 83–112.

Ishii Ryōsuke. "Gunji, keisatsu oyobi kōtsu seido." In Ishii, *Nihon hōseishi gaisetsu*, pp. 128–34. Tokyo: Kōbundō, 1948.

Ishii Susumu. "Bushidan no hatten." In *Kanagawa-kenshi, tsūshihen*, vol. 1, pp. 347–442. Yokohama: Kanagawa-ken, 1981.

————. *Chūsei bushidan.* Tokyo: Shōgakukan, 1974.

————. "Chūsei seiritsuki gunsei kenkyū no isshiten: kokuga o chūshin to suru gunjiryoku soshiki ni tsuite," *Shigaku zasshi,* 78, no. 12 (1969): 1–32.

————. *Kamakura bushi no jitsuzō.* Tokyo: Heibonsha, 1987.

Ishimoda Shō. "Chūsei seiritsu no 2-3 mondai." In Ishimoda, *Zōhō chūseiteki seikai no keisei,* pp. 372–97. Tokyo: Itō shoten, 1950.

————. *Kodai makki seijishi josetsu.* Tokyo: Matsuraisha, 1956.

————. "Taira Tadatsune no ran ni tsuite." In Ishimoda, *Kodai makki seijishi josetsu,* pp. 182–96. Tokyo: Miraisha, 1956.

Ishio Yoshihisa. "Nichitō gunbōryō no hikaku kenkyū." In Ishio, *Nihon kodai hō no kenkyū.* Tokyo: Hōritsu bunka sha, 1959.

Itō Haruyuki. "7-8 seiki emishi shakei no kisō kōzō," *Iwate shisaku kenkyū,* 70 (1987): 27–62.

Itō Jun. "Nihon kodai ni okeru shiteki tōchi shōyū keisei no tokushitsu," *Nihonshi kenkyū,* no. 225 (1981): 1–34.

Itoga Shigeo. "Hitachi heishi ronyōsetsu," *Shigaku,* no. 50 (1980): 269–88.

Iyanaga Teizō. "Ritsuryōseiteki tōchi shōyū." In *Iwanami kōza Nihon rekishi kodai 3,* pp. 33–78. Tokyo: Iwanami shoten, 1962.

de Jomini, Baron. *Art of War.* Westport, Conn.: Greenwood Press. Originally published in 1862.

Jones, Archer. *The Art of War in the Western World.* Chicago: University of Illinois Press, 1987.

Kadowaki Teiji. "Ritsuryō taisei no henbō." In *Iwanami kōza Nihon rekishi kodai 3,* pp. 187–228. Tokyo: Iwanami shoten, 1962.

Kanda, James. "Methods of Land Transfer in Medieval Japan," *Monumenta Nipponica,* 23, no. 4 (1978): 379–405.

Kawahara Hideo. "Ritsuryō ikaisei to zaichi shakai," *Kokushi-gaku*, no. 121 (1983): 1–57.

Kawane Yoshiyasu. "Nihon hōken kokka no seiritsu o meguru futatsu no kaikyū." In Kawane, *Chūsei hōkensei seiritsu shiron*, pp. 19–93. Tokyo: Tōkyō daigaku shuppan kai, 1971.

Kikuchi Katsumi. "Nihon ritsuryō izen keibatsu seido no tokushitsu," *Tōyō bunka*, no. 68 (1988): 219–37.

Kiley, Cornelius J. "Estate and Property in the Late Heian Period." In John W. Hall and Jeffrey P. Mass, eds., *Medieval Japan: Essays in Institutional History*, pp. 109–26. New Haven, Conn.: Yale University Press, 1974.

———. "The Imperial Court as a Legal Authority in the Kamakura Age." In Jeffrey P. Mass, ed., *Court and Bakufu in Japan*, pp. 29–44. New Haven, Conn.: Yale University Press, 1982.

———. "Property and Political Authority in Medieval Japan." Ph.D. dissertation, Harvard University, 1970.

———. "State and Dynasty in Archaic Yamato," *Journal of Japanese Studies*, 3, no. 1 (1973): 25–49.

Kindai Ashikaga-shi shi, shiryō hen. Vol. 1. Ashikaga, Japan: Ashikaga-shi, 1977.

Kindai Ashikaga-shi shi, tsūshihen: genshi-kindai. Vol. 2. Ashikaga, Japan: Ashikaga-shi, 1977.

Kishi Toshio. "Ritsuryō taiseika no gōzoku to nōmin." In *Iwanami kōza Nihon rekishi kodai 3*, pp. 79–115. Tokyo: Iwanami shoten, 1962.

Kita Keita. "Gundanshi no kunren ni kansuru ikkōsatsu," *Shokunihongi kenkyū*, no. 224 (1982): 13–28.

———. "Hashimoto Hiroshi 'Ritsuryō gunsei no kenkyū,'" *Rekishi kenkyū*, no. 557 (1986): 45–51.

———. "Seii gunhen ni tsuite no ikkōsatsu," *Shorikubu kiyō*, no. 39 (1988): 1–19.

Kitayama Shigeo. "Sekkan seiji." In *Iwanami kōza Nihon reki-shi kodai 4*, pp. 1–40. Tokyo: Iwanami shoten, 1962.

Knutsen, Roald M. *Japanese Polearms*. London: Hollard Press, 1963.

Kobayashi Hiroko. *The Human Comedy of Heian Japan: A Study of the Secular Stories in the 12th Century Collection of Tales, Konjaku Monogatarishu*. Tokyo: Centre for East Asian Cultural Studies, 1979.

Kobayashi Yukio. "Jōdai Nihon ni okeru jōba no fūshū," *Shirin*, 34, no. 3 (1951): 173–90.

Koguchi Yasuo. "Ritsuryō gundansei no gunji kunren seido," *Shokunihongi kenkyū* (3 parts), no. 211 (1980): 14–16; no. 216 (1981): 1–18; no. 222 (1982): 15–34.

———. "Sekichō ni miru ritsuryō gundan heishi no bugi kun-ren," *Shokunihongi kenkyū*, no. 225 (1983): 29–40.

Koyama Yasukazu. "Nihon chūsei seiritsu no mibun to kaikyū," *Rekishigaku kenkyū*, no. 328 (1967): 26–40.

Kudō Masaki. "Kodai emishi no shakai: kōeki to shakai so-shiki," *Rekishi hyōron*, no. 434 (1986): 13–35.

———. "Tōhoku kodaishi to jōsaku," *Nihonshi kenkyū*, no. 136 (1973): 17–33.

Kurita Hiroshi. "Gundan no seifu kondei no sei." In Kurita Tsutomu, ed., *Kurita sensei zasshō*. Tokyo: Yoshikawa han'itsu shobō, 1901.

Kuroda Kōichirō. "Jingū kebiishi no kenkyū," *Nihonshi kenkyū*, no. 107 (1969): 1–20.

Ledyard, Gari. "Galloping Along with the Horseriders: Look-ing for the Founders of Japan," *Journal of Japanese Studies*, 1, no. 2 (1975): 217–54.

McCullough, Helen C. "A Tale of Mutsu," *Harvard Journal of Asiatic Studies*, no. 25 (1964–65): 178–211.

———. "Yoshitsune: The Historical Figure, the Legend,

Yoshitsune Himself." In McCullough, *Yoshitsune: A 15th-Century Japanese Chronicle*, pp. 3–68. Tokyo: Tokyo University Press, 1966.

————, tr. *Okagami, the Great Mirror: Fujiwara Michinaga and His Times*. Princeton, N.J.: Princeton University Press, 1980.

————. *The Tale of the Heike*. Stanford, Calif.: Stanford University Press, 1988.

McCullough, William. "Japanese Marriage Institutions in the Heian Period," *Harvard Journal of Asiatic Studies*, no. 27 (1967): 103–67.

McCullough, William H., and Helen Craig McCullough. "Some Notes on Rank and Office." In McCullough and McCullough, trs., *A Tale of Flowering Fortunes: Annals of Japanese Aristocratic Life in the Heian Period*, vol. 2, pp. 789–832. Stanford, Calif.: Stanford University Press, 1980.

Mass, Jeffrey P. *The Development of Kamakura Rule, 1180–1250: A History with Documents*. Stanford, Calif.: Stanford University Press, 1979.

————. "The Early Bakufu and Feudalism." In John W. Hall and Jeffrey P. Mass, eds., *Court and Bakufu in Japan: Essays in Kamakura History*, pp. 123–42. New Haven, Conn.: Yale University Press, 1982.

————. "The Kamakura Bakufu." In *The Cambridge History of Japan*, vol. 3: *Medieval Japan*, ed. Kozo Yamamura, pp. 46–88. New York: Cambridge University Press, 1990.

————. *The Kamakura Bakufu: A Study in Documents*. Stanford, Calif.: Stanford University Press, 1976.

————. *Lordship and Inheritance in Early Medieval Japan: A Study of the Kamakura Sōryō System*. Stanford, Calif.: Stanford University Press, 1989.

————. "Patterns of Provincial Inheritance in Late Heian Japan," *Journal of Japanese Studies*, 9, no. 1 (1983): 67–96.

———. *Warrior Government in Medieval Japan: A Study of the Kamakura Bakufu, Shugo and Jitō*. New Haven, Conn.: Yale University Press, 1974.

Masuda Toshinobu. "Shōmonki ron." In Inoue Tatsuo, ed., *Kodai chūsei no seiji to chiiki shakai*, pp. 164–97. Tokyo: Oyama kyaku, 1986.

Matsuhara Hironobu. "Gyōmin, kaizoku, soshite Sumitomo no ran," *Shakai kagaku kenkyū*, no. 14 (1987): 1–21.

Matsumoto Masaharu. "Gundan kihei to kondei," *Shokunihongi kenkyū*, no. 222 (1982): 35–44.

———. "Gundan no tōkyū ni tsuite." In Naoki Kōjirō sensei koki kinenkai, ed., *Kodaishi ronshū*, pp. 265–92. Tokyo: Haniwa shobō, 1988.

———. "Gunji no gunji shidō to sono kiban," *Hisutoria*, no. 113 (1986): 18–36.

———. "Nakamarō no ran to heiko," *Shokunihongi kenkyū*, no. 210 (1980): 31–38.

———. "Ritsuryōka shokoku gundan to sono kikō," *Shakaika kenkyū*, no. 16 (1973): 2–16.

———. "Ritsuryō seika shokoku dansu ni tsuite," *Kodai bunka*, 32, no. 6 (1980): 45–60.

———. "Seiishi to seitōshi," *Nihon rekishi*, no. 477 (1987): 20–39.

Matsumoto Shinpachirō. "Shōmonki no inzō," *Bungaku*, 19, no. 10 (1951): 6–21.

Mayu Hiromichi, ed. *Chūō shūken kokka e no michi: senran Nihonshi*. Vol. 1. Tokyo: Daiichi hōgen shuppan, 1988.

Miller, Richard J. *Ancient Japanese Nobility: The Kabane Ranking System*. Berkeley: University of California Press, 1973.

———. "A Study of the Development of a Centralized Japanese State Prior to the Taika Reform, AD 645." Ph.D. dissertation, University of California, Berkeley, 1953.

Minamoto Yasushi. *Gekiroku Nihon no kassen: Masakado to*

Sumitomo no hanran. Tokyo: Tōkyō supōtsu shinbunsha, 1979.

Minegishi Sumio. "Tōgoku bushi no kiban: Kōzuke no kuni no Arata no shō." In Inagaki Yasuhiko, ed., *Shōen no seikai,* pp. 33–68. Tokyo: Zaidan hōnin Tōkyō daigaku shuppankai, 1973.

Minobuya Tetsuichi. "Kebiishi to kiyome," *Hisutoria,* no. 87 (1980): 57–78.

Miyagawa Mitsuru with Cornelius J. Kiley. "From Shōen to Chigyō: Proprietary Lordship and the Structure of Local Power." In John W. Hall and Toyoda Takeshi, eds., *Japan in the Muromachi Age,* pp. 89–107. Berkeley: University of California Press, 1977.

Miyahara Takeo. "Ritsuryō seika no nōmin tōsō." In *Kōza Nihonshi,* ed. Rekishigaku kenkyūkai to Nihonshi kenkyūkai, vol. 1, pp. 217–40. Tokyo: Tokyo Daigaku shuppankai, 1970.

Miyanaga Tetsuo and Morita Tei. "Heian zenki tōgoku no gunji mondai ni tsuite," *Kanezawa daigaku kyōiku gakubu kiyō,* no. 24 (1975): 49–61.

Mizuno Yū. "Jinshin no ran." In Ōbayashi Taryō, ed., *Ikusa,* pp. 179–204. Tokyo: Shakai shisōsha, 1984.

———. *Nihon kodai ōchō shiron jōsetsu.* Tokyo: Komiyama shoten, 1954.

———. "Origin of the Japanese People," *Understanding Japan,* no. 22 (1968): 1–74.

Morita Tei. "Heian chūki kebiishi ni tsuite no kakusho," *Nihonshi kenkyū,* no. 12 (1972): 51–63.

———. "Heian zenki o chūshin shita kizoku no shiteki buryoku ni," *Shigen,* no. 15 (1972): 70–84.

———. "Heian zenki tōgoku no gunji mondai ni tsuite." In Morita, *Kaitaiki ritsuryō seiji shakaishi no kenkyū.* Tokyo: Kokusho kangyōkai, 1983.

———. "Kebiishi no kenkyū," *Shigaku zasshi*, 78, no. 9 (1969): 1–44.

———. "Kebiishi seiritsu no zentei," *Nihon rekishi*, no. 255 (1969): 62–77.

———. *Kenkyūshi ōchō kokka*. Tokyo: Kadokawa kōbunkan, 1980.

———. "Kodai sentō ni tsuite." In Morita, *Heian shōki kokka no kenkyū*, pp. 170–90. Tokyo: Gendai sōzōsha, 1970.

———. *Ōchō seiji*. Tokyo: Kyōikusha, 1979.

———. *Zuryō*. Tokyo: Kyōikusha, 1978.

Morris, Dana Robert. "Peasant Economy in Early Japan, 650–950." Ph.D. dissertation, University of California, Berkeley, 1980.

Morris, Ivan. *The World of the Shining Prince: Court Life in Ancient Japan*. New York: Knopf, 1964.

Murai Yasuhisa, ed. *Heian ōchō no bushi*. Vol. 2 of *Senran Nihonshi* series. Tokyo: Daiichi hōgen shuppan, 1988.

Murakami Yasusuke. "Ie Society as a Pattern of Civilization," *Journal of Japanese Studies*, 10, no. 2 (1984): 281–363.

Muraoka Kaoru. "8 seikimatsu 'seii' saku no saikentō: ritsuryō gunsei to no kakawari de." In Takeuchi Rizō, ed., *Kodai tennōsei to shakai kōzō*, pp. 123–46. Tokyo: Azekura shobō, 1980.

———. "Enryaku 11 nen shokoku gundan heishisei teihai no ikkōsatsu." In *Minshū shi no kadai to hōkō*, ed. Minshū shi kenkyūkai, pp. 19–42. Tokyo: San'itsu shobō, 1978.

Murdoch, James. *A History of Japan*. 3 vols. New York: F. Unger, 1964. Originally published 1910–26.

Mushakoji Minoru. "Ikusa monogatari ni tsuite," *Nihon bungaku*, 4, no. 1 (1955): 1–7.

Mutō Kōichi. "Gundan heishisei ni kansuru jakkan no mondai," *Chūō shigaku*, no. 9 (1986): 105–204.

Nagahara Keiji. "Land Ownership Under the Shoen-

Kokugaryo System," *Journal of Japanese Studies*, 1, no. 2 (1975): 269–96.

———. *Nihon hōken shakai ron*. Tokyo: Tōkyō daigaku shuppankai, 1956.

———. *Shōen*. Monograph series *Wakai seidai to gataru Nihon no rekishi*, no. 12. Tokyo: Hyōronsha, 1978.

———. "The Social Structure of Early Medieval Japan," *Hitotsubashi Journal of Economics*, 1, no. 1 (1960): 90–97.

Nagai Hajime. "Gundansei teihaigo no heishi," *Kokugakuin zasshi*, 89, no. 9 (1988): 46–59.

———. "Kondeisei ni tsuite no saikentō: heianki kondei o chūshin to shite," *Shigaku kenkyū shūroku*, no. 8 (1983): 30–39.

Nakaguchi Hideo. "8–9 seiki no maku ni tsuite," *Shigaku zasshi*, 95, no. 1 (1986): 1–37.

Nakamura Akizō. "Fujiwara Hirotsugu no ran." In Ōbayashi Taryō, ed., *Ikusa*, pp. 205–24. Tokyo: Shakai shisōsha, 1984.

Nakata Katsumi. "Gundan heishisei ni tsuite: heishi yakumu o chūshin to shite," *Shigaku kenkyū shūroku*, no. 6 (1981): 27–40.

Naoki Kōjirō. "Gundan no hyōsū to haibi no han'i ni tsuite," *Shokunihongi kenkyū*, 7, no. 8 (1960): 1–5.

———. "Ikkō, ichi heishi no gensoku to tenpeisotsu," *Nihon rekishi*, no. 175 (1962).

———. *Jinshin no ran*. Tokyo: Hanawa shobō, 1961.

———. "Kodai tennō no shiteki heiryoku," *Shirin*, 45, no. 3 (1962): 1–32.

———. *Nihon kodai heiseishi no kenkyū*. Tokyo: Kadokawa kōbunkan, 1968.

———. "Tōgoku no seijiteki chii to sakimori," *Kokubungaku kaishaku to kanshō*, no. 245 (1956): 54–59.

Niino Naoyoshi. *Kenkyūshi kuni no miyatsuko*. Tokyo: Yoshikawa kōbunkan, 1974.

Nishioka Toranosuke. "Bushi kaikyū kessei no ichi yoin to shite no 'maki' no hatten." In Nishioka, *Shōenshi no kenkyū*, vol. 1, pp. 301–407. Tokyo: Iwanami shoten, 1953. Originally published in 1928.

———. *Shin Nihonshi nenpyō*. Tokyo: Chūō kōronsha, 1955.

Nishiyama Ryōhei. "Ritsuryōsei shakai no henyō." In *Kōza Nihonshi*, ed. Rekishigaku kenkyūkai to Nihonshi kenkyūkai, vol. 2, pp. 129–68. Tokyo: Tokyo daigaku shuppankai, 1984.

Noda Reishi. "Nihon ritsuryō gunsei no tokushitsu." *Nihonshi kenkyū*, no. 76 (1965): 31–54.

———. "Ritsuryō gunji kikō no seiritsu to sono yakuwari," *Nihonshi kenkyū*, no. 150/151 (1975): 43–54.

———. *Ritsuryō kokka no gunjisei*. Tokyo: Yoshikawa kōbunkan, 1984.

———. "Ritsuryō kokka no seiritsu to jinmin tōsō," *Nihonshi kenkyū*, no. 104 (1969): 3–24.

———. "Sakimori to eji," *Shigen*, no. 15 (1972): 2–12.

———. "Sasayama Haruo sensho 'Nihon kodai efu seido no kenkyū,'" *Nihonshi kenkyū*, no. 284 (1986): 81–86.

Noguchi Minoru. *Bandō bushidan no seiritsu to hatten*. Tokyo: Kōseisho rinseishūsha, 1982.

Nojiri Fusao. "Efu kenkyū no seika to mondaiten: ryō–gekan to shite no efu o chūshin ni," *Shigen*, no. 19 (1975): 84–96.

Ōae Akira. *Ritsuryō seika no shihō to keisatsu: kebiishi seido o chūshin to shite*. Tokyo: Daigaku kyōikusha, 1979.

Ōbayashi Taryō. "Uji Society and Ie Society from Prehistoric to Medieval," *Journal of Japanese Studies*, 11, no. 1 (1985): 3–28.

———, ed. *Ikusa*. Tokyo: Shakai shisōsha, 1984.

Oboroya Hisashi. *Seiwa genji*. Tokyo: Kyōikusha, 1984.

Ogura Akio. "Jūtō toneri ryō ni tsuite: sono setchiki o chūshin ni shite," *Shokunihongi kenkyū*, no. 244 (1986): 1–8.

Okuno Nakahiko. "Heian jidai no guntō ni tsuite." In *Minashū undō to sabetsu-jōsei*, ed. Minshūshi kenkyūkai, pp. 5–27. Tokyo: Ōyama kaku, 1985.

———. "Nihon no sakimorisei ni tsuite," *Minshūshi kenkyū*, no. 30 (1986): 17–29.

Ōmori Kingorō. *Buke jidai no kenkyū*. 3 vols. Tokyo: Fukuyamabō, 1924.

Ōyama Kyōhei. "Shōensei to ryōshūsei." In *Kōza Nihonshi*, ed. Rekishigaku kenkyūkai to Nihonshi kenkyūkai, vol. 2, pp. 75–105. Tokyo: Tōkyō daigaku shuppankai, 1970.

Oyama Yasunori. "Kodai makki no tōgoku to saigoku." In *Iwanami kōza Nihonshi kodai 4*, pp. 231–69. Tokyo: Iwanami shoten, 1976.

———. "Nihon chūsei seiritsuki no mibun to kaikyū," *Rekishigaku kenkyū*, no. 328 (1967): 26–41.

Phillipi, Donald L., tr. *Kojiki*. Tokyo: Tokyo University Press, 1968.

Piggott, Joan R. "Tōdaiji and the Nara Imperium." Ph.D. dissertation, Stanford University, 1987.

Pulleyblank, Edwin. "The An Lu-shan Rebellion and the Origins of Chronic Militarism in Late T'ang China." In John Perry and Bardwell Smith, eds., *Essays on T'ang Society*, pp. 32–61. London: Brill, 1976.

Rabinovitch, Judith N. *Shōmonki: The Story of Masakado's Rebellion*. Tokyo: Monumenta Nipponica Monograph, 1985.

Reischauer, Edwin O. "Heiji Monogatari." In Edwin Reischauer and Joseph Yamagiwa, eds., *Translations from Early Japanese Literature*, pp. 269–353. Cambridge, Mass.: Harvard University Press, 1972.

———. *Japan: The Story of a Nation*. 3d ed. Rutland, Vt.: Tuttle, 1981.

Reischauer, Robert K. *Early Japanese History*. 2 vols. Gloucester, Mass.: Peter Smith, 1967. Originally published in 1937.

Saeki Arikiyo, Sakaguchi Tsutomo, Sekiguchi Akira, and Oishiro Chihiro. *Masakado no ran*. Tokyo: Yoshikawa kōbunkan, 1976.

Saitō Toshio. "11-12 seiki no gunji, tone to kokuga shihai," *Nihonshi kenkyū*, no. 205 (1979): 28–59.

Sansom, George. *A History of Japan to 1334*. Stanford, Calif.: Stanford University Press, 1958.

Sasaki Ken'ichi. "Masakado no ran to tōgoku gōzoku: toku ni Musashi Takeshiba o chūshin to shite." In Takeuchi Rizō, ed., *Kodai tennōsei to shakai kōzō*, pp. 235–56. Tokyo: Kōsō shobō, 1980.

Sasaki Muneo. "10-11 seiki no zuryō to chūō seifu," *Shigaku zasshi*, 96, no. 9 (1987): 1–36.

Sasaki Tsunebito. "Chinpei shokō," *Tōhoku rekishi shiryōkan kenkyū kiyō*, no. 11 (1985): 1–17.

Sasama Yoshihiko. *Nihon kōchū-bugu jiten*. Tokyo: Kashiwa shobō, 1981.

Sasayama Haruo. "Bunken ni mirareru senjutsu to buki." In Ōbayashi Taryo, ed., *Ikusa*, pp. 123–55. 1984.

———. "Chūefu setchi ni kansuru ruijū sandai kyaku shosai choku ni tsuite," *Shokunihongi kenkyū*, 2, no. 9 (1955): 201–12.

———. "Hyōe ni tsuite no ikkōsatsu: toku ni kinai buryoku no kankei o megutte." In *Nihon kodai seiji to bunka*, ed. Aoki Kazuo sensei kanreki kinen kai, pp. 97–137. Tokyo: Yoshikawa kōbunkan, 1987.

———. *Kodai kokka to guntai*. Tokyo: Chūkō shinsho, 1975.

———. *Nihon kodai efu seido no kenkyū*. Tokyo: Tokyo daigaku shuppankai, 1985.

———. "Nihon kodai no gunji soshiki." In Ishimoda Shō et

al., eds., *Kodaishi kōza*, vol. 5, pp. 307–37. Tokyo: Gaku-seisha, 1962.

Sato, Elizabeth. "Early Development of the Shoen." In John W. Hall and Jeffrey P. Mass, eds., *Medieval Japan: Essays in Institutional History*, pp. 91–108. New Haven, Conn.: Yale University Press, 1974.

———. "Oyama Estate and Insei Land Policies," *Monumenta Nipponica*, 34, no. 1 (1979): 73–99.

Satō Shin'ichi. *Nihon no chūsei kokka*. Tokyo: Iwanami shoten, 1983.

Seki Yukihiko. *Bushidan kenkyū no ayumi: gakusetsu shiteki ten-kai*. 2 vols. Tokyo: Shinjinbutsu ōraisha, 1988.

Sekiguchi Akira. "Ezo no hanran to sono rekishiteki igi," *Re-kishigaku kenkyū*, no. 390 (1972): 35–45.

———. "Kodai ni okeru kengun to jōsaku: Dewa no kuni Yū-shō gun o chūshin ni," *Shokunihongi kenkyū*, no. 202 (1979): 10–31.

Sekiguchi Hiroko. "Kodai kazoku to kon'in keitai." In *Kōza nihonshi 2*, ed. Rekishigaku kenkyūkai to Nihonshi kenkyū-kai, pp. 287–326. Tokyo: Tōkyō daigaku shuppan kai, 1984.

Shima Setsuko. "Masakado no ran no zaichi kōzō," *Nara shien*, no. 13 (1965): 1–11.

Shimizu Mitsuo. "Kokugaryō to bushi." In Shimizu, *Jōdai no tochi kankei*, pp. 133–61. Tokyo: Itō shoten, 1943.

Shimizu Osamu, tr. "Nihon Montoku Tenno Jitsuroku: An Annotated Translation, with a Survey of the Early Ninth Century in Japan." University Microfilms, 1951.

Shimomukai Tatsuhiko. "Nihon ritsuryō gunsei no kihon kōzō," *Shigaku kenkyū*, no. 175 (1987): 17–43.

———. "Ōchō kokka gunsei kenkyū no kihon shikaku: 'tsuibu kanpu' o chūshin ni." In Sakamoto Shōzō, ed., *Ōchō kokka seishi*, pp. 285–345. Tokyo: Yoshikawa kōbunkan, 1987.

———. "Ōchō kokka kokuga gunsei no kōzō to tenkai," *Shigaku zasshi*, no. 151 (1981): 44–67.

———. "Ōchō kokka kokuga gunsei no seiritsu," *Shigaku kenkyū*, no. 144 (1979): 1–27.

———. "Ōryōshi, tsuibushi no shoruikei," *Hisutoria*, no. 94 (1982): 17–33.

———. "Shokuku ōryōshi-tsuibushi shiryō shūseitai: shokoku ōryōshi-tsuibushi ni tsuite" *Hiroshima daigaku bungakubu kiyō*, no. 45 (1986): 1–41.

Shinoda Minoru. *The Founding of the Kamakura Shogunate*. New York: Columbia University Press, 1960.

———. "Victory in Battle and Family Tragedy: Minamoto No Yoritomo and Yoshitsune." In Murakami Hyoe and Thomas J. Harper, eds., *Great Historical Figures of Japan*, pp. 79–90. Tokyo: Japan Culture Institute, 1978.

Shioda Yōichi. "Tenpyō shōhō ki no sakimorisei." In *Nihon rekishi no kōzō to tenkai*, ed. Nagashima Fukutarō sensei taishoku kinnenkai, pp. 161–82. Tokyo: Yamakawa shuppansha, 1983.

Shirakawa Tetsurō. "Heishi ni yoru kebiishi chō shōaku ni tsuite," *Nihonshi kenkyū*, no. 298 (1987): 52–75.

Shōji Hiroshi. "Heian shōki kebiishi buryoku no ikkōsatsu," *Gunji shigaku*, 23, no. 4 (1988): 17–22.

———. *Henkyō no sōran*. Tokyo: Kyōikusha, 1977.

Snellen, J. B. "Shoku Nihongi," *Transactions of the Asiatic Society of Japan* (2 parts), no. 11 (1934): 151–239, no. 14 (1937): 209–78.

Sogabe Shizuo. "Tōgoku shusshin no sakimori tachi," *Shirin*, 44, no. 2 (1961): 129–39.

Sonoda Kōyō. "Waga jōdai no kiheitai," *Shigen*, no. 23/24 (1962): 5–22.

Stramigioli, Giuliana. "Preliminary Notes on the Masakadoki and Taira No Masakado Story," *Monumenta Nipponica*, 28, no. 3 (1973): 261–93.

Sugimoto Keizaburō. "Konjaku monogatari no bushi setsuwa: heike monogatari to no kanren ni oite," *Hōsei daigaku bungakubu kiyō*, no. 9 (1963): 26–53.

Sugiwara Akira. "Shōki shōen no hakkai to zaichi gōzoku," *Shikai*, no. 26 (1979): 21–30.

Suzuki Hideo. "Kaken to sōryō ni kansuru kakusho." In Yasuda Motohisa, ed., *Shoki hōkensei no kenkyū*, pp. 281–310. Tokyo: Yoshikawa kōbunkan, 1963.

Suzuki Kunihiro. "Ichi gekyū kanri no kazoku to seikatsu: 'shinsaru gakki' no seikai." In *Nihon chiikishi kenkyū*, ed. Murakami Nao sensei kanreki kinen kai, pp. 1–37. Tokyo: Bunken shuppan, 1986.

Suzuki Susumu. *Nihon kassenshi hyakubanashi*. Tokyo: Tatsukaze shobō, 1982.

Suzuki Takeo. "Heian jidai ni okeru nōmin no uma," *Nihon rekishi*, no. 239 (1968): 42–55.

Tabata Yasuko. "Kodai, chūsei no 'ie' to kazoku: yōshi o chūshin to shite," *Tachibana jōshi daigaku kenkyū kiyō*, no. 12 (1985): 41–67.

Takada Minoru. "10 seiki no shakai henkaku." In *Kōza Nihonshi*, ed. Rekishigaku kenkyūkai to Nihonshi kenkyūkai, vol. 2, pp. 17–46. Tokyo: Tokyo daigaku shuppankai, 1970.

Takahashi Masaaki. "Bushi no hassei to sono seikaku," *Rekishi koron*, 2, no. 7 (1976): 54–65.

———. *Kiyomori izen*. Tokyo: Heibonsha, 1984.

———. "Masakado no ran no hyōka o megutte," *Bunka shigaku*, no. 26 (1971): 25–44.

Takahashi Takashi. "Kodai kokka to emishi," *Kodai bunka*, 38, no. 2 (1986): 13–24.

———. "Mutsu-Dewa no gunsei," *Shigen*, no. 15 (1972): 22–30.

———. "Ritsuryō kyōsei ni okeru gundansū to heishisū," *Shokunihongi kenkyū*, 10, no. 4/5 (1963): 20–28.

Takahashi Tomio. *Bushidō no rekishi*. 3 vols. Tokyo: Shin jinbutsu ōraisha, 1986.

———. *Hiraizumi no sekai: Fujiwara Kiyohira*. Tokyo: Kiyomizu shinsho, 1983.

———. "Kodai kokka to henkyō." In *Iwanami kōza Nihon rekishi kodai 3*, pp. 229–60. Tokyo: Iwanami shoten, 1962.

———. "Mononofu no michi: bushidō no rekishi," *Gekkan budō*, Sept. 1978–July 1979.

———. "Tōhoku kodai shijō no kibe to chinpei," *Nihon rekishi*, no. 90 (1962): 36–41.

Takayama Kahoru. "Shirakawa inseiki ni okeru kebiishi no issokumen: bunin jōetsu kara mite," *Shōnan shigaku*, no. 7/8 (1986): 64–98.

Takayanagi Mitsutoshi and Suzuki Tōru. *Nihon kassenshi*. Tokyo: Gakugei shorin, 1968.

Takegawa Seijirō. *Hōseishijō yori kentaru Nihon nōmin no seikatsu: kondei jidaika*. Tokyo: Dōjinsha shoten, 1927.

———. "Ritsuryōsei no mondai ten," *Rekishi kyōiku*, 11, no. 5 (1963): 1–10.

Takeuchi Rizō. *Bushi no tōjō*. Vol. 6 of *Nihon no rekishi*. Tokyo: Chūō kōronsha, 1965.

———. "History and the Present State of the Study of the Shoen in Japan." In Asakawa Kan'ichi, ed., *Documents of Iriki*, pp. xiii–xix. Westport, Conn.: Greenwood Press, 1974.

———. "Shōki no bushidan." In Kawasaki Yasuyuki, ed., *Ni-*

hon jinbutsu shi taikei, vol. 1, pp. 194–214. Tokyo: Asakura shoten, 1961.

———. "Zaichō kanjin no bushika." In Takeuchi Rizō, ed., *Hokensei seiritsu no kenkyū,* pp. 1–42. Tokyo: Yoshikawa kōbunkan, 1955.

———, ed. *Kodai tennōsei to shakai kōzō.* Tokyo: Azekura shobō, 1980.

Takeuchi Rizō hakasei kanreki kinenkai, ed. *Shōensei to bushi shakai.* Tokyo: Yoshikawa kōbunkan, 1969.

Tanaka Takashi. "Sakimori," *Shokunihongi kenkyū,* 3, no. 10 (1956): 19–22.

Toby, Ronald P. "Why Leave Nara? Kammu and the Transfer of the Capital," *Monumenta Nipponica,* 40, no. 3 (1985): 331–48.

Tochigi-kenshi, tsūshihen, vol. 3: *Chūsei.* Tochigi, Japan: Tochigi-ken, 1984.

Toda Yoshimi. "Chūsei seiritsuki no kokka to nōmin," *Nihonshi kenkyū,* no. 97 (1968): 18–33.

———. "Kokuga gunsei no keisei katei." In *Chūsei no kenryoku to minshū,* ed. Nihonshi kenkyūkai shiryō kenbukai, pp. 5–44. Tokyo: Sōgensha, 1970.

———. "Shōki chūsei bushi no shokunō to shoyaku." In *Nihon no shakai shi,* vol. 4: *Futan to zōyo,* pp. 247–71. Tokyo: Iwanami shoten, 1986.

Toyama-kenshi, tsūshihen, vol. 1: *Genshi-kodai.* Toyama, Japan: Toyama-ken kyōkasho kyōkyūsho, 1976.

Tsurumi, Patricia. "Male Present vs. Female Past," *Bulletin of Concerned Asia Scholars,* 14, no. 4 (1982): 71–75.

Turnbull, Stephen R. *The Samurai: A Military History.* New York: Macmillan, 1976.

Ueda Hironori. "Nihon kodai no buki." In Ōbayashi Taryo, ed., *Ikusa,* pp. 43–122. Tokyo: Shakai shisōsha, 1984.

Uemura Seiji. "Empress Jingu and the Conquest of Silla," *Memoirs of the Tōyō Bunkō*, no. 35 (1977): 75–83.

Ury, Marian, tr. *Tales of Times Now Past: 62 Stories from a Medieval Japanese Collection*. Berkeley: University of California Press, 1979.

Uwayokote Masataka. "Heian chūki no keisatsu jōtai." In *Ritsuryō kokka to kizoku shakai*, ed. Takeuchi Rizō hakase kanrekikinenkai, pp. 511–40. Tokyo: Yoshikawa kōbunkan, 1969.

————. "Heian jidai no nairan to bushidan." In Toda Yoshimi, ed., *Shinpojium Nihon rekishi 5 chūsei shakai no keisei*, pp. 141–291. Tokyo: Gakuseisha, 1972.

————. "Kodai makki nairan kenkyū no mondaiten," *Rekishi hyōron*, no. 88 (1957).

Vargo, Lars. *Economic Conditions for the Formation of the Early Japanese State*. Stockholm: Almquist and Wiksell, 1982.

Varley, H. Paul. *Japanese Culture*. Honolulu: University of Hawaii Press, 1973.

————, tr. *A Chronicle of Gods and Sovereigns: Jinnō Shōtōki of Kitabatake Chikafusa*. New York: Columbia University Press, 1980.

Wada Hidematsu. "Tsuibushi kō," *Nyoran shawa*, no. 6 (1888).

Watanabe Naohiko. "Kebiishi no kenkyū." In *Nihon kodai kan'i seido no kisoteki kenkyū*, pp. 295–384. Tokyo: Yoshikawa kōbunkan, 1972.

Wilson, William R. "The Way of the Bow and Arrow: The Japanese Warrior in the Konjaku Monogatari," *Monumenta Nipponica*, 28, no. 1/4 (1973): 177–233.

————, tr. *Hōgen Monogatari: A Tale of the Disorder of Hogen*. Tokyo: Monumenta Nipponica Monograph, 1971.

Yamagishi Tokuhei and Takahashi Teiichi, eds. *Hōgen monogatari (nakaraibon) to kenkyū*. Toyohashi: Mikan kokubun shiryō kankokai, 1959.

Yamamura Kozo. "Decline of the Ritsuryo System: Hypothesis on Economic and Institutional Change," *Journal of Japanese Studies*, 1, no. 1 (1974): 3–37.

Yamanouchi Kunio. "Kondeisei o meguru shomondai." In *Nihon kodaishi ronsō*, pp. 348–70. Tokyo: Endō Yukio hakasei kanreki kinen Nihon kodaishi ronsō kangyōkai, 1970.

———. "Ritsuryō gundan ni kansuru kenkyū no dōkō," *Shigen*, no. 7 (1969): 30–68.

———. "Ritsuryō gundansei no suii," *Shigen*, no. 15 (1972): 13–21.

———. "Ritsuryōsei gundan heishi no kanten hōhō ni tsuite: ikkō ichi heishi setsu no kenten o chūshin to shite," *Meiji daigaku daigakuin kiyō*, no. 4 (1966): 709–16.

———. "Ritsuryōsei gundan no seiritsu ni tsuite," *Gunji shigaku*, no. 11 (1967): 24–38.

———. "Sakimori no shubichi to shusshinchi: Ikemori Seikichi no 'shokoku sakimori to Tsukushi sakimori' no kentō o tsūjite," *Sendai shigaku*, no. 25 (1969): 20–56.

Yamashita Takashi. "Ritsuryō gunseiron jōsetsu," *Nihon shisōshi kenkyūkai kaihō*, no. 6 (1987): 38–48.

Yamazato Jun'ichi. "Ritsuryō chihō zaisei ni okeru gunji kankeihai ni tsuite," *Risshō shigaku*, no. 58 (1985): 7–24.

Yashiro Kazuo. "Shōmonki no sekai: Sadamori, Masakado o chūshin ni." In Yashiro, *Shōmonki: kenkyū to shiryō*, pp. 8–44. Tokyo: Shindoku shosha, 1963.

Yasuda Motohisa. "Bushi hassei ni kansuru kakusho." In Yasuda, ed., *Nihon hōkensei seiritsu no shozentei*, pp. 84–111. Tokyo: Yoshikawa kōbunkan, 1960.

———. *Bushi sekai no jōmaku*. Tokyo: Yoshikawa kōbunkan, 1973.

———. *Bushidan*. Tokyo: Hanawa shobō, 1964.

————. "Bushidan no keisei." In *Iwanami kōza Nihon rekishi kodai 4*, pp. 132–60. Tokyo: Iwanami shoten, 1962.

————. *Gempei no sōran*. Tokyo: Shin jinbutsu ōraisha, 1987.

————. *Senran*. Tokyo: Kintō shuppansha, 1984.

————, ed. *Chūō shūken kokka e no michi*. Senran Nihonshi series. Tokyo: Daiichi hōgen, 1988.

————. *Gempei no sōran*. Senran Nihonshi series. Tokyo: Daiichi hōgen, 1988.

————. *Heian ōchō no bushi*. Senran Nihonshi series. Tokyo: Daiichi hōgen, 1988.

Yokota Ken'ichi. "Tenpyō jūni nen Fujiwara Hirotsugu no ran no ikkōsatsu." In *Ritsuryō kokka no kiseki kōzō*, ed. Ōsaka rekishi gakkai, pp. 293–312. Tokyo: Yoshikawa kōbunkan, 1960.

Yoneda Yūsuke. *Kodai kokka to chihō gōzoku*. Tokyo: Kyōikusha, 1979.

————. "Ritsuryō seika no gōzoku." In *Kōza Nihonshi*, ed. Rekishigaku kenkyūkai to Nihonshi kenkyūkai, vol. 1, pp. 241–64. Tokyo: Tōkyō daigaku shuppankai, 1970.

————. "Taihō ryō zengo no heisei," *Shokunihongi kenkyū*, 9, no. 4/6 (1962): 33–44.

————. "Tōgoku sakimori to sono seiritsu." In *Kodai no chihōshi*, vol. 5, pp. 142–66. Tokyo: Asakawa shoten, 1977.

Yoshida Akira. "Heian chūki no buryoku ni tsuite," *Hisutoria*, no. 47 (1967): 1–16.

————. "Masakado no ran ni kansuru 2, 3 no mondai," *Nihonshi kenkyū*, no. 50 (1960): 6–26.

Yoshie Akio. "Shōki chūsei sonraku no keisei." In *Kōza Nihonshi*, ed. Rekishigaku kenkyūkai to Nihonshi kenkyūkai, vol. 2, pp. 105–30. Tokyo: Tōkyō daigaku shuppankai, 1970.

Yoshimura Shigeki. "In hokumen kō," *Hōseishi kenkyū*, no. 2 (1953): 45–71.

————. "Takiguchi no kenkyū," *Rekishi chiri*, 53, no. 4 (1929): 1–30.

Yoshizawa Mikio. "9 seiki no Mutsu-dewa seisaku ni tsuite," *Tōhoku rekishi shiryōkan kenkyū kiyō*, no. 11 (1985): 19–34.

Yumino Masatake. "Ritsuryō seika no 'buryō' to 'ōryō.'" In Takeuchi Rizō, ed., *Kodai tennōsei to shakai kōzō*, pp. 215–35. Tokyo: Kōsō shobō, 1980.

INDEX

In this index an "f" after a number indicates a separate reference on the next page, and an "ff" indicates separate references on the next two pages. A continuous discussion over two or more pages is indicated by a span of page numbers, e.g., "57–59." *Passim* is used for a cluster of references in close but not consecutive sequence.

Abe, Princess, 61–63
Abe Sadatō, 115
Abe Yoritoki, 115
Alliances, military/political, 76–81, 98–101, 112–19, 203
An Lu-shan, 44
Anna incident, 91n
Anrakuji, 103
Antoku, Emperor, 2
Archery skills, 50, 71, 193
Armor, 36
Armories, 28n
Army, imperial, *see* Military, imperial
Asaka, Prince, 62
Asakawa Kan'ichi, 4ff, 169
Ashikaga District, 102f
Ashikaga Estate, 200

Ashikaga military network, 104, 199
Ashikaga Nariyuki, 102
Ashikaga Tadatsuna, 102, 104–5
Ashikaga Toshitsuna, 102–5, 199
Ashikaga Yasutsuna, 105
Ashikaga Yoshikane, 103, 105
Aterui (Emishi leader), 48–49
Awaji province, 45
Awa province, 106, 111f, 145
Azuma kagami, 90, 103, 112, 117
Azuma toneri, 60

Bandits, 82–84, 96–97, 138. *See also* Pirates
Bandō region, 23
Batten, Bruce, 57

Bizen province, 156
Buryōshi, 142
Bushi, 3–7; defined, 181. See also Military networks, private; Military personnel
Bushidan, 93–95, 197. See also Military networks, private

Capital Region (kinai), 135, 164
Cavalry, 35–40 passim, 50–52, 172–73, 187
Censorate (danjōdai), 132ff
Chiba of Shimōsa, 105
Chiba Peninsula, 105f
Chiba Tsunetane, 108
Ch'ih Yu, 145n
China, T'ang: influence on imperial military, 8–11 passim; military threat of, 11
Chinjō, 24
Chinjufu, 24
Chinpei, 21, 24–25, 49, 51
Chōnai, 67–68
Chūefu, 59–64 passim, 68, 191
Chūnagon, 27
Classical age, transition from, 2, 4–7, 167–71
Class structure, 66f, 77–78
Conscription, 12–15 passim, 34–35, 38n, 124–28 passim
Council of State (daijōkan), 26, 132, 134f, 140, 161ff
Court, imperial: scholarship on, 5–7, 168–71; activist policy of, 7; relations with provinces, 72–76; alliances of, 76–81, 98, 100–101; warriors in the, 88–93; and warriors, 156, 165–66. See also Council of State; State, imperial
"Court Army," 128

Court rank system, 18n, 192

Daijōkan, see Council of State
Daiki, 18
Danjōdai (Censorate), 132ff
Dannoura, Battle of, 1f
Dazaifu, 23, 47, 124
Deer hunting, 71n
Dewa province, 47f, 124
District officials, see Gunji
Dōkyō, 68

Ebisu, see Emishi
Echizen province, 55, 156
Eji, 28–29f
Ejifu, 27–30 passim, 64
Emishi, 21n, 47–49, 51
Emonfu, 27–30 passim, 64, 129, 133
Emperor, see Court, imperial
Emperor's army, see Military, imperial; Ritsuryō military
Expeditionary forces, see Ritsuryō expeditionary forces
Ezo, see Emishi

Families, noble, see Noble houses
Five Guards (goefu), 27–30, 40, 58, 65, 68f, 132f. See also Six Guards
Former Nine Year's War (1055–62), 109n
Frontier garrisons, 20–25, 46–49. See also Chinpei; Sakimori
Fujiwara, bandō, 88–93, 99, 102–5
Fujiwara Akimitsu, 92
Fujiwara Arihira, 151
Fujiwara Fubito, 60f
Fujiwara Fujinari, 90

Fujiwara Fusasaki, 61, 191
Fujiwara Haruaki, 145
Fujiwara Harutsugu, 81
Fujiwara Hidesato, 88n, 90f,
    102, 146–48, 152, 210
Fujiwara Kanetaka, 213
Fujiwara Kiyohira, 91
Fujiwara Kōmyō, 60f
Fujiwara Korechika, 145
Fujiwara Kuromaro, 81
Fujiwara Maro, 61
Fujiwara Masao, 85, 87
Fujiwara Morotō, 115
Fujiwara Motonaga, 76, 84
Fujiwara Muchimaro, 61, 63, 86
Fujiwara Murao, 90
Fujiwara Nakamaro, 63, 68
Fujiwara Sanekiyo, 101n
Fujiwara Sumitomo, 149f, 152f
Fujiwara Tadabumi, 151
Fujiwara Tadahira, 100
Fujiwara Tadakiyo, 108
Fujiwara Tadanobu, 210
Fujiwara Takenori, 91n
Fujiwara Toyozawa, 90
Fujiwara Tsunekiyo, 91
Fujiwara Umakai, 61
Fujiwara Uona, 89
Fujiwara Yoshinao, 81, 85f
Fukushōgun, 26
Fun'ya Makio, 85, 87

Gaiefu, 63–64, 68. See also Five
    Guards; Six Guards
Gempei War, 3, 107, 113, 168.
    See also Dannoura, Battle of
Genealogy, 202
Genmei, Empress, 59–60
Genshō Ashikaga, 102f, 105
Goefu (Five Guards), 27–30, 40,
    58, 65, 68f, 132f

Gokenin (shōgunal vassals), 113.
    See also Kamakura shōgunate
Go (squads), 17
Governor, provincial, see Pro-
    vincial governors
Guerilla tactics, 51
Gun (army), 26
Gundan, see Provincial regi-
    ments
Gunji (district officials), 19, 66
Gunken, 26
Gunki, 18ff
Gunshi, 127
Gunsō, 26

Hachiman, 92
Hall, John W., 5f, 9, 169–70
Haniwa figurines, 35–36
Hatakeyama, 112
Hatakeyama Shigetada, 110
Heian-kyō, 122
Heiji Incident, 3, 93, 169
Heijō, Emperor, 87
Heijō (capital), 122
Heike monogatari, 104, 117
Heishi, 15–17, 51, 127. See also
    Military personnel
Hirano Tomohiko, 205
Hitachi province, 51, 101, 104n,
    144f
Hōgen Incident, 3, 93, 169
Horse-and-bow warfare, 50. See
    also Cavalry
Horses, 28, 39–40
Hotai, 17. See also Infantry
Houses, noble, see Noble
    houses
Hurst, G. Cameron, 78
Hyōbushō (Ministry of Military
    Affairs), 14
Hyōefu, 27–30 passim, 64, 191.

See also Five Guards; Six
Guards
Iga house, 91
Iji no Azumaro, 48
Ikusa, 93. *See also* Military net-
works, private
Imperial court, *see* Court, impe-
rial
Imperial house, 58–64
Imperial Police, Office of, *see*
Kebiishi-chō
Imperial succession, 58–63, 191
Imperial Sword, 2
Infantry, 37–41 *passim*, 44, 50,
172–73
Inheritance, 115–16
Inland Sea, 149
Inoue Mitsuo, 143, 146f, 152,
157
Ise Morotsuga, 137
Ise province, 55
Ishimura Ishitate, 68
Ishio Yoshihisa, 38n
Itō Sukechika, 111n
Iyo province, 149
Izu province, 145

Jien, 2
Jingū, Empress Regent, 42
Jinpei system, 125–28
Jinshin War (672), 12, 44
Jitō, Empress, 12–13, 59
Junnin, Emperor, 62–63
Jutōe, 63, 68
Jutō toneri, 62
Jutō toneri ryō, 59–61, 68, 191

Ka (campfire), 17. *See also Ritsuryō* military
Kadobe, 28

Kaga province, 162
Kai province, 85
Kamakura Gongorō Kagemasa,
110
Kamakura shōgunate, 3, 124,
168f, 175
Kammu, Emperor, 88n, 90
Kammu Heishi, 88, 90, 93, 99,
106, 108f. *See also* Taira house
Kanada Yoritsugu, 111n
Kanezawa Stockade, 109
Kanpei, 127
Karu, Prince, 59
Kasagake, 71, 192
Katsurahara, Prince, 90
Kazusa Hirotsune, 105–8
Kazusa house, 107
Kazusa province, 51, 81, 90,
104–11 *passim*, 127, 138, 145
Kazusa Tsunezumi, 108, 201
Kebii-dokoro, 136f
Kebiishi, 123
Kebiishi, provincial, 136–40
Kebiishi bettō, 206–7
Kebiishi-chō, 123, 128–36, 164,
205f
Kii province, 176
Kiley, Cornelius, 77
Kinai (capital region), 131–
36 *passim*, 164
Kinmasa, 117
Kinohe (stockade), 48
Kinugasa Stockade, 112
Kiryū Rokurō, 105
Kitai, 17. *See also* Cavalry
Kiyowara Iehira, 109, 175
Kiyowara Kanetoki, 135
Kiyowara Norikiyo, 101n
Kiyowara Sanehira, 109
Kiyowara Takehira, 109
Kōga Koreshige, 155

Kōken, Empress, 62
Kondei, 51–56, 190
Kon'efu, 61–64, 68. See also Six
  Guards
Konjaku monogatari shū, 96, 114f
Korea, 11, 44, 54
Kōzuke province, 51, 102, 104,
  104n, 145
Kun'i (merit rank) system, 66–
  67
Kuni no miyatsuko (provincial
  patriarchs), 10f, 19f, 37, 44
Kurihara Estate, 81
Kusakabe, Prince, 59
Kyōi, 18
Kyōshiki (Offices of the Capi-
  tal), 131–32
Kyushu, 149

Land commendation, 79, 92
Latter Three Years' War (1083–
  87), 109, 175

Mass, Jeffrey, 89, 114f
Matsuda house, 91
Medieval age, transition to, 2,
  4–7, 167–71
Mercenaries, 71. See also Military networks, private
Merit rank (kun'i) system, 66–
  67
Mibu Yorihira, 135
Military, imperial, 13–15, 31,
  125, 165. See also Ritsuryō
  military; privatization of, 69–
  72, 96–97, 119–28 passim,
  156, 171–74 passim; modifications to, 123–24, 139–40,
  144, 165; and court, 160–64;
  organization of, 160–66
Military networks, private, 71,

93–121 passim, 174; alliances
  within, 76, 98–101, 112–19,
  203; as "bushidan," 93–95;
  genesis of, 95–98; power of,
  98, 148, 168–77 passim; structure of, 98–101, 118; leadership of, 99–100; rewards in,
  116–17; loyalty in, 117–19;
  and the state, 146ff, 165–66
Military personnel: characteristics of, 14, 23ff, 28–31 passim,
  45–55 passim; duties of, 15–
  17, 23–30 passim, 39f, 53–54,
  126, 183, 191; supplies for,
  16, 29, 41; numbers of, 17–
  18, 26ff, 38n, 46, 51–55 passim, 62, 64, 184; schedules of,
  183; supplies, 187
Military skills, 81–88, 96–97,
  119
Militia, 31
Minamoto house, 88n, 89, 91–
  93, 197
Minamoto Kunifusa, 117
Minamoto Mitsumasa, 92
Minamoto Mitsunaka, 87, 89,
  91
Minamoto Tameyoshi, 117
Minamoto Tsunemoto, 89
Minamoto Yorichika, 89, 92,
  162
Minamoto Yorifusa, 162
Minamoto Yorimitsu, 89
Minamoto Yorinobu, 89, 92,
  101, 106
Minamoto Yoritomo, 3, 93,
  103–8 passim, 113, 170, 176,
  213
Minamoto Yoriyoshi, 92, 118–
  19
Minamoto Yoshichika, 159

Minamoto Yoshiie, 92, 101n, 109, 113, 159, 175–76, 196
Minamoto Yoshikuni, 103
Minamoto Yoshitomo, 3, 110
Minamoto Yoshitsuna, 101n
Minamoto Yoshitsune, 1–2
Minamoto Yoshiyasu, 103
Minamoto Yoshizumi, 108–12 passim
Ministry of Justice (gyōbushō), 132f
Ministry of Military Affairs (hyōbushō), 14
Mino province, 55
Minoru Shinoda, 8
Miura, naval resources of, 112
Miura Estate, 111
Miura network, 108–12
Miura Peninsula, 111
Miura Tametsugu, 109f
Miura Yoshiaki, 108–12, 202
Miura Yoshimune, 112
Miura Yoshitsugu, 110
Miura Yoshizumi, 110, 111n
Miyako no musha 88–93, 100–101
Miyoshi Kiyotsura, 42f
Monmu, Emperor, 59
Mononobe, 28
Montoku, Emperor, 87
Morita Tei, 126f
Morris, Dana, 74
Muraoka Kaoru, 38n
Murasaki Shikibu: The Tale of Genji, 168
Murdoch, James: History of Japan, 216
Musashi province, 51, 99, 138, 145, 147
Mutō house, 91

Mutsu province, 47f, 91, 109, 124
Mutsuwaki, 115, 118

Nagaoka, 48
Nagato province, 47
Nakata Katsumi, 45
Nara (capital), 122
Naval warfare, 112
New Emperor, 144–45. See also Taira Masakado
Nihon shoki, 21, 23, 54
Nishioka Toranosuke, 52
Nitta Estate, 104
Nitta Yoshishige, 103f
Noble houses, 77–79, 88; power of, 11, 57; private warriors of, 57–58, 86–87; and provinces, 74–75, 80–81; and outlaws, 82, 96–97

Ōae Akira, 137
Obito, Prince, 59–60
Office of Imperial Police, see Kebiishi-chō; Police
Offices of the Capital (kyōshiki), 131–32
Ōishi, 54
Okiyo Fuminushi, 129
Okura Harusane, 149
Omi Ihohara no Kimi, 54
Ōmi province, 54f
Ōno no Azumabito, 48
Ono Yoshifuru, 149, 151
Ōryōshi, 123, 140–59 passim, 164, 209
Ōsaka, 54
Ōta house, 112
Ōtomo house, 60, 91
Ōtomo Surugamaro, 48

Outlaws, 82–84, 96–97, 138, 149–53 passim
Owari province, 76, 84, 117
Oyama house, 91
Oyama Tomomasa, 103
Ōyumi, 41–43, 50

Paekche, 54
Palace, 30n
Peasants, 8f, 14–15, 30, 34–35, 39, 45, 54, 73, 165
Pirates, 149–53 passim
Police, 44, 59, 128–36, 215; and provinces, 126–27; organization of, 160–66. See also Ōryōshi; Tsuibushi; Tsuitōshi
Population registers, 13, 34, 38n
Provinces, 47n; relations with court, 72–76
Provincial elites, 67, 74, 202; advancement through military, 64–69, 72, 165; alliances of, 76–81, 98–101
Provincial government, 123, 162f. See also Provincial governors
Provincial governors, 73–86 passim, 126ff, 154–55, 161
Provincial military, 160–64 passim, 215
Provincial patriarchs (kuni no miyatsuko), 10f, 19f, 37, 44
Provincial regiments, 13–20, 68–69, 184; abolished, 45–52, 124, 173; shortcomings of, 46–47, 49; and kondei, 51–56

Religious institutions, 74–75, 82
Ritsuryō codes, 9n, 13n, 78. See also Ritsuryō military; Taihō codes; Yōrō codes
Ritsuryō expeditionary forces, 25–27
Ritsuryō military: characteristics of, 8, 11–12, 31–32, 37–41 passim, 50; peasants in, 8f, 14–15, 30, 34–35, 39, 45, 54, 69, 124–25; failure of, 8–9; influence of China on, 8–11 passim, 44; creation of, 10–13; organizational structure of, 11–12, 17–20, 25–28, 39, 42, 44, 51–52, 60–61, 63–64, 184; separated from civil power, 20; frontier garrisons of, 20–25, 46–49; and troop mobilization, 26; modifications of, 34, 45, 68–69, 124f, 139, 144, 172–73; shortcomings of, 34–45; and cavalry, 35–40 passim, 50–52, 172–73, 187; purpose of, 37, 44; and infantry, 37–44 passim, 50, 172–73; abuses in, 44–45, 49; court pressures on, 57–59; and provincial elites, 64–69
Rokuefu (Six Guards), 56–61, 64f
Rokuji, 26
Rosochi, 18
Roster, regimental, 15, 183
Rōtō, 83–86. See also Military networks, private; Provincial regiments
Ryō no gige, 66
Ryūge, 54

Sadazumi, Prince, 89
Sado, 47, 124

Saeki house, 60
Saeki Tsunenori, 118–19
Sagami province, 108, 110ff, 145
Saikaidō, 55
Sakanoue Tamuramaro, 49
Sakimori, 20–24 *passim*, 185
Sakko (stockade), 48
Sangi, 27
San'indō, 55
Sano house, 91
Sansom, George, 4–6ff
San'yōdo, 55
Sanzaku, 71, 193
Satō house, 91
Seiwa, Emperor, 88n, 89
Seiwa Genji, 88–93 *passim*, 99, 107–8, 110, 195
Sekkanke, 89
Settō, 26, 185
Shiden, 67
Shieiden ryōshu, 95
Shields, 41
Shijin, 67–68
Shikida Estate, 156
Shima province, 45f
Shimokabe house, 91
Shimōsa province, 51, 106f, 111, 144f
Shimotsuke province, 102f, 145ff
Shinano province, 85
Shōen, 79, 112, 163
Shōgun, 26f
Shōki, 18
Shoku nihongi, 23, 51, 63, 67
Shōmonki, 96. *See also* Taira Masakado
Shōmu, Emperor, 59–62 *passim*
Shōtoku, Empress, 63–64
Shuchō, 18

Silla, 44
Six Guards (*rokuefu*), 56–61, 64f. *See also* Five Guards
Smallpox, 46, 61
Standing army, 31f
State, imperial, 5–7, 12–13, 71, 168–71; power of, 10–13, 26, 31, 37–38, 57–58, 165–66; and provinces, 69, 72–76. *See also* Council of State; Court, imperial
Stockade, 48
Suruga province, 84–85

Tachibana Moroe, 61
Tachibana Tōyasu, 149
Tahasami, 71, 193
Tai (company), 17
Taihō codes, 13, 66. *See also Ritsuryō* codes
Taika Reforms, 10–12, 20
Taira house, 88, 90, 93, 103f, 106, 159n, 196f. *See also* Kammu Heishi
Taira Kanetada, 114–15
Taira Kiyomori, 3, 93, 104, 108
Taira Koremochi, 114f
Taira Koremoto, 101
Taira Kunika, 90
Taira Masakado, 96, 100, 128, 144–47, 152f
Taira Masamori, 93, 159
Taira Naokata, 106
Taira Sadamori, 90, 145f
Taira Shigetoki, 117
Taira Tadatsune, 101, 106
Taira Takamochi, 90
Taira Tokiko, 2
Taira Tomomori, 1–2
Taira Tsunechika, 106–7
Taira Tsuneharu, 107, 201

Taira Tsunemasa, 106–7
Taira Tsunezumi, 107
Taira Yoshifumi, 106
Taira Yukinaka, 117
Taishō, 18
Taishōgun, 26
Tajima, 159
Takami, Prince, 90
Takamochi, Prince, 106
Taxation, 73f, 76, 79
Tenji, Emperor, 10
Tenmu, Emperor, 12–13, 37, 59
Titles: empowerment of, 12,
    123
Toba, Emperor, 103
Tōkaidō, 55
Tōkaidō route, 111
Tōsandō, 55
Tōshō Ashikaga, 102–5. See also
    Fujiwara, bandō
Tsuibu kanpu, 161–62
Tsuibushi, 123, 148–59, 164; appointments of, 150–55 passim,
    211–14
Tsuitōshi, 159–60, 163
Tsushima, 159
Turnbull, Stephen, 175

Uda, Emperor, 90

Uji, Battle of, 104

Wakasa province, 45
Warrants: from Council of
    State, 161–62
Warrior class, 2–7 passim, 88–
    93, 120, 181, 197; alliances of,
    100–101; loyalty of, 117–19;
    power of, 168–77 passim. See
    also Bushi
Weapons, 13, 41–43, 50
Wilson, William R., 93

Yabusame, 71, 193
Yamanouchi Kunio, 45
Yamato province, 161f
Yamato house, 10–12, 23
Yang Yu-chi, 71, 72n
Yasuda Motohisa, 94–95
Yatsumato, 71, 193
Yi I, 72, 72n
Yōrō Codes, 13, 142. See also
    Ritsuryō codes; Jinpei system
Yui-no-ura, Battle of, 110
Yumino Masatake, 142

Zaichi ryōshu, 95
Zaichō kanjin, 136f

Library of Congress Cataloging-in-Publication Data

Friday, Karl F.
    Hired swords : the rise of private warrior power in early Japan /
Karl F. Friday.
        p.   cm.
    Includes bibliographical references and index.
    ISBN 0-8047-1978-0 (cl.) : 0-8047-2696-5 (pbk.)
        1. Japan—History, Military—To 1868.   2. Samurai—History.
I. Title.
DS838.5.F75   1992
952—dc20   91-24615
                                                        CIP